The Impact of International Television
A Paradigm Shift

LEA'S COMMUNICATION SERIES
Jennings Bryant/Dolf Zillmann, General Editors

Several titles in Communication Theory and Methodology subseries (Jennings Bryant, Series Advisor) include:

Berger • Planning Strategic Interaction: Attaining Goals Through Communicative Action

Bryant/Zillmann • Media Effects: Advances in Theory and Research, Second Edition

Dennis/Wartella • American Communication Research: The Remembered History

Elasmar • The Impact of International Television: A Paradigm Shift

Ellis • Crafting Society: Ethnicity, Class, and Communication Theory

Greene • Message Production: Advances in Communication Theory

Heath/Bryant • Human Communication Theory and Research: Concepts, Contexts, and Challenges, Second Edition

Riffe/Lacy/Fico • Analyzing Media Messages: Using Quantitative Content Analysis in Research

Salwen/Stacks • An Integrated Approach to Communication Theory and Research

For a complete list of titles in LEA's Communication Series, please contact Lawrence Erlbaum Associates, Publishers, at www.erlbaum.com.

The Impact of International Television

A Paradigm Shift

Michael G. Elasmar, PhD
Boston University

LAWRENCE ERLBAUM ASSOCIATES, PUBLISHERS
2003   Mahwah, New Jersey   London

Copyright © 2003 by Lawrence Erlbaum Associates, Inc.
All rights reserved. No part of this book may be reproduced in any form, by photostat, microfilm, retrieval system, or any other means, without prior written permission of the publisher.

Lawrence Erlbaum Associates, Inc., Publishers
10 Industrial Avenue
Mahwah, NJ 07430

Cover design by Kathryn Houghtaling Lacey

Library of Congress Cataloging-in-Publication Data

The impact of international television : A paradigm shift / edited by Michael G. Elasmar
   p. cm. —(LEA's communication series)

Includes bibliographical references and index.
ISBN 0-8058-4219-5 (cloth : alk. paper)
ISBN 0-8058-4220-9 (pbk. : alk. paper)
1. Foreign television programs.   I. Elasmar, Michael G.   II. Series

PN1992.8.F67 I48 2002
791.45—dc21   2002075977
                                                             CIP

Books published by Lawrence Erlbaum Associates are printed on acid-free paper, and their bindings are chosen for strength and durability.

Printed in the United States of America
10 9 8 7 6 5 4 3 2 1

Contents

Preface		vii
1	The Cultural Imperialism Paradigm Revisited: Origin and Evolution *Michael G. Elasmar and Kathryn Bennett, Boston University*	1
2	Impacts of Cross-Cultural Mass Media In Iceland, Northern Minnesota, and Francophone Canada In Retrospect *David E. Payne, Sam Houston State University*	17
3	Socialization Effects of American Television on International Audiences *Alexis S. Tan, Gerdean Tan and Todd Gibson, Washington State University*	29
4	Perceived Foreign Influence and Television Viewing In Greece *Thimios Zaharopoulos, Washburn University*	39
5	The Influence of Television and Media Use on Argentines About Perceptions of the United States *Mary Beadle, John Carroll University*	57

6	Choosing National TV: Cultural Capital, Language, and Cultural Proximity in Brazil *Joseph Straubhaar, University of Texas*	77
7	Cultural Proximity On the Air in Ecuador: National, Regional Television Outperforms Imported U.S. Programming *Linda Lee Davis, University of Kansas*	111
8	A Meta-Analysis of Crossborder Effect Studies *Michael G. Elasmar, Boston University and John E. Hunter, Michigan State University*	133
9	An Alternative Paradigm for Conceptualizing and Labeling the Process of Influence of Imported Television Programs *Michael G. Elasmar, Boston University*	157
10	The Impact of International Audio-Visual Media: An Expanded Research Agenda for the Future *Michael G. Elasmar, Boston University*	181
Contributors		191
Author Index		195
Subject Index		201

Preface

My interest in developing this book can be traced to an observation I first made during the course of my doctoral studies at Michigan State University when I was reviewing the literature on imported TV effects. I found out that most writers, including those of books, articles, and conference papers, assumed that imported TV programs have a strong cultural influence on local viewers. However, when sorting articles according to their method of inquiry, I could only find a very few empirical studies about this topic. Where was the systematic evidence that was being relied on for assuming strong influence? I figured that the evidence must have been profuse as the writers were so confident in their contentions of strong influence. I was determined to find it. The more I searched, the more disappointed I became. As a student of both international communication and empirical methods of inquiry, I could not believe that there were only very few empirical studies about this topic. Over time, I collected both published and unpublished manuscripts that followed an empirical approach. This effort eventually led me to prepare the first meta-analytic effort in this subject area, the earliest outcome of which was a paper presented during the Speech Communication Association (now National Communication Association) conference in 1993. A later version of this meta-analysis (co-authored with John Hunter) was published in *Communication Yearbook* in 1997 and is reprinted in this book.

My effort to understand the process and effect of crossborder television gave me the opportunity to meet several empirical researchers with similar interests. Some of these researchers had active programs of study in this area and had conducted seminal investigations about this topic long before my interest in it had ever transpired. Others were my contemporaries. Without knowing it, we were all independently examining the same questions using similar methods.

This book brings together the works of multiple researchers in an effort to shed some light on the premise of strong and homogenous international television effects. It aims at filling a void in the literature of international communication concerning empirical perspectives for explaining the influence of imported television.

This book is narrow in scope as it approaches this topic by focusing on the local viewer of imported TV programs that are designed to entertain. It neither pretends to cover the entire field of international communication nor the effects of other forms of crossborder information flows. It also neither claims to uncover the intentions of international government policies nor the covert objectives of multinational companies. It focuses on the viewer of imported entertainment TV.

Some readers might object to the use of the word paradigm in the title of this book, considering a modification of a paradigm to be too pretentious a goal for a single book. The reality is that, for several decades, cultural imperialism has been the dominant paradigm for conceptualizing, labeling, predicting, and explaining the effects of international television. The cultural imperialism paradigm has been used as an unchallenged premise on which were built hundreds of essays about the topic of imported television influence. By bringing the work of several independent researchers together, this book bridges over 40 years of research efforts that, altogether, challenge the de facto homogenous and strong effects assumed by those who subscribe to the cultural imperialism paradigm. By doing so, this book indeed offers an alternative paradigm that researchers might wish to consider when conceptualizing the effects of crossborder TV.

I certainly do not contend that the definite answer concerning the effects of crossborder TV lies within the pages of this book. Instead, my hope is that this volume will inspire the future generations of researchers to further our knowledge of this issue by approaching this topic with an open mind and by considering more than one paradigm.

In the first chapter of this book, we (Elasmar and Bennett) review the historical factors that have led to the emergence of the cultural imperialism theoretical framework. We also extract and detail the key assumptions of this theory. The purpose of this chapter is to provide a background for the reader to understand the contentions of cultural imperialism and the context in which its assumptions emerged and developed.

In the second chapter, David Payne reviews the results of his research program, the earliest one that exists about this topic. Payne takes a retrospective view of the studies he conducted. These studies have inspired many researchers to begin their own research programs about this topic. Payne's studies were the first to yield findings inconsistent with the assumptions of the cultural imperialism theory.

The third chapter also reviews the results from yet another early research program that examined the influence of imported TV shows. Alex Tan and his colleagues extract results from Tan's early studies, integrate them with newer findings, and then discuss the relevance of their results to several theoretical perspectives about the process of television influence. This chapter illustrates the complexities of the relationship between exposure to foreign TV and its subsequent effects on local audience members and the difficulty of achieving strong and homogenous effects.

In chapter 4, Thimios Zaharopoulos details the results of a recent study he conducted in Greece. Zaharopoulos illustrates the inadequacy of cultural imperialism theory in explaining the variation in the culturally specific behaviors of Greek adolescents. He observes the complexities of the process of influence on culturally specific behaviors and the limited role that imported TV plays in it.

In chapter 5, Mary Beadle focuses on the impact of imported American television on the beliefs that adult professionals in Argentina have of the United States. Beadle finds that imported U.S. television has limited direct effects on the beliefs of the participants in her study.

In chapter 6, Joseph Straubhaar integrates the findings of his many years of studying the process by which local audiences select imported television programs. Selection and exposure are a prerequisite for influence. Straubhaar integrates the results of his previous studies with a more recent case study of Brazil. He finds that language, cultural capital, and cultural proximity are predictors of television program selection and exposure. Local viewers prefer programs that share their language, that are compatible with their cultural capital, and that represent content that is imbedded with elements close to their own culture. Given the similarity between the culture of the locals and the culture imbedded in the imported programs they prefer to watch, one cannot argue that imported television programs can have homogenous and strong cultural effects on local viewers. Further, this chapter also refutes the tacit assumption made by many subscribers to the cultural imperialism theory that the mere presence of imported television programs in domestic television schedules is evidence of cultural influence.

In chapter 7, Linda Davis focuses on the selection of television programs by local viewers in Ecuador. She finds results consistent with Straubhaar's contentions concerning language, cultural capital, and cultural proximity as predictors of television program selection. Davis shows that the simple presence of American television programs in the schedules of Ecuadorian television stations cannot be taken as evidence that the local viewers are exposed to them. This chapter therefore confirms the finding that imported television programs cannot have homogenous and strong cultural effects on local viewers.

In chapter 8, we (Elasmar and Hunter) present a very systematic approach for examining the strength of the effect of imported television. This chapter integrates the results of over three decades of study findings using meta-analytic procedures. The results of the meta-analysis are totally inconsistent with the assumption of homogenously strong effects contended by cultural imperialism proponents.

Chapter 9 observes that although the previous studies find no evidence that imported television programs have strong and homogenous effects, they do not rule out the possibility that they can be influential some of the time and for certain local audience members. However, the cultural imperialism theoretical framework is not useful in understanding under what circumstances these effects are possible. In this chapter, I propose an alternative process to that which is implicit in the cultural imperialism theoretical framework. I call this new process the model of *Susceptibil-*

ity to Imported Media (SIM). I also propose a new label for labeling an effect stemming from this process. The new label is *Media-Accelerated Culture Diffusion* (MACD). This chapter explains which local viewers are most likely to be influenced by imported television, illustrates and labels the process of influence, and by doing so, demonstrates the reason why strong and homogenous effects cannot be found.

Chapter 10 looks ahead beyond the current body of research. Its purpose is to help future researchers build upon the current findings to advance the knowledge in this field.

CHAPTER

1

The Cultural Imperialism Paradigm Revisited: Origin and Evolution

Michael G. Elasmar
Kathryn Bennett
Boston University

In the field of international communication, the concept of cultural imperialism (Schiller, 1976, 1991) has fueled many debates. When it comes to conceptualizing the impact of international television messages, cultural imperialism (CI) has been the theoretical framework of choice for most researchers. For this chapter, international television is defined as entertainment television programs originally produced for an audience in country A then exported to country B. The term international television is used interchangeably with the terms imported TV and foreign TV. We are interested in international TV regardless of how this foreign TV content reaches its audience (e.g., traditional broadcast, cable, satellite, etc.).

CI has been described as "a verifiable process of social influence by which a nation imposes on other countries its set of beliefs, values, knowledge and behavioral norms as well as its overall style of life"(Beltran, 1978, p. 184). The prominence of this theoretical framework in the literature leads us to conclude that, by far, it is the dominant paradigm when it comes to explaining and predicting the impact of international television (Elasmar & Hunter, 1996).

This chapter traces the roots of the CI paradigm in order to gain a better understanding of its contentions concerning the role and effects of international TV. We first identify and review the building blocks of the underlying rationale of CI. We then focus on the mindset of the CI proponents and use an interpretive approach for understanding how CI advocates have framed and linked historical events in order to generate their contentions regarding the effects of international TV. Many scholars have documented the historical developments reviewed in this chapter and their work will be cited throughout this manuscript. Thus, this chapter does not claim to be a historical research effort but rather is an interpretive effort that focuses on the mindset of CI advocates that has led to their conceptualizing about the effects of international TV.

FROM CONSPIRACY TO CULTURAL DOMINATION: THE COMPONENTS OF THE CI PARADIGM IN BRIEF

CI proponents utilize an inductive process for drawing conclusions about the contemporary international intentions and behaviors of states, using conspiracy theory as their premise (see Schiller, 1976). Conspiracy is assumed and never questioned. CI advocates set out to document the presumed conspiracy that underlies the behavior of powerful states in their quest to dominate weaker states (see Roach, 1993). The conspiracy assumption, itself, is most probably based on the historical motivations of rulers (e.g., kings, princes, emperors, and governments) as observed via their documented behaviors throughout human history (see Diamond, 1999). CI advocates, however, are especially interested in the era of European colonialism that is seen as an extension of the crossborder realities of intergroup behaviors throughout history. Colonialism, therefore, is an important concept in the CI paradigm (see Roach, 1993). CI draws on the realities of the economic relationships that existed between European colonizers and their colonies: Economic dependency is another important concept in the CI paradigm (see Tomlinson, 1991). Colonialism is seen as a direct antecedent of the economic dependency that prevailed during the colonial era (see Berger, 1974). Furthermore, the economic inequities among states observed in the postcolonial era that followed World War II are seen as a direct effect of the desire of more powerful states to maintain their control over weaker states (see King, 1997). Here is where CI advocates begin interpreting the intentions of states by projecting past behavioral trends in order to explain the causes of contemporary economic inequities among states. Still assuming conspiracy and aiming to uncover it in the postcolonial era, CI advocates perceive stronger states as intending to perpetuate the economic dependency that prevailed during colonialism (King, 1997). CI proponents believe the mass media to be the remote control tools with which more powerful states control the populations of weaker states (see Tomlinson, 1991). The mass media are said to achieve their mission by altering the culture of the local inhabitants of weaker states and affecting their behaviors in ways that benefit the more powerful states (Tomlinson, 1991). Hence the definition of CI by Beltran (1978) quoted earlier.

Figure 1.1 illustrates the underlying rationale and building blocks of the CI framework vis-à-vis the impact of international TV. Figure 1.1 is designed to be read from top to bottom.

The relationships among the building blocks illustrated in Fig. 1.1 are implicit in the CI literature. It is beyond the scope of this chapter to test out the relationships illustrated in Fig. 1.1. In fact, many of these relationships cannot be tested as they are

1. THE CI PARADIGM REVISITED 3

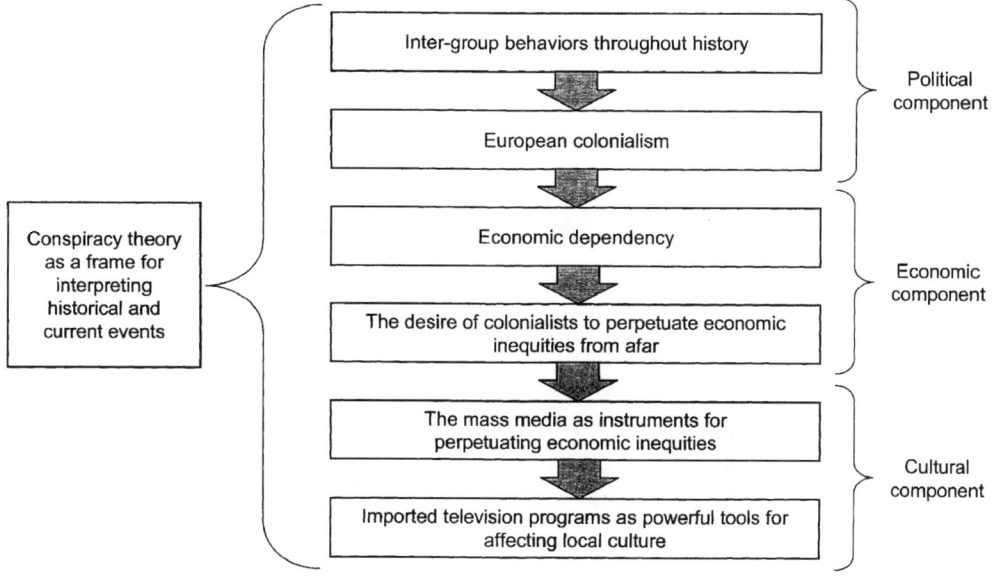

FIG. 1.1. The underlying rationale of the CI paradigm.

based on ideological interpretations and assume conspiracy. It is fairly clear, however, that the early links in Fig. 1.1 are based on undisputed historical facts whereas the latter links are based on ideological interpretations of historical and current events. The main focus of this book is on the last component of Fig. 1.1, that which concerns the effects of international or imported television on local viewers. However, in order to better understand the role that this component plays in the CI framework, one needs to examine the components that precede it. This chapter briefly reviews each of the building blocks of Fig. 1.1 and the interrelationships among them as advocated by CI.

Conquests and Empires—Setting the Stage

There is no doubt that the history of human civilization is full of wars and conquests. Ever since the dawn of civilization, humans have attacked each other and attempted to control each other (Diamond, 1999). Early on, these conquests occurred on a smaller scale. For example, a tribe attacked another tribe; a village loyal to one prince attacked a neighboring village loyal to another prince (Korman, 1996). These conquests eventually developed into wars that involved organized armies and spanned very large geographical territories (Diamond, 1999). Every time that a group of people felt powerful, they would expand their control over neighboring geographical areas. Organized groups of humans (whether they were tribes, nations, countries, or others) would invade other groups, occupy their lands, kill some, enslave others and impose on the rest their norms, laws, and ways of life (Adams, Langer, Hwa, Stearns, & Wiesner-Hanks, 2000; McNeil, 1987). This pattern of international relations was the unchallenged norm of international behavior (Jacks, 1938; Phillips, 1920; Williams, 1929).

Throughout our history, many of these invasions were very successful at subordinating large groups of people (Diamond, 1999). By doing so, the invaders built their empires. Historians describe in detail the rise and fall of many empires such as the Egyptian, Roman, Ottoman, French, British, and others (Fieldhouse, 1966; Herold, 1963; Inalcik & Quataert, 1994; Rodolfo, 1925; Rowell, 1922). In summary, conquests, wars, empire creation, and predatory behavior have been at the roots of international behavior ever since the dawn of human civilization. This very fact seems to be the source of inspiration for CI advocates' belief that conspiracy underlies the international behaviors of states today.

THE EMERGENCE AND DIFFUSION OF IDEOLOGICAL SEEDS FOR INTERPRETING HUMAN HISTORY

In order to discuss the many events that have shaped human history, historians and critics have adopted labels to represent certain types of historical events. Three of these labels are central for our understanding of the emergence of the CI framework: colonialism, imperialism, and dependency.

Colonialism

The term "colonialism" is a label that has had many meanings in modern history. The origins of the colonialism label can be traced to the establishment of a settlement or colony by one group of humans in a geographical area inhabited by another group of humans (Emerson, 1968). Over time, however, this label has acquired a different meaning: "… the establishment and maintenance, for an extended time, of rule over an alien people that is separate from and subordinate to the ruling power" (Emerson, 1968, p. 1).

The most common meaning of "colonialism" is associated with the European invasions beginning in the 15th century (Emerson, 1968; Roach, 1993). Although there were invasions and conquests for many centuries before European countries emerged as centers of power (Diamond, 1999), the term "colonialism" is fairly confined to the international behavior of countries of Europe.

As with the invasions that preceded them, European conquests brought with them control over the language, teachings, economics, trade, natural resources, norms, values, and other aspects of the group of humans who were colonized (Roach, 1993). Historians report that European colonialism was fueled by theories such as those of Kipling, who believed it was the "white man's burden" to offer civilization to these "backwards" nations (Daalder, 1968, p. 101). The European colonial relationship is said to have been characterized by a civilization with Christian origins, that is, superior technologically and economically, imposing itself on a non-Christian civilization that was inferior materially, economically, and technologically (Emerson, 1968). With total control imposed on them, colonies naturally developed dependencies on the colonizers. These dependencies were facts of life regardless of whether they were intended by the colonizers (Verlinden, 1970).

In addition to labeling the behaviors of European countries that controlled other countries, other labels were also developed to describe the extent of these countries' breadth of control and the effects that this control had on the population living within the controlled territories. Two labels emerged: imperialism and dependency.

Imperialism and Dependency

Imperialism. As a word, it originally comes from the word empire and was inspired by the large-scale invasions that led to the creation of immense centers of power. Most notably it was used to describe the territorial expansion of the French empire under the leadership of Napoleon (Daalder, 1968). During the 19th century, the term *imperialism* was also used to describe a formal policy, first begun by the British, to expand their markets by invading weaker countries and creating colonies (Simnett, 1942). Such expansions were credited for giving the British a powerful economic edge over other European countries. Imperialism was advocated for achieving economic power by many prominent British leaders of the time (Daalder, 1968). The belief that the colonies contributed to the powerful economic edge of the British led other European countries to begin establishing colonies (Daalder, 1968; Townsend, 1941).

In the 20th century, the connotation of the term significantly changed and acquired a negative meaning. Although the expansion of the British and others, through the creation of colonies, was in line with the international behavior of states known until that time, the concept of colonialism progressively came under attack. Scholars, most notably Hobson (1902), spoke vehemently against colonialism. In his book titled *Imperialism* he linked European colonialism to capitalism and economics. At the start of the 20th century Hobson formalized the idea that colonialism was an undesirable state of existence.

In addition to labeling the breadth of control that European countries had over others, the effect of their control was also given a label: Dependency.

Dependency. It is a label that formalizes the relationship between the invader and those invaded. The latter group becomes dependent on the former (Tomlinson, 1991). This type of relationship was present throughout human history, whenever invasions occurred. It gained a particular importance in the 20th century as more observers began conceptualizing the relationships among countries with a critical eye on colonialism. According to these observers, dependency was the means that colonialists used for achieving their economic power: They exploited those whom they had colonized (Galtung, 1971). Building upon Hobson's (1902) work, Lenin (1916) further developed the argument against colonialism and its link to capitalism. In one of his most famous critiques of the United States, Lenin argued that capitalism in its highest monopolistic stage was, in fact, imperialism. He argued that this advanced stage of capitalism, which had taken on the form of "international cartels" was responsible for the current "peculiar epoch of world colonial policy" (Lenin, 1916, p. 235). Lenin drew on the ideas of Marx, who had begun criticizing capitalism in the mid-19th century.

The recording of historical events and reflections on these events allowed observers of international relations to make important links between events and theories. By connecting certain concepts with each other, they were laying down the seeds of a theoretical framework later known as *cultural imperialism*. By the end of World War I, imperialism, colonialism, and capitalism had been linked by those who subscribed to a neo-Marxist ideology. The observers of the time had looked at the trend in international behavior and extracted a type of model that makes certain predictions about international relations. This model that is imbedded in Marxist writing makes the following predictions:

> Powerful countries will invade and exploit others for their own benefits. Their goal is to create empires. They will first attempt to take control over their neighbors. Then they will expand further by taking over other weaker countries. Their military control is designed to put into place a system that later allows the invader to withdraw militarily while still retaining control over the various establishments of the invaded country by creating a dependency. The dependency that remains after military withdrawal benefits the economy of the invader.

In the early 20th century, these observations were not widely disseminated outside their ideological circles and the educated elites. However, as the century progressed, an increasingly larger number of people had the appropriate level of education and could now devote time for thinking about these issues and communicating their thoughts to others in writing. The culmination of these observations about the facts of world history, the behavior of powerful countries, the creation of empires, the motivations of colonialists, and the resulting effects on those who were invaded were utilized to develop an ideological framework for interpreting the international behavior of states during the post World War II era.

IDEOLOGICAL SEEDS AS FRAMES FOR INTERPRETING CONTEMPORARY WORLD EVENTS FOLLOWING WORLD WAR II

The end of World War II ushered in a new international order: The United States emerged as a superpower whereas many of the countries that were powerful before the war suffered significant destruction (Katz & Wedell, 1977). After the war, there

1. THE CI PARADIGM REVISITED

were severe economic disparities among countries. Some were progressively becoming centers of economic activity, others were in desolate conditions. More often than not, countries that were not doing well economically were those that were or had been colonies. Many of the colonizers began letting their colonies gain their independence (Lee, 1980). At about the same time, the United States and the Soviet Union, the world's superpowers of the time, began what has been termed the Cold War (Walker, 1993). Note here that the Soviet Union was built on the ideology of Marx and Lenin. The emergence of the Soviet Union as a world superpower put the ideas of Marx and Lenin in the limelight. Outside the Soviet Union, neo-Marxist schools of thought became quite popular in certain academic circles in both the United States and Latin America. These schools of thought developed an ideological framework based on the work of Marx and Lenin for interpreting contemporary world events.

Following World War II, many observers were concerned about the economic discrepancies among countries. Although some were concerned about how to remedy these economic discrepancies, others set out to explain the reason behind these inequities. The effort of the former led to the development of the modernization hypothesis (Higgott, 1980), whereas the latter resulted in the re-formulation of the dependency hypothesis (Sinclair, 1982).

Modernization: A Misinterpreted Effort

American social scientists were among those who were concerned about the economic discrepancies that were witnessed following World War II. They believed that the inequities could be remedied if developing countries adopted the more developed nations' technologies and ways of life, thus modernizing themselves (Berger, 1974; McAnany, Schnitman, & Janus, 1981). The idea of modernization was conceived by American social scientists and was supported and funded by the U.S. government (Katz & Wedell, 1977). It was thought that the prevailing cultures in underdeveloped countries prevented them from moving ahead. Therefore, an immediate goal of modernization was to alter the cultural fabric of countries that were in need of economic development. For modernization, the mass media were the chosen tools for social change (Berger, 1974; Wells, 1972). Modernization assumed a powerful media effect (discussed later): It concentrated on the "internal social processes" (Fejes, 1981, p. 283) of the developing countries and assumed that all individuals in the country would be strongly effected by mass media. Such was a popular view of American social science at the time that modernization was being promoted.

For conspiracy theorists, however, many aspects of the modernization effort were framed and interpreted using Marxist ideology (McQuail, 1987). Conspiracy theorists began looking for evidence that would confirm their suspicions that, consistent with the European colonial goals that preceded them, modernization efforts were somehow self-serving to the United States. The critics of modernization used their knowledge of pre-World War II trends in international behaviors to frame and interpret the efforts of the United States. They saw striking similarities between the assertion by modernization advocates that efforts should be concentrated on changing the cultures of developing countries and those of colonialists who advocated similar goals. Colonial states were perceived by conspiracy theorists to have plotted against the people that they controlled for the benefit of their own economies. By association, critics also perceived the United States as conspiring against those countries where modernization efforts were taking place for the benefits of the U.S. economy.

Conspiracy theorists looked at the activities of American social scientists who were involved in modernization efforts and were suspicious about the objectives of their studies. American social scientists were closely following the progress of modernization efforts. They did so by collecting quantitative data to monitor the effects of the modernization interventions on the beliefs and behaviors of the residents of less-developed countries. Critics saw these data collection efforts as evidence of collusion between the United States government and the social scientists associated with the modernization programs for the purpose of controlling the minds of the people in the countries where these programs were implemented (Schiller, 1983). American social scientists were accused of being "more interested in individual actions and reactions than in the overall social system and its communication fabric" (Beltran, 1976, p. 116). Analysis of the effect of mass media on individual viewers was seen by critics as a tool for fostering American economic superiority by making "findings about the less powerful ... available to the more powerful" (Schiller, 1983, p. 256). In summary, the modernization efforts were misinterpreted and rejected.

Whereas American social scientists focused on using modernization techniques to remedy the economic discrepancies following World War II, others set out to explain the reason for the prevailing economic discrepancies and focused specifically on Latin America. Led by Latin American observers, critics began using the early concept of dependency for framing and interpreting more contemporary events occurring in Latin America. They extended the concept of "dependency" to encompass an explanation of the prevailing economic discrepancies and also as an interpretation of the modernization efforts undertaken by the United States.

An Extension of the Concept of Dependency

The first attempts to challenge the goals of modernization theory came from Latin America. It is not surprising that Latin America was the source of this challenge. Given the expectation that powerful countries always conquered their weaker neighbors, and because the United States had emerged after World War II as a super power, its Latin American neighbors became quite fearful of being invaded. Modernization efforts were perceived by Latin American observers as an attempt by the United States to achieve influence by changing the cultural fabric of Latin America, not for the sake of improving the lives of Latin American people, but for the purpose of making these people dependent on the United States (McAnany et al., 1981;

Nordenstreng & Schiller, 1979). This interpretation was reached through the looking glass of conspiracy theory.

As a result, a movement of resistance emerged and focused on the need to free Latin America from what was perceived to be attempts by the United States to control it. Latin American academics rejected modernization theory and all that was associated with it. They also rejected the methodologies and quantitative analytic techniques that American social scientists had been utilizing (Curran, Guerevitch, Woollacott, Marriott, & Roberts, 1977).

Latin American academics and their U.S. colleagues decided to adopt a totally different paradigm for conceptualizing and interpreting the modernization efforts. They chose a Marxist critical–cultural approach, and drew on the work of Althusser, Gramsci, and the Frankfort School (Roach, 1997). This critical–cultural paradigm resulted in conceptualizing modernization as an effort to formalize dependency. "The dependency model can be seen as a counterpart of earlier theories of imperialism, particularly the Marxist–Leninist concept of imperialism, reformulated from the point of view of the underdeveloped countries" (Fejes, 1981, p. 284). By the mid-20th century, conspiracy theorists had yet another international development to contend with: widely diffused electronic communication.

The Electronic Media as Tools for Control

Although Marx had written his thoughts before the advent of electronic mass media, his ideas about capitalism and his approach for analyzing international events were adopted by Latin American scholars for framing and interpreting the role and effects of modern communications. A group of academics were central to the formalization of these neo-Marxist analytic approaches. They belonged to the Frankfort School, which stemmed from Marxism, and comprised German theorists who fled to the United States during World War II. Members of this school sought to explain why the "revolutionary social change predicted by Marx" did not occur. In doing so, they analyzed the mass media as a means through which economic change within developing countries was being prevented (McQuail, 1987, p. 65). Members of the Frankfort School believed that mass media could be used to eliminate diversity in an audience by "homogeniz[ing it] into [an] unthinking mass" (Fiske, 1986, p. 392).

The Marxist approach to media analysis adopted by dependency theorists focused on "attempting to detect the ideologies of the communicators behind the manifest content of their mass media messages [and] taking these as expressions of the pro-status quo interests of the power structures that dominate society" (Beltran, 1976, p. 127). Such an approach ignored the analysis of the effects of media on individuals, which was the methodological approach used by American social scientists. It rather concentrated on the analysis of media flow and the messages embedded within the content of media. Conspiracy was assumed to be the main motivation for the exportation of U.S. television programs and efforts were concentrated on revealing their underlying messages.

Critics uncovered capitalist values within American media content (Dorfman & Mattelart, 1975; Goldsen & Bibliowicz, 1976). They believed that these values would be instilled in the foreign audiences who consumed such media by the mere fact that these values were present in the programs that filled the schedules of local television channels. This type of analysis was often referred to as the critical–cultural approach.

The critical–cultural school of thought linked American economic prosperity and capitalism and U.S. involvement in Latin America with the large influx of American mass media into Latin America. By relying on Marxist theories of economic determinism, supporters drew a direct link between the quantity of American mass media being exported and the way an "American world hegemony" (Schilller, 1978, p.185) was maintained. Dependency theorists believed that capitalism was supported and maintained by the cultural influences of developing countries brought up through modern communications (Roach, 1997). In contrast to the functional analytic approaches of American social scientists, Latin American scholars used structural analysis to interpret the economic discrepancies among nations in the postwar era. This resulted in a modern conception of dependency theory: Developed countries act intentionally to keep developing countries in economically and politically inferior positions for the benefit of the developed countries (Fejes, 1981). Electronic media play a major role in perpetuating the dependency.

To summarize, dependency theory was re-formulated as a Latin American reaction to a perceived American influence in the form of (a) modernization efforts, (b) efforts by American social scientists to quantify the effects of modernization efforts by studying individuals receiving modernization messages, and (c) the widespread presence of U.S. media content in Latin American countries. Dependency was perceived to be a function of a conspiracy for controlling Latin American countries remotely through American mass media. Those who subscribed to this perspective looked for evidence about the motives of the United States consistent with their points of view.

MEDIA POWER AND TRANSNATIONAL CORPORATIONS: FEEDING THE FEARS OF CONSPIRACY THEORISTS

In the post World War II era, the United States also emerged as a major producer of audio-visual products. By the late 1940s, television had become a mass medium in the United States. Without a context, these facts, by themselves, should not have been a source of concern to international observers. However, in the first decade of the 20th century, new theories about the effects of mass communication had emerged. The most notable of these theories contended that mass mediated messages, especially those transmitted audio-visually, had strong and homogenous effects on those who received them (Sproule, 1989). This "strong effects" theory, which was developed in the United States, had gained credibility during both World War I and World War II, when many countries spent considerable money and effort developing engines of propaganda (DeFleur & Ball-Rokeach, 1989; Roetter, 1974). Governments were convinced that mass communication could be used as a weapon against the enemy. Believers in this theory also existed outside of government. They reasoned that because the government was spending so much money and effort for using communication as a weapon against the enemy, this theory must be true.

Between the 1950s and 1970s, the era of audiovisual mass communication progressively flourished worldwide as, in most countries, television stations began broadcasting to local audiences. Television stations required content to fill their schedules. As most countries were not capable of producing enough local television programs, they resorted to importing television content from the United States (Noam, 1993). By the 1970s, most countries had a substantial proportion of their television schedules filled with programs produced in the United States (Nordenstreng & Varis, 1974).

The U.S. exportation of television programs was seen by critics as additional evidence of a conspiracy to control developing countries (Masmoudi, 1979; Schiller, 1983). The flow of media from the United States to developing countries was interpreted by using the dependency frame developed before the Second World War but reformulated by subscribers to the critical–cultural school of thought.

At the same time that the United States was exporting TV programs, American and European companies were exporting another type of business: the transnational corporation (Mattelart, 1983). A transnational corporation is a business entity headquartered in one country that branches out into other countries for the purpose of selling a product or service. The vast majority of early transnational corporations were American and European. They were seen by critics as another piece of the conspiracy by primarily the United States for achieving world control (McAnany et al., 1981). Critics who subscribed to this point of view reasoned as follows: After influencing the local inhabitants with their television programs and convincing them to adopt the American ways of life, the United States sends its transnational corporations to take their country's natural resources, convinces them to provide cheap labor for manufacturing U.S. goods, sells these same products back to them and brings the profits back to the United States (Masmoudi, 1979; Salinas & Paldan, 1979). Conspiracy was the frame through which critics interpreted everything that the United States was doing.

From Neo-Colonialism to Cultural Imperialism

From the early writings of Hobson, imperialism has been linked to dependency. In the early 20th century, countries labeled as imperialistic, such as Great Britain, began to let go of their colonies. Structural theories of imperialism were established. According to these theories, there are "Center Nations" and "Periphery Nations" and the Center nations maintain relationships with the Periphery nations that benefit the Center nations (Galtung, 1971, p. 81). These relationships have been characterized by unequal flows of goods. To ensure its economic prosperity, a Center nation keeps its Periphery nations dependent on it and by doing so maintains the economic inequalities (Wallerstein, 1979).

After World War II, when colonialism was brought to an end, economic disparities among states remained. The idea of neo-colonialism was born. It was argued that through neo-colonialism, the colonial relationships of the past were maintained through forms subtler than forceful military control. In the past, colonial powers had instilled their cultures on the people within their colonies. This act may have been partly due to a feeling of obligation to help a "backwards" culture and it could have resulted from a desire to maintain "remote control" over their colonies. During the post-World War II period, the United States was exporting large quantities of mass media. This one-way flow of media was seen by critics as an effort to create neo-colonialism through electronic media. For believers in conspiracy theory, the simple presence of U.S. television programs in domestic television schedules was equated with cultural influence.

THE EFFECTS OF TELEVISION AS SEEN THROUGH THE CULTURAL IMPERIALISM FRAMEWORK

The theory of cultural imperialism is derived through the linking of several circumstances occurring at specific points in time within the ideological framework established by certain schools of thought. Supporters of cultural imperialism theory study the relationships among nations on a macro level. Doing so leads to the discovery of two important contentions of cultural imperialism theory with respect to imported TV:

1. Flow of media is indicative of the exporter's desire to affect and control the developing nation that receives this media.
   This belief has been fueled by an interpretation of the historical events summarized in this chapter.
2. Presence of media content is equated with strong effects on the people who consume this media content.

Interestingly, this belief was borrowed from the hypodermic model or magic bullet theory that had helped conceive modernization theory. By the 1950s, this theory was deemed invalid by the American social scientists who developed it. However, supporters of cultural imperialism theory still rely on the assumptions of the magic bullet theory (Tracey, 1985).

Linking these two contentions along with the emergence of transnational corporations leads to cultural imperialism theory: Western powers (mainly the United States) export mass media to developing countries with the deliberate intention of corroding the traditional cultures of these countries and convincing the people of these countries to adopt Western cultural values which will lead to their purchase of Western products (Salinas & Paldan, 1979).

1. THE CI PARADIGM REVISITED

The theory of cultural imperialism gained prominence in the 1970s, as Third World nations fought to resist attack on their indigenous cultures by preventing the excessive influx of American media. The Non-Aligned movement was created to maintain the cultural integrity of these nations and the UNESCO studies were commissioned to examine the international communication flow (Gunter, 1978).

Summarizing the various concerns expressed about imported TV programs, Lee (1980) concluded that the vast majority of critics widely believe that the values embodied in these programs will indeed influence the values structures of audience members. Those who are fearful of this influence claim that, as a result of the spread of crossborder media, "the indigenous cultures of the Third World disintegrate consistently and without resistance" (Goonasekara, 1987, p. 11). Others believe that international television is used by industrialized countries as a device to broaden their domestic commercial activities (Hadad, 1978). Hadad (1978) asserted that this goal is best achieved "by launching a 'cultural invasion' of developing nations" (p. 19). The vast majority of authors who have published articles about this topic hold these beliefs about de facto effects of foreign television. The influence assumption has prompted them to be suspicious of any imported TV programs, including those that are educational. Commenting about the importation of Sesame Street into Latin America, Goldsen and Bibliowicz (1976) stated that it will "lay down an important part of the cultural scaffolding that Latin American children will build on. They expose the continent's children to a massive cultural assault whose consequences are incalculable" (p. 125).

Goonasekara (1987) contended that CI refers to an effect that stems from the documented flow of television programs from Western countries into Third World television schedules. Critics of imported TV programs use the term CI to label a process of influence and the influence that is assumed to result from such a process. The contentions of CI are at the roots of all international legislation to protect indigenous cultures from influence through foreign television. The CI arguments are also used as a basis for international debates and resolutions about the same topic (for a discussion of these debates, see McPhail, 1987). In addition to focusing on the role of television and other media, it is worth noting that more recent CI research efforts have centered on using the CI framework for studying the effects of interpersonal communication contact between Westerners and non-Westerners through such means as travel, education, missionary work, and others (Sreberny-Mohammadi, 1997).

Extracting the Assumptions of Cultural Imperialism Relevant to Imported Television

By examining the interacting developments that have led to the formulation of the cultural imperialism paradigm, we are now able to extract its assumptions about the role and effect of imported television:

1. Imported television programs present in domestic television schedules are placed there as part of a conspiracy against the local population. These TV

programs are used to lure viewers and entice them to watch content that has foreign cultural values imbedded within it;
2. The object of this conspiracy is to erode the local values and replace them with those imbedded in the foreign TV content;
3. This foreign TV content is then imposed on local viewers;
4. The foreign TV content has strong effects on those who watch it;
5. The ample presence of foreign TV content in domestic television schedules is evidence of the conspiracy;
6. Associations between exposure to foreign TV content and adoption of foreign attitudes, behaviors, and the like on the part of local residents are further evidence of the conspiracy.

As noted at the beginning of this chapter, it is beyond the scope of this book to test out the contentions that have led to the CI paradigm. CI proponents contend that international television programs have powerful (strong and homogenous) effects on the local viewers who are exposed to them. The focus of this book is on determining the impact of international television as revealed by the empirical literature. Are the empirical research results consistent with CI's contentions about the power of international TV? Is CI a useful paradigm for explaining and predicting the effects of imported TV on local viewers? In the next chapters, several researchers examine these questions from multiple dimensions.

REFERENCES

Adams, P. V., Langer, E. D., Hwa, L., Stearns, P. N., & Wiesner-Hanks, M. E. (2000). *Experiencing world history*. New York: New York University Press.
Beltran, L. R. (1976). Alien premises, objects and methods in Latin American communications research. *Communications Research, 3*(2), 107–134.
Beltran, L. R. (1978). Communication and cultural domination: USA–Latin American case. *Media Asia, 5,* 183–192.
Berger, P. L. (1974). *Pyramids of sacrifice: Political ethics and social change.* New York: Basic Books.
Curran, J., Guerevitch, M., Woollacott, J., Marriott, J., & Roberts, C. (1977). *Mass communication and society.* Beverly Hills, CA: Sage Publications.
Daalder, H. (1968). Imperialism. *International encyclopedia of the social sciences* (pp. 101–109). New York: Macmillan & The Free Press.
DeFleur, M. L., & Ball-Rokeach, S. (1989). *Theories of mass communication.* New York: Longman.
Diamond, J. (1999). *Guns, germs and steel.* New York: Norton.
Dorfman, A., & Mattelart, A. (1975). *How to read Donald Duck: Imperialism ideology in the Disney comic* (D. Kunzle, Trans.). New York: International General. (Original work published 1971)
Elasmar, M. G., & Hunter, J. E. (1997). The impact of foreign TV on a domestic audience: A meta-analysis. *Communication Yearbook, 20,* 47–69.
Emerson, R. (1968). Colonialism: Political aspects. *International Encyclopedia of the Social Sciences* (pp. 1–6). New York: Macmillan & The Free Press.
Fejes, F. (1981). Media imperialism: An assessment. *Media, Culture, & Society, 3,* 281–289.

Fieldhouse, D. K. (1966). *The colonial empires: A comparative survey from the eighteenth century.* New York: Delacorte Press.
Fiske, J. (1986). Television: polysemy and popularity. *Critical Studies in Mass Communication, 3*(4), 391–408.
Galtung, J. (1971). A structural theory of imperialism. *Journal of Peace Research, 8*(2), 81–117.
Goldsen, R. K., & Bibliowicz, A. (1976). Plaza Sesamo: "Neutral" language or "cultural assault." *Journal of Communication, 26*(2), 124–125.
Goonasekara, A. (1987). The influence of television on cultural values—With special reference to Third World countries. *Media Asia, 14,* 7–12.
Gunter, J. (1978). An introduction to the great debate. *Journal of Communication, 28,* 141–156.
Hadad, I. (1978). Media and international misunderstanding. *Phaedrus, 5,* 17–19.
Herold, J. C. (1963). *The age of Napoleon.* New York: American Heritage.
Higgott, R. A. (1980). From modernization theory to public policy: Continuity and change in the political science of political development. *Studies in Comparative International Development, 15*(4), 26–58.
Hobson, J. A. (1902). *Imperialism: A study.* London: Allen & Unwin.
Inalcik, H., & Quataert, D. (Eds.). (1994). *An economic and social history of the Ottoman empire, 1300–1914.* New York: Cambridge University Press.
Jacks, L. P. (1938). *Co-operation or coercion? The League at the crossways.* London: Heinemann.
Katz, E., & Wedell, G. (1977). *Broadcasting in the Third World.* Cambridge, MA: Harvard University Press.
King, A. D. (1997). *Culture, globalization, and the world-system: Contemporary conditions for the representation of identity.* Minneapolis: University of Minnesota Press.
Korman, S. (1996). *The right of conquest: The acquisition of territory by force in international law and practice.* New York: Oxford University Press.
Lee, C. (1980). *Media imperialism reconsidered: The homogenizing of television culture.* Beverly Hills, CA: Sage.
Lenin, V. I. (1916). *Imperialism, the highest stage of capitalism (abridged)* in *Lenin on the United States* (pp. 210–287). New York: International Publishers.
Masmoudi, M. (1979). The new world information order. *Journal of Communication, 29,* 172–185.
Mattelart, A. (1983). *Transnationals and the Third World: The struggle for culture* (D. Buxton, Trans.). South Hadley, MA: Bergin & Garvey.
McAnany, E. G., Schnitman, J., & Janus, M. (1981). *Communication and social structure.* New York: Praeger.
McNeil, W. H. (1987). *A history of the human community: Prehistory to the present* (2nd ed.). Englewood, NJ: Prentice-Hall.
McPhail, T. L. (1987). *Electronic colonialism: The future of international broadcasting and communication.* Newbury Park, CA: Sage.
McQuail, D. (1987). *Mass communication theory: An introduction.* Beverly Hill, CA: Sage.
Noam, E. M. (1993). Media Americanization, national culture and forces of integration. In E. M. Noam & J. C. Millonzi (Eds.), *The international market in film and television programs* (pp. 41–58). Norwood, NJ: Ablex.
Nordenstreng, K., & Schiller, H. I. (1979). *National sovereignty and international communication.* Norwood, NJ: Ablex.
Nordenstreng, K., & Varis, T. (1974). Television traffic—A one-way street. *Reports and Papers on Mass Communication,* No. 70. Paris: UNESCO.

Phillips, W. A. (1920). *The confederation of Europe; A study of the European alliance, 1813–1823, as an experiment in the International Organization of Peace.* London: Longmans, Green.
Roach, C. (1993). *Communication and culture in war and peace.* Newbury Park, CA: Sage.
Roach, C. (1997). Cultural imperialism and resistance in media theory and literary theory. *Media, Culture, and Society, 19*(1), 47–66.
Rodolfo, L. (1925). *Ancient and modern Rome.* Boston: Marshall Jones.
Roetter, C. (1974). *The art of psychological warfare, 1914–1945.* New York: Stein & Day.
Rowell, N. W. (1922). *The British empire and world peace; Being the Burwash Memorial Lectures, delivered in Convocation Hall, University of Toronto, November, 1921, by the Hon. Newton W. Rowell.* Toronto: College Press.
Salinas, R., & Paldan, L. (1979). Culture in the process of dependent development: Theoretical perspectives. In K. Nordenstreng & H. I. Schiller (Eds.), *National sovereignty and international communication* (pp. 82–98). Norwood, NJ: Ablex.
Schiller, H. I. (1976). *Communication and cultural domination.* Armonk, NY: International Arts and Sciences Press.
Schiller, H. I. (1978). Computer systems: Power for whom and for what? *Journal of Communication, 28*(4), 184–193.
Schiller, H. I. (1983). Critical research in the information age. *Journal of Communication, 33*(3), 249–257.
Schiller, H. I. (1991). Not yet the post-imperialist era. *Critical Studies in Mass Communication, 8,* 13–28.
Simnett, W. E. (1942). *The British colonial empire.* New York: Norton.
Sinclair, J. (1982, February). From "modernization" to cultural dependence: Mass communication studies and the Third World. *Media Information Australia, 23,* 12–18.
Sproule, J. M. (1989). Progressive propaganda critics and the magic bullet myth. *Critical Studies in Mass Communication, 6*(3), 225–246.
Sreberny-Mohammadi, A. (1997). The many faces of imperialism. In P. Golding & P. Harris (Eds.), *Beyond cultural imperialism* (pp. 48–68). Thousand Oaks, CA: Sage.
Tomlinson, J. (1991). *Cultural imperialism.* Baltimore: Johns Hopkins University Press.
Townsend, M. E. (1941). *European colonial expansion since 1871.* Chicago: Lippincott.
Tracey, M. (1985). The poisoned chalice? International television and the idea of dominance. *Proceedings of the American Academy of Arts and Sciences, USA, 114,* 17–56.
Verlinden, C. (1970). *The beginnings of modern colonization.* Ithaca, NY: Cornell University Press.
Walker, M. (1993). *The Cold War: A history.* New York: Henry Holt.
Wallerstein, I. (1979). *The capitalist world economy.* Cambridge, UK: Cambridge University Press.
Wells, A. (1972). *Picture tube imperialism.* Maryknoll, NY: Orbis Books.
Williams, J. F. (1929). *Chapters on current international law and the League of Nations.* London: Longmans, Green.

CHAPTER

2

Impacts of Cross-Cultural Mass Media In Iceland, Northern Minnesota, and Francophone Canada in Retrospect

David E. Payne
Sam Houston State University

This chapter is an overview with the perspective of time. It lacks some of the sharp detail of intense contemporary involvement and puts broad ideas in perspective, and, it is hoped, adds the richness and appreciation that comes with a little distance.

This chapter summarizes research done 15 or more years ago, and makes a few observations that are tempered by time. Because it summarizes dozens of variables and several papers, detailed exposition of the individual variables and their reliability and validity is not included in this chapter. The information for each variable is available in the original reports.

DATA SETS EMPLOYED

The following is a summary from data gathered in three settings: Iceland, Northern Minnesota, and Quebec. This chapter draws extensively from the original studies (Broddason, 1970; Dunn & Josepsson, 1972; Payne, 1978a, 1978b; Payne & Caron, 1982, 1983; Payne & Peake, 1977) and does not give detailed reference to them in each paragraph.

Icelandic data that were analyzed came from two sources. The first source was a study initially conducted by Thorbjörn Broddason with preliminary results made available by the University of Iceland Press in 1970. The second source was a study by Thomas Dunn and Bragi Josepsson with partial results reported to the National

Science Foundation in 1972. Data from these two projects were reanalyzed, compared, and reported in 1977 and 1978.

The second set of data comes from Northern Minnesota. Data were gathered by sociology methods students and the author in 1977 and were first published in 1978. The third set of data was collected in Quebec in late 1979 by sociology students and professional interviewers under the direction of Dr. André Caron and the author and analyzed and first reported in 1980. Each of these data sets show a common design characteristic. Exposure to television signals was controlled by geographic location, not viewer choice. In those days when direct satellite broadcast was mostly a glint in homeowners' and media moguls' eyes, it was possible to select matched areas, some of which had TV signals available and some of which did not. Respondents from these areas could be matched and differences in their information levels, attitudes, and behaviors attributed to television affects isolated from the contamination of self-selected viewing and all the predispositional, economic, and class baggage that accompanies those differences. With a little careful site selection, the impact of one culture's television could be examined as it spilled over into other cultures' reception areas. Today, because of direct satellite broadcast, such naturally controlled studies can only be conducted by examining the impact of media from developed countries on the most underdeveloped countries. This introduces a whole new set of methodological complications.

Iceland Studies

Two sets of data providing material about cross-cultural mass media impact were gathered in Iceland, one by Thorbjörn Broddason and one by Thomas Dunn and Bragi Josepsson. This data was recoded and reanalyzed. This analysis was then compared with the original analysis. Broddason's data were from 601 Icelanders ages 10 to 14. They came from three locations, one received no television (Akureyri), one U.S. TV only (Vestmannaeyjar), and one both U.S. and recently initiated Icelandic TV (Reykjavik). The author's reanalysis of the Broddason data used four indicators of exposure to U.S. TV (geographic availability of signal, length of TV ownership, frequency of watching, and name recognition of U.S. programs). Correlations between these independent variable measures varied from .4 to .61 and the geographic location was most central to the underlying variable. Dependent variables included positive attitude toward the United States (desire to immigrate to the United States), knowledge of U.S. political leaders compared to those not covered on U.S. TV, and feelings of fear, anger, or sadness that Broddason had hypothesized would be produced by U.S. TV. In each case after the analysis had been performed on the total sample, a separate analysis was conducted for each age, gender, and socioeconomic group, and no substantial differences were found between the findings in each of these subgroups or the total sample.

The Dunn–Josepsson data were collected from 1,314 young people between the ages of 9 and 17 in areas that were supposed to have no Icelandic TV (Northwest) or only Icelandic TV (Southwest). Although the data about sampling are less clear in this study, almost 70% of the people living in the no-TV area reported having TVs in their homes for over a year. Further analysis indicated that many of these locations could receive U.S. television from an American air base in Iceland. Rather than being non-Icelandic TV-receiving locations, they were probably U.S. TV-receiving locations. Icelandic TV was just beginning to be received in a few of these areas and probably played a much less important role.

Eliminating from the Broddason sample those who had actually visited the United States, there was some indication that high viewing of United States TV was associated with preference for the U.S. as a migration site ($Tau_b = .12\ p < .05$) but this was not true for all measures of the independent variable and, therefore, should be accepted with caution (Payne & Peake, 1977). Dunn and Josepsson measured positive attitude toward the United States using an adjective checklist. Thirteen of 60 possible relationships were statistically significant ($p < .05$), but the relationships were weak with none exceeding .08 (Tau_b), which again indicated the marginal nature of TV's influence in this study. Further, the attitude shifts were about equally split between positive and negative (Payne, 1978). A careful analysis of signals available at their sites suggests a reinterpretation of their data indicating that watching U.S. TV may have a slight negative effect on attitudes about Americans (Payne, 1978a, p. 179).

The author's analysis of the Broddason data indicated a very slight and irregular positive effect of U.S. TV watching on knowledge of leaders covered on U.S. TV (Payne & Peake, 1977). The Dunn–Josepsson data about information acquisition indicated that there was no consistent evidence that watching U.S. TV was related to knowledge of political leaders. Given the tenuous nature of the finding in the Broddason data, perhaps Dunn and Josepsson's conclusions are the most accurate ones about information acquisition from the Icelandic data.

Using the Broddason data we also addressed the question of whether U.S. TV produced feelings of fear, anger, or sadness in viewers. Broddason reported that watching U.S. TV was related to increased levels of fear in young males only. As this is reported by only 13 of 466 possible cases, it should not be over-interpreted. However, the most surprising result from the data was that such feelings were reported more commonly among those viewing the recently inaugurated Icelandic than U.S. TV. We proposed that Icelandic TV, because of its language familiarity, might have had more influence. It is also possible that, because it had only been in operation a few months, those viewing it (and TV) for the first time were more affected than their more media-experienced, American media-viewing countrymen.

The Minnesota Study

Data were obtained in rural northern Minnesota from three matched (age, income, occupation, education, religion, ethnic origin) sites; one received only Canadian TV, one received both Canadian and U.S. TV, and one received only U.S. TV. An interview was conducted with one adult in each household in the selected areas.

Completion rates for the three areas were between 90% and 92% (n = 414). In addition the questionnaire was given to all 9th, 10th, and 11th-grade students in attendance on a given day in four area high schools. Completion rate was 88% (n = 280). Migration into these rural areas was very low, hence most respondents had spent most of their lives in the same location.

Three independent variables were employed: geographic location, percentage of time viewing Canadian TV, and percentage of time viewing Canadian news programs. The last two variables allowed media viewing variation in the geographic area that received both U.S. and Canadian signals, but introduced self-selection as a confounding effect. The correlations (r) between the three independent variable measures ranged from .84 to .76.

The development of dependent variables was much more extensive and sophisticated in this study than in either of the Icelandic studies. Cognitive and affective measures relating to the sending country (Canada), the receiving country (United States), and both countries were employed.

In the cognitive area, respondents were asked to name the most important issues facing each country and both countries (the number of issues named was coded as a cognitive measure and the relative placement of them as an agenda setting measure); then to select which was most important for each setting; then to provide some facts about the issue, people involved, and possible solutions. They were also asked to identify the American meaning of seven Canadian words.

In the attitudinal area the author used a large number of scales, many of which had been developed and employed by Sparks (1977) and M. McCombs (personal communication, 1976) in their studies in New York and Ontario. They measured shift in national identification, attitudes toward ethnic groups in countries, agenda setting (open ended and paired comparison), and a variety of cultural items such as attitudes about nudity and violence, socialized medicine, and government-supported housing, which had been proposed in the literature as being different in U.S. and Canadian cultures. A detailed analysis of all questions and their reliability is provided by Payne (1978) and is beyond the scope of this chapter.

Twenty-four control variables organized in three areas (other exposure to Canadian media, other exposure to Canada, and socioeconomic status) were employed. Correlation analysis was conducted with 0 order and 24th order partial correlations reported with significant other partial data commented on.

The data indicate that there was a minimal affect for adults and high school students on cognitive measures relating to the United States (reception country) with only 2 of 12 relationships being above .1 (r). The majority of these small correlations were negative. However, moderate affects were found on cognitive measures about Canada (sending country) with all 18 possible correlations being above .22, eight above .32, and the highest .51. Correlations relating to cognitive issues relating the two countries were generally between those for the separate countries. Tests of significance were not calculated because a population rather than a sample was interviewed, but if significance tests had been used, all of the cognitive variable relationships relating to knowledge of Canada and most of them relating to knowledge of the two countries would have been significant. The application of the 24 control variables had minimal effect on any of the relationships except for the recognition of the American equivalent of Canadian words among high school students, where the relationship was substantially reduced by listening to Canadian radio that provided the same information.

Generally speaking, the adult sample attitudes toward the United States were unaffected by watching Canadian TV, with the following exceptions. Those who watched Canadian TV were slightly more favorable toward blacks than those who watched American TV, and there was some difference in the importance given to specific issues by watchers of Canadian and U.S. TV. These data give some support to the notion that media set people's agendas and that U.S. media portray blacks in an unfavorable light. Viewing Canadian TV was somewhat more related to attitudes about Canada, but generally speaking, attitudinal differences were still not strong. Adult viewers of Canadian TV were somewhat less favorable toward Canada ($r = .13$) and had moderately different views about the most important issue facing Canada ($r = .29$ to $.36$ depending on the independent variable). Insertion of control variables had little effect on the correlations.

For the high school population, the correlations were less consistent and more susceptible to controls. Correlations relating to the United States were all small and not substantively significant. Correlations relating to attitudes about Canada did, however, show some important relationships. Viewers of Canadian TV had more negative evaluations of Canada ($r = .27$ to $.39$) and these increased with the addition of the controls. They also had slightly more negative attitudes about French and English Canadians. Finally, like their adult counterparts, they had different views about the most important issue facing Canada ($r = .24$ to $.34$).

Two final comments on the Minnesota study are useful. Moderate affects were found relating to cognitions and attitudes about Canada despite the fact that at the time 36% of the material being transmitted over Canadian TV came from the United States. If the material had all been of Canadian origin the effect on viewers' knowledge and attitudes about Canada could have been stronger. Second, it may be possible that the lack of affect from watching Canadian TV on attitudes and cognitions about the United States results from the 36% of U.S. material that was broadcast over Canadian TV. Thus, they were getting substantial American media exposure from Canada. If the content of Canadian TV had been all-Canadian there might have been stronger effects relating to the United States.

The Quebec Study

The Quebec study built on the Minnesota study and used many of the same measures translated into French and adapted to local cultural circumstances. Data were gathered in September of 1979. Two demographically matched cities were selected, one that had only Francophone television and one that had Francophone and

Anglophone Canadian and American television available over cable. A systematic random sample of persons over 18 years of age in each city was selected and 814 usable interviews were collected (89% return rate).

One measure of TV use grouped viewers into those who had only Francophone TV available in their city, those who had signals of both languages in their city but only Francophone in their homes, and those who had both language TV signals in their homes. Other TV-use measures included percentage of time viewing U.S. TV and percentage of time viewing Anglophone Canadian TV. The range of independent variables was expanded in this study to other media. These measures were language of radio listened to and magazines and newspapers read.

Controls were employed for visiting or having relatives or friends in Anglophone Canada or the United States, familiarity with English, and socioeconomic status.

Measures of knowledge and attitudes were similar to those used in the Minnesota study except they were extended to Quebec and Europe as well as the United States and Canada. In addition, semantic differential items measuring the evaluation, activity, and potency dimensions, and five items that measured relative preference for Francophone, Anglophone, or American cultural features were included. Discussion of reliability and other statistical issues is contained in Payne and Caron (1982).

The relationship between media use (Francophone, Anglophone, American) and the dependent variables was examined separately for each medium except newspapers where use of the Anglophone medium was minimal. The composite relationship of media to dependent variables was then compared with the relationships resulting from socioeconomic background and from intercultural interpersonal contact.

Nine of 18 relationships between viewing non-Francophone television (geographically determined measure) and knowledge variables were statistically significant ($p < .05$), and all but one of these dealt with non-Quebec people or issues. The correlations were low (r from .1 to .06) and almost all became nonstatistically significant when controls were introduced. Thus, there appears to be little to no effect of increasing knowledge about the United States, Canada, and Europe from having available non-Francophone television.

Availability of non-Francophone TV was positively and significantly related to 6 of 12 attitudes toward Canada and 8 of 16 toward the United States but only 1 of 12 toward Quebec measures. Those with non-Francophone TV available tended to see Canada and the United States more favorably than those who did not. The correlations, though statistically significant, were low (r values between .06 and .12) and were further diminished by controls with only half as many remaining statistically significant.

The same basic pattern appeared to hold when using percentage of time viewing U.S. TV as the independent variable. The strongest relationships were with willingness to select American rather than Francophone Canadian food, entertainment, and lodging alternatives.

Correlations between listening to Anglophone radio and the various measures of cognition and attitudes were rare, nonsystematic, and small. It was concluded that they were probably the result of chance.

Two thirds of the correlations between reading Anglophone information magazines and knowledge indicators were significant. As with television, these relationships clustered around knowledge of the United States and Europe. Only about a fifth of the relationships between reading English language magazines and attitudes were statistically significant and the rather small correlations were further reduced by the addition of controls.

The multiple correlations between the combined media measures and each dependent variable were also calculated. Ten of the 18 relating to the knowledge dimension were significant, four of four for the United States, three of four for Europe, two of four for Canada, and only one of four for Quebec. This supports the notion that media have the largest impact on information about less familiar areas. However, when controls are added only two of the correlations remain significant and the highest multiple correlation is .10. Thus, affects that cannot be explained by status and interpersonal contact are small and mostly tied to television. Fewer of the multiple correlations with attitudes were significant, the level of association was smaller and more completely eliminated by controls; thus, it is concluded that the influence not explainable by status, and interpersonal contact is even smaller.

This finding led to the conclusion that a separate analysis should be conducted to determine the relative impact of media, interpersonal contact, and socioeconomic status on different types of dependent variables. Data from both the Minnesota and the Quebec studies were relevant to this question.

In both studies, cross-cultural media exposure had more impact on agenda ranking than did interpersonal contact. Intercultural media was also more strongly related to international information acquisition than interpersonal contact in the Minnesota study but less strongly in the Quebec study. The Minnesota data show little intercultural media or interpersonal contact effect on attitudes, but the Quebec data show both, with the media exposure being slightly stronger. None of the differences between intercultural media and intercultural interpersonal exposure was striking.

The impact of socioeconomic status on all the dependent variables was also examined. For the Quebec study, the effect of familiarity with the English language was examined. Generally speaking, socioeconomic status in both studies was related to the amount of information respondents acquire, to their attitudes, and to a lesser degree, to their agendas. In the Quebec study where language was an important variable, it was also associated with the full range of variables. The effects of language and socioeconomic status were, generally speaking, stronger or as strong as those of media or interpersonal contact.

In the Quebec study, controlling for language does not significantly reduce the effects of status indicating separate effects. However, when language and status are controlled for, the effects of interpersonal and media cross-cultural contact were substantially reduced and, in most cases, became insignificant.

In a few specific cases interpersonal and media contact retained their significance and were among the strongest relationships in all the data; however, these cases differed across the two settings and for the different measures of the media and interpersonal contact variables, indicating the complexity and specificity of the relationships.

Several conclusions suggested by Payne and Caron (1983) resulted from comparing these studies. These seem to remain legitimate today. First, even using the same measures, different cultural settings resulted in different outcomes. Overgeneralization from data in one or even several settings to other settings is dangerous.

Second, the effects of media, interpersonal, and sociolinguistic variables are not uniform for different categories of dependent variables. The results lead to the belief that better theory and better measurement will yield more rather than less complexity of findings.

Third, changes in attitudes, agendas, and information levels have complex causes with many contributing factors. Assessment of the role of media in these changes should always be in the context of sophisticated controls for linguistic, socioeconomic, and interpersonal contact variables. None of these variables should be taken out of context.

THOUGHTS AND REFLECTIONS

It is not claimed that this review of the current literature is complete or that all the latest theoretical frameworks have been carefully examined. That is the purpose of the other chapters in this compilation. The following is a discussion of the roadblocks and closed doors encountered 15 years ago and how they have been passed or opened.

Fifteen years ago, studies of media effects were being conducted in a variety of settings around the world and results were being reported much as they are now. The studies generally had four problems: (a) the findings across settings, and sometimes even in the same studies, were not consistent; (b) the theoretical frameworks were not useful in explaining these inconsistencies in a way that allowed for future prediction; (c) obtaining sufficient control over independent and extraneous sources of variance and attributing causation rather than simply association was difficult; and (d) the strength of effect was small.

Inconsistent Findings

The findings in the studies reviewed in this chapter remain relatively inconsistent. Media effect on attitudes was sometimes positive (Snyder, Roser, & Chaffee, 1991), sometimes negative (Snyder et al., 1991; Tan, Tan, & Tan, 1987), sometimes both (Tan, Li, & Simpson, 1986; Varan, 1998), and sometimes neither (Snyder et al., 1991). Sometimes intercultural media use appears to increase information levels (Weimann, 1984), sometimes not. Sometimes media effects are toward the programming source country (Tan et al., 1986; Tan & Suarchavarat, 1988; Weimann,

1984), sometimes toward the receiving country (Pingree & Hawkins, 1981; Tan et al., 1987). Sometimes they are related to heavy viewing (Gerbner, Gross, Morgan, & Signorielli, 1980, p. 14; Weimann, 1984), sometimes to moderate or light viewing, sometimes to both (Weimann, 1984, p. 188). Sometimes the effect is greatest when other exposure is lacking (Tan et al., 1986; Tan & Suarchavarat, 1988; Zhao, 1989), and sometimes when it is present (Pingree & Hawkings, 1981, p. 104). Sometimes associations are reduced by controls (Zhao, 1989), and sometimes not (Tan et al., 1986). The lack of consistent pattern continues for numerous other dimensions and seems to have a familiar ring.

Weak Theoretical Framework

The great variety of findings underlines the importance of a simple, clear, accurate theory to organize the findings and provide predictive power. First reactions to reviewing the literature for theory were positive. Especially impressive were the notions of "mainstreaming" (really a media version of regression toward the mean) and "resonance" (Gerbner, Gross, Morgan, & Signorielli, 1980). The notion of "cultivation" which was used in several articles (e.g., Weimann, 1984) and the notion that the influence of media is more in structuring our perceptual and organizational processes than in the content of any item or group of items (Altheide & Snow, 1991), were also attractive. The theory that media is a small part of a complex set of internal and external forces that act on each person, and therefore any media impact must be considered in that complex context (Höijer, 1992), matched the author's data well. Finally, the use of the erosion metaphor and its four subcomponents as a conceptual and perhaps theoretical basis for cross-cultural mass media effects research (Varan, 1998) was of interest.

But when these various theories were utilized to understand the author's data, it felt as if some theory components of the material being read were constructed and almost artificially attached to the first of each article and to the discussion section. Others were central to the article or book, but too general to have predictive power. They provided a rationale for what had been found in the study or refuting them formed such a rationale, but little was given that would help much with prediction for new sites and circumstances. In short, the theoretical orientations were more sophisticated than the old notions that American media were all-powerful and generally bad, but not much more useful in practical scientific research or policy development. In short, I found new words but few new insights.

Methodological, Statistical, and Control Problems

There are many difficult methodological problems in conducting cross-cultural research. One of the most difficult methodological problems for intercultural media research is developing independent variables that are free from contamination and sufficiently strong to produce an effect. Experimental studies eliminated the problem of viewer self-selection by randomly assigning them to different treatment conditions, but such treatments (media exposure) were typically limited, and hence, produced little effect. The strategy of having viewers self-select the amount and nationality of media they use over the years allows the treatment to be much more extensive but confounds the treatment with existing predispositions. Thus, a person's existing predisposition may cause them both to view U.S. TV and have an attitude or piece of knowledge that is also transmitted over U.S. TV. Separating out that which media use caused and that which is a predisposition is especially difficult and has become more rather than less problematic over the last two decades. The alternate strategy of simply analyzing media content and assuming impact on people remains an unattractive option.

A second methods problem is the discovery and inclusion of appropriate control variables. Snyder et al. (1991, pp. 118, 129) correctly said, "The effects of foreign media content depend on structural factors, social factors, and individual variables such as an audience member's education, sex, and age." Over the past 15 years there appears to be development in these areas. Some studies now control for language familiarity, socioeconomic status, and interpersonal contact with people from other cultures, and allow for exposure to the full range of media rather than just television. Still some studies, because of limited variation in these variables, may over-interpret the relative effect of media.

There are, of course, many other methodological and statistical issues that continue to be problematic, especially the appropriate match between statistical technique and level of measurement and the assessment of causation in cross-sectional data (Snyder et al., 1991; Weimann, 1984). Nevertheless, it seems that the level of sophistication has increased somewhat.

Strength of Relationship

One of the striking consistencies across the years is the relatively low level of association between mass media use and the variety of attitudes, behaviors, and levels of information acquisition that are analyzed. Studies using correlation techniques typically report most correlations are less than .2. Levels of statistical significance for even the most strongly correlated variables are achieved more through large sample sizes than substantive meaning. Changes in mean distribution or Beta scores employed in other studies also continue to be relatively low. It was heartening to see some cases where these were appropriately labeled as modest (Tan et al., 1987), "on the weak side of moderate" (Pingree & Hawkins, 1981), and so on.

It may be as Gerbner et al. (1980) said:

> ... The observable independent contributions of television can only be relatively small. But just as an average temperature shift of a few degrees can lead to an ice age or the outcomes of elections can be determined by slight margins, so too can a rela-

tively small but pervasive influence make a crucial difference. The "size" of an "effect" is far less critical than the direction of its steady contribution. (p. 14)

But more caution is urged. Weimann's (1984, p. 195) conclusion that "... cultural invasion and TV imperialism may operate through the one way flow of programs [from the United States]" should have a heavy emphasis on "may," especially given the dubiousness of the "one way" hypothesis (Haynes, 1984; Stevenson & Cole, 1984). The observation of Ferguson (1993) and of Gans (1993) that media effects may be over employed seems still appropriate.

CONCLUDING THOUGHTS

It remains convincing that there are effects of intercultural mass media whether it is from the United States to Mexico, China, India, or Iceland or from any of those countries to the United States or each other. Little has been found to change the author's feeling of 15 years ago that we do not have a clear, useful framework for understanding and predicting the complexity that characterizes those relationships in a variety of intercultural settings. Perhaps such a theory will be provided today or tomorrow, but in its absence, avoiding dogmatic overgeneralization of findings across settings and across variables is urged. We need to continue to explore thoroughly the nonmedia variables that are part of the interconnected causal network.

REFERENCES

Altheide, D. L., & Snow, R. P. (1991). *Media worlds in the postjournalism era*. New York: de Gruyter.
Broddason, T. (1970). *Children and television in Iceland: A study of ten to fourteen year old children in three communities*. Reykjavik: University of Iceland Press.
Dunn, T., & Josepsson, B. (1972). *Assessing the personal and social impact of a recently established national television system*. New York: Final Report to the National Science Foundation.
Ferguson, M. (1993). Invisible divides: Communication and identity in Canada and the U.S. *Journal of Communication, 43*, 42–57.
Gans, H. (1993). Reporting the black box: Limited effects theory. *Journal of Communication, 43*, 29–35.
Gerbner, G., Gross, L., Morgan, M., & Signorielli, N. (1980). The "mainstreaming" of America: Violence profile no. 11. *Journal of Communication, 30*, 10–29.
Haynes, R. D., Jr. (1984). Test of Galtung's theory of structural imperialism. In R. L Stevenson & D. L. Shaw (Eds.), *Foreign news and the new world information order* (pp. 200–216). Ames: Iowa State University Press.
Höijer, B. (1992). Socio-cognitive structures and television reception. *Media Culture and Society, 14*, 583–604.
Payne, D. E. (1978a). U.S. TV in Iceland: A synthesis of studies. *Gazette, 14*, 173–180.
Payne, D. E. (1978b). Cross national diffusion: The effects of Canadian TV on rural Minnesota viewers. *American Sociological Review, 43*, 740–756.

Payne, D. E., & Caron, A. H. (1982). Anglophone Canadian and American mass media: Use and effects on Quebecois adults. *Communication Research, 9,*113–144.

Payne, D. E., & Caron, A. H. (1983). Mass media, interpersonal and social background influences in two Canadian and American settings. *Canadian Journal of Communication, 9,* 33–63.

Payne, D. E., & Peake, C. A. (1977). Cultural diffusion: The role of U.S. TV in Iceland. *Journalism Quarterly, 54,* 523–531.

Pingree, S., & Hawkins, R. (1981). U.S. programs on Australian television: The cultivation effect." *Journal of Communication, 31,* 97–105.

Snyder, L., Roser, C., & Chaffee, S. (1991). Foreign media and the desire to emigrate from Belize. *Journal of Communication, 41,*117–132.

Sparks, V. M. (1977). TV across the Canadian border: Does it matter? *Journal of Communication, 27,* 40–47.

Stevenson, R. L., & Cole, R. R. (1984). Issues in foreign news. In R. L. Stevenson and D. L. Shaw (Eds.), *Foreign news and the new world information order* (pp. 5–20). Ames: Iowa State University Press.

Tan, A., Li, S., & Simpson, C. (1986). American TV and social stereotypes of Americans in Taiwan and Mexico. *Journalism Quarterly, 63,* 809–814.

Tan, A., & Suarchavarat, K. (1988). American TV and social stereotypes of Americans in Thailand. *Journalism Quarterly, 65,* 648–654.

Tan, A., Tan, G. K., & Tan, A. S. (1987). American TV in the Philippines: A test of cultural impact. *Journalism Quarterly, 64,* 65–72.

Varan, D. (1998). The cultural erosion metaphor and the transcultural impact of media systems. *Journal of Communication, 48,* 58–85.

Weimann, G. (1984). Images of life in America: The impact of American TV in Israel. *International Journal of Intercultural Relations, 8,* 185–197.

Zhao, X. (1989). Effects of foreign media use, government and traditional influences on Chinese women's values. *Revue Europeenne des Sciences Sociales, 27,* 239–251.

CHAPTER

3

Socialization Effects of American Television on International Audiences

Alexis S. Tan
Gerdean Tan
Todd Gibson
Washington State University

Considerable attention has been given recently to television as a source of social reality perceptions and as a transmitter of culture. Because television is a major source of information and entertainment in the United States and in a growing number of foreign countries, expectations are that audience perceptions of social realities will closely correspond to the "realities" portrayed in television, and that audiences will adopt values and behaviors emphasized in television. Information presented in television is readily available; little effort is needed to process it; realities are presented in summary forms, with simple solutions to problems and even simpler portrayals of cultural groups and their environments.

Several theories can explain the influence of television on the culture and social realities of viewers. In this chapter we discuss three theories which have been influential in describing the influence of American television on American audiences. We apply these theories in an international context, and present data from a study of American television in Russia.

CULTIVATION THEORY

Cultivation theory (Gerbner, Gross, Morgan, & Signorielli, 1982) suggests that television presents a distorted but uniform picture of reality that is internalized and accepted by heavy viewers, primarily because of the pervasiveness of the images.

Television, according to Gerbner, leads to a "commonality of outlooks and values," an effect he called "mainstreaming." In this theory, the important predictor is total television viewing (i.e., a gross measure of frequency of TV viewing.) There is evidence that heavy television viewing in the United States is related to many real-world perceptions such as fear of crime and estimates of real-life violence, and to common perceptions of economic class membership, political ideology, and opinions on social and economic issues (Gerbner, Gross, Morgan, & Signorielli, 1986).

In its early form, cultivation theory followed the stimulus–response model of media effects (i.e., frequency of TV viewing leads to internalization of contents), with little attention to intervening cognitive and motivational processes. More recent derivations of the theory have considered viewer motivations and processing of television information in explaining cultivation effects. However, total frequency of television viewing continues to be the favored predictor.

SOCIAL COGNITIVE THEORY

Another explanation of television's influence on values and behaviors of audiences is provided by Bandura's *social cognitive theory* (Bandura, 1986), which maps out a process by which viewers learn through observation. Social cognitive theory suggests that behaviors and values are learned when they are repeated, simple, vicariously or directly reinforced, and when the viewer feels competent in adopting them. Because most of the realities presented in television fulfill these criteria, many viewers learn and accept them, In social cognitive theory, specific contents of television are first identified, and equivalent behaviors are then matched to these contents (Tan, 1986).

Social cognitive theory emphasizes not only the nature of the television stimulus (realities, values and behaviors depicted in specific programs), but also the intervening cognitive (i.e., learning) and motivational (e.g., estimates of self-efficacy) processes. Learning is matched to behaviors and values depicted in specific television programs.

COGNITIVE FUNCTIONAL THEORY

Cognitive functional theory (Tan, Nelson, Dong, & Tan, 1997) extends the cognitive and reinforcement principles of social cognitive theory and the perceived realism concept from cultivation theory to the analysis of how specific values and behaviors are learned and internalized.

The basic postulate of cognitive functional theory is that television audiences accept and adopt values, behaviors, and norms portrayed in television when these cultural forms are easily learned and when they are perceived to be functional or useful in obtaining rewards. A basic assumption is that humans are "economic" beings—goal driven and using available resources to their advantage. Homans (1974) suggested two general principles of economic human behavior. The value principle states that "the more valuable to a person is the result of action, the more likely he is to perform the action" (p. 25). The success principle states that "for all actions taken by persons, the more often a particular action of a person is rewarded, the more likely the person is to perform that action" (p. 25). An exchange occurs when a society rewards its members for accepting certain cultural forms that are necessary for its continued existence (Merton, 1957).

These principles from behavioral exchange theories are the basis of cognitive functional theory (Tan et al., 1997). They can be used to explain the socialization effects of American television on international audiences, as follows:

1. Motivation for accepting American culture: Foreign audiences will show differential degrees of motivation for accepting American culture. The greater the perceived rewards (or functionality) for accepting American norms, behaviors, and values within their native cultures, the stronger this motivation will be. Perceived rewards may take the form of manifest functions (such as economic prosperity) or latent functions (such as higher self-esteem or social approval) (see, e.g., Merton, 1957).

2. Learning about socialization: Foreign audiences learn about American culture from personal contact with Americans, schools, their governments, and the American mass media, particularly television. The stronger a person's motivation, the more he or she will learn about American culture.

3. Evaluating manifest and latent functionality of American norms, behaviors, and values: Foreign audiences evaluate functionality on the basis of information provided by socialization agents, including American television. When American norms, values, and behaviors are portrayed or presented as functional, the individual will consider them to be functional for him or her.

4. Adopting American culture: The acceptance of American norms, behaviors, and values is a function of motivation, knowledge (learning), and perceived reward value (manifest and latent functions.) There is a greater probability of acceptance when motivation is high, American culture is learned, and perceived reward value is high.

5. Persistence of socialization: The persistence of American norms, behaviors, and values depends on their continued reinforcement, vicariously (as in media portrayals) or through the individual's experiences within his or her native culture. The more often they are rewarded, the longer they will persist.

These principles are the foundation of a cognitive functional analysis of television's effects on foreign audiences (Tan et al., 1997). The assumption that television use and evaluations of its contents precede value acceptance is suggested by previous observations that in many foreign countries, the major source of American culture is American television, which is readily available, whereas other sources of socialization to American culture (e.g., personal contact with Americans) are not (Umble, 1990).

PREVIOUS RESEARCH

Some studies have used social cognitive theory to analyze the influence of American television programs on foreign audiences. These studies tested whether viewing specific programs would influence foreign audiences to accept the values and social realities emphasized in those programs. In Thailand, frequent viewers of specific American television entertainment programs were more likely than infrequent viewers to characterize Americans as aggressive, arrogant, impulsive, mercenary, sensual, and pleasure loving. These social stereotypes of Americans corresponded to how Americans were portrayed in American television programs watched frequently by Thai respondents (Tan & Suarchavarat, 1988). In Taiwan and Mexico, frequency of viewing *Dallas* and *Dynasty* was related to stereotyping of Americans as aggressive, cruel, dishonest, and pleasure loving, characteristics that had been used by other respondents to describe the portrayals of Americans in those television programs (Tan, Li, & Simpson, 1986). In the Philippines, frequent viewers of American television were more likely than infrequent viewers to rate "pleasure" as an important value, and "salvation" and "wisdom" to be less important. Also, frequent viewers were less likely than infrequent viewers to rate the instrumental value "forgiving" to be important. "Pleasure" was not considered by the average Filipino to be an important value, whereas "salvation," "wisdom," and "forgiving," were considered to be important. The study concluded that frequent viewing of American television led to some erosion of traditional Filipino values (Tan, Tan, & Tan, 1987).

AMERICAN TELEVISION IN RUSSIA

Data were collected from a convenience sample of Russians between June 15 and July 26, 1992. Of the total sample, 224 were from Camp Ruski Mir, about 50 miles from Moscow. The camp is owned by the state and is used as a summer facility. According to the camp director, all Russian students are given the opportunity to attend the camp. Questionnaires were also distributed to members of two classes at the Moscow Institute of Steel and Alloys, a major trade school in Moscow. The 46 student participants in the study were taking a course on semiconductors. The third group of respondents were Russian host families for Americans visiting Moscow and St. Petersburg. Ninety-three family members completed the questionnaire.

Given the constraints on data collection in Russia at the time the study was conducted, a random sample was not possible. According to our Russian collaborators, our student samples are fairly representative of Moscow "college" students. Age, gender, and other demographic variables are controlled for in the analysis.

Questionnaires (translated into Russian) were filled out by respondents in classes at Camp Ruski Mir and the Moscow Institute of Steel and Alloys, with Russian in-

3. SOCIALIZATION EFFECTS

structors and one of the authors present to answer questions. Host family members completed the questionnaire at home and returned them to one of the authors.

Measures

Use of American media was measured by asking respondents how often they watched each of the following American television program genres, on a five-point scale (from 1, never, to 5, more than once a day): comedy, adventure, movies, drama other than movies, sports, music, and news. They were also asked how often (five-point scales) they watched American movies on VCRs, read American magazines, read American newspapers, and had contact with Americans. We also asked them how many hours in the past week they had listened to Voice of America and American music, and had watched Russian television.

We measured agreement with *democratic and other American values* using 14 items adopted from Robinson, Rusk, and Head (1968) and Rokeach (1980). We asked our respondents to agree or disagree on a five-point scale (5 = strongly agree) with each of the following statements:

"One should be tolerant of other opinions."
"Equality for all is important."
"I should be free to do what I want."
"Being competitive is important to me."
"Democracy is the best form of government."
"One should be able to be wealthy."
"It is important to be individualistic."
"Working hard is important to me."
"Strong family ties are important to me."
"Change is good."
"The press (newspapers, television, and radio) should be free to criticize the government and its leaders."
"The minority should be free to criticize government decisions."
"Public officials should be chosen by majority vote."
"Every individual should have an equal chance to influence government policy."

To measure *perceived themes in American television,* we asked our Russian respondents:

"Think about the American television programs and American movies that you watch frequently. How often do you see each of these themes portrayed in these programs?" The 14 themes (just mentioned) were listed, followed by a five-point scale from 1 (almost never) to 5 (very often.) These items measured thematic contents of American television and movies, as perceived by Russian viewers.

The questionnaire was written in English, translated into Russian, and pretested in Russia.

Results

Of the 363 respondents, 46.1% were male and 53.9% were female. The average age was 21.13 years, with a mode of 16. Only 11.1% had contact with Americans "often"; 46.6% had contact with Americans "rarely"; 11.9% had visited the United States. On the English proficiency measure, 18.2% reported no English reading ability; 4.4% said they could read English "very well"; 30% reported they could read English "moderately well."

Concerning media use, our respondents saw an average of 7.48 movies in the previous month (theatres, VCRs, and television), with a median and mode of five. The most frequently watched American movies were "Pretty Woman," "Terminator," "Terminator II," "Double Impact," "Ghost," "Silence of the Lambs," "Police Academy," and "Wild Orchid."

Reading of American magazines was infrequent: 76.1% rarely or never read an American magazine; 22.5% said they read American magazines "sometimes." The most frequently read American magazines were *America, Time, Playboy, Readers Digest,* and *Newsweek*. American newspapers were rarely read: 60.1% had never read an American newspaper; 9.7% read them "sometimes." The most frequently read American newspapers were *The New York Times* and *USA Today*.

Respondents reported listening to Voice of America .92 hours per week, and to American music 11.59 hours per week. They watched Russian television an average of 17.87 hours per week.

The frequencies of viewing American program types were, on a five-point scale (1 = never; 2 = once a week; 3 = 2 to 4 times weekly; 4 = daily; 5 = more than once a day) were, in descending order: Music TV (2.93), Movies (2.92), News (2.76), Adventure (2.65), Comedy (2.51), Sports (2.23), and Drama (1.99). On the average, all program types were viewed at least once a week. The most popular programs were *Donohue* and CNN. A factor analysis of the responses yielded two factors: Comedy (.77), Adventure (.73), Movies (.68) and Drama (.63) clustered in Factor 1, with Cronbach's alpha = .71. In Factor 2 were Sports (.80), Music TV (.53) and News (.11), with Cronbach's alpha = .60.

Concerning acceptance of democratic and other American values, the values with the highest acceptance scores (on a five-point scale) were Wealth (4.42), Working Hard (4.39), Strong Family Ties (4.38), and Tolerance (4.28). In general, respondents expressed strong agreement with democratic values. A factor analysis of the 14 items yielded 4 factors: Factor A included tolerance of other opinions (.47), equality (.44), working hard (.51), and strong family ties (.43.) Factor B included change (.44), equal influence (.57), public officials chosen by vote (.65), and minority criticism (.67.) Factor C included democracy (.46), wealth (.53), and press criticism (.67.) Factor D included "free to do what I want" (.73), competition (.47), and individualism (.44.) Cronbach's Alphas were .55 for Factor A, .51 for Factor B, .51 for Factor C, and .45 for Factor D.

Concerning themes in American television, the themes most frequently perceived by our Russian respondents were individualism (3.91; 5 = very often), independence (3.88), competition (3.82), working hard (3.66), and freedom (3.57.) The themes least frequently perceived in American television were tolerance of other races (2.9), obedience (2.8), and equality (2.8). The average for the 14 themes was 3.4, indicating that Russians perceived the values to be portrayed in American television and movies "often."

Tests of Hypotheses

The cultivation hypothesis predicts that aggregate frequency of viewing American television is positively related to acceptance of American values; that is, frequent viewing leads to acceptance of American values. We tested the cultivation hypothesis using a standard regression model with the four value subscales as dependent variables and an aggregated measure of frequency of American television viewing as predictor, along with demographic control variables. As Table 3.1 shows, the aggregate measure of American TV viewing did not predict any of the value subscales. Agreement with value subscale A (tolerance, equality, working hard, and strong family ties) was predicted by English proficiency, "been to the United States," and reading of American newspapers. Agreement with value subscale B (change, equal influence, public officials chosen by vote, and minority criticism) was predicted by respondent gender, "been to the United States," and listening to American music. Agreement with value subscale C (democracy, wealth, and press criticism) was predicted by English proficiency and "been to the United States." Agreement with value subscale D (competition, freedom, and individualism) was predicted by respondent gender and reading newspapers. These results show that English proficiency and personal contact with American culture ("been to the United States), rather than aggregate viewing of American television, predicted acceptance of democratic and related American values.

The social cognitive hypothesis predicts that frequency of viewing specific television genres, rather than aggregate viewing, will be positively related to acceptance of American values. To test this hypothesis, we used standard regression models with viewing of specific American television program types as predictors (along with demographic and other control variables), and the value subscales as dependent variables. As Table 3.2 shows, frequency of viewing American television drama significantly predicted acceptance of value subscales A, B, and C, whereas frequency of viewing American news predicted subscales A and C. These are the program types most likely to portray democratic and related American values (Selnow, 1990). Comedy, sports, and music programs were not significant predictors of acceptance of American values.

TABLE 3.1
Acceptance of Democratic Values by Total Media Use;
Cultivation Hypothesis, Russian Sample[1]

PREDICTORS	DEMOCRATIC VALUES SUBSCALES			
	A	B	C	D
Gender (M = 1; F = 2)		2.36 (.02)		2.29 (.02)
Age				
English proficiency	2.34 (.02)		1.91 (.05)	
Been to the United States	2.05 (.04)	2.10 (.03)	2.56 (.01)	
# of movies past month				
Frequency of reading newspapers	2.25 (.02)			2.05 (.04)
Frequency of watching American VCR movies				
Hours Russian TV				
Frequency of listening, Voice of America				
Frequency of listening, American music		2.60 (.01)		
Frequency of viewing American TV Comedy/ Adventure/Drama				
Contact with Americans				

[1]Table entries are *t*-values from a standard regression model. Only *t*s significant at $p = .05$ are shown; *p*s are in parentheses.

These data show strong support for the social cognitive predictions. Specific program types most likely to depict American values predicted acceptance of those values. Aggregate television viewing did not have any effects.

SUMMARY AND CONCLUSIONS

In this chapter we presented three theories of communication and socialization that can explain the socialization effects of American television on international audiences. Cultivation theory suggests that aggregate viewing of television, as measured by total frequency, is sufficient to explain the acceptance of American culture as portrayed in television. Television presents a uniform view of American culture.

TABLE 3.2
Acceptance of Democratic Values by Frequency of Watching TV Content Types; Social Learning Hypotheses, Russian Sample[1]

PREDICTORS	A	B	C	D
Gender (M = 1; F = 2)		1.9 (.05)		
Age	1.9 (0.5)		3.6 (.0004)	2.06 (.04)
English proficiency	2.03 (.04)			
Been to the United States				
Frequency of viewing American comedy				
Frequency of viewing American adventure				
Frequency of viewing American drama	2.89 (.004)	2.38 (.01)	2.28 (.02)	
Frequency of viewing American news	2.45 (.01)		2.08 (.03)	
Frequency of viewing American sports				
Frequency of viewing American music TV				

[1]Table entries are *t*-values from a standard regression model. Only *t*s significant at *p* = .05 are shown; *p*s are in parentheses.

Therefore, the more frequently American television is watched, the more likely international audiences will accept its contents and adopt American culture.

Social cognitive theory suggests that learning and adoption of American culture depends on specific cultural forms learned. Therefore, the critical predictors are frequencies of viewing those American television programs that depict American culture. We presented data from Russia that indicate that television drama and news, programs that are more likely to portray American culture than other program genres, predicted acceptance of American values.

Cognitive–functional theory extends social cognitive theory by taking into account the functionality of observed values, norms, and behaviors. Research on Anglo American, Native American, and Hispanic adolescents has confirmed several predictions from a cognitive–functional theory of television's socialization effects (Tan et al., 1997.) Learning and functionality evaluations of observed values led to acceptance of those values. Adolescents from these American ethnic groups accepted values observed in television when they recognized them (a measure of learning) and when they evaluated the values to be important in "being successful" in the United States (a measure of functionality.) We suggest that similar analyses can be applied to the study of the effects of American television on international audiences. Socialization research in general can inform socialization research abroad. We believe that the same underlying principles apply, whether the socialization effects of television are studied abroad or at home.

However, our results suggest that the relationships between television use and socialization are quite complex, requiring the identification of other variables such as family and peer influence. Also, the direction of causality should be tested more rigorously to address the possibility that television use is the effect of pre-existing values, norms, and behaviors.

REFERENCES

Bandura A. (1986). *Social foundations of thought and action: A social cognitive theory.* Englewood Cliffs, NJ: Prentice-Hall.

Gerbner, G., Gross, L., Morgan, M., & Signorielli, N. (1982). Charting the mainstream: Television's contributions to political orientations. *Journal of Communication, 32,* 100–127.

Gerbner, G., Gross, L., Morgan, M., & Signorielli, N. (1986). Living with television: The dynamics of the cultivation process. In J. Bryant & D. Zillman (Eds.), *Perspectives on media effects* (pp. 17–20). Hillsdale, NJ: Lawrence Erlbaum Associates.

Homans, G. C. (1974). *Social behavior: Its elementary forms* (Rev. ed.). New York: Harcourt Brace Jovanovich.

Merton, R. K. (1957). *Social theory and social structure.* Glencoe, IL: The Free Press.

Robinson, J., Rusk, J., & Head, K. (1968). *Measures of political attitudes.* Ann Arbor, MI: Institute for Social Research, University of Michigan.

Rokeach, M. (1980). *Beliefs, attitudes and values.* San Francisco: Jossey-Bass.

Selnow, G. (1990). Values in prime-time television. *Journal of Communication, 40,* 64–74.

Tan, A. (1986). Social learning of aggression from television. In J. Bryant & D. Zillman (Eds.), *Perspectives on media effects* (pp. 41–55). Hillsdale, NJ: Lawrence Erlbaum Associates.

Tan, A., Li, S., & Simpson, C. (1986). American television and social stereotypes of Americans in Taiwan and Mexico. *Journalism Quarterly, 64,* 809–814.

Tan, A., Nelson, L., Dong, Q., & Tan, G. (1997). Value acceptance in adolescent socialization: A test of a cognitive–functional theory of television effects. *Communication Monographs, 64,* 82–97.

Tan, A., & Suarchavarat, K. (1988). American television and social stereotypes of Americans in Thailand. *Journalism Quarterly, 65,* 648–654.

Tan, A., Tan, G., & Tan, A. (1987). American television in the Philippines: A test of cultural impact. *Journalism Quarterly, 64,* 65–72.

Umble, D. (1990). International cultivation analysis. In N. Signorielli & M. Morgan (Eds.), *Cultivation analysis.* Newbury, CA: Sage.

CHAPTER

4

Perceived Foreign Influence and Television Viewing in Greece

Thimios Zaharopoulos
Washburn University

The purpose of this chapter is to look at Greek adolescents' television viewing in terms of its relationship to their perception of foreign influence on Greek culture and to their consumption of foreign products. The approaches used here are social construction of reality and cultivation analysis.

The cultivation hypothesis states that the more television people watch, the more likely they are to hold a view of reality that is closer to television's depiction of reality. This is characterized by the work of George Gerbner and his colleagues (Gerbner et al., 1977). Their work starts with the cultural indicators project, which looks at the content of television programming, and relates it to differences in perceptions, about various societal topics, between heavy and light viewers (Gerbner, Gross, Jackson-Beeck, Jeffries-Fox, ,& Signorielli, 1978). This process shows that heavy TV viewing cultivates a television-shaped view of the world (Hawkins, Pingree, & Alter, 1987). The cultivation hypothesis generally assumes that light viewers tend to be exposed to more varied and diverse information sources, whereas heavy viewers, by definition, tend to rely more on TV (Signorielli & Morgan, 1990, p. 17).

However, Adoni and Mane (1984) stated that television's influence will be greater when direct experience with the response to be learned is limited. Thus, as the social learning theory also suggests, we learn from television, but viewers without direct experience with what is to be learned may be most influenced by television. In settings where foreign television programs play a dominant role, this programming may also be most influential, as viewers do not have direct experience with the content depicted by foreign programs.

CULTURAL IMPERIALISM: THE OLD PARADIGM

The influence of foreign television content has been discussed for over three decades now, usually in the context of the cultural/media imperialism debates. However, as Sreberny-Mohammadi (1997) stated, the concept of cultural imperialism "was broad and ill-defined, operating as evocative metaphor rather than precise construct" (p. 49). Furthermore, researchers may not have devised the methodological tools to study this concept.

Cultural imperialism is defined by Prosser (1978) as:

> The tendency of members of a culture to seek dominance over other members of the culture or over members of different cultures.... The cultural imperialist is expansive in pushing outward his or her own values, beliefs, assumptions, and often his or her codes of communication, such as language ... Cultural imperialism requires dependency and often seeks control over others. (p. 295)

The International Commission for the Study of Communication Problems (1980) described cultural domination as taking the "form of dependence on imported models reflecting alien life-styles and values" (p. 31). Keeping in mind the media's role in transmitting such values and life styles, the media then have been seen as tools of cultural imperialism and domination.

McPhail (1981) coined the term *electronic colonialism*, which he defined as "The dependency relationship established by the importation of communication hardware, foreign-produced software, ... that vicariously established a set of foreign norms, values and expectations, which in varying degrees may alter the domestic cultures and socialization processes" (p. 20).

The introduction of imported media hardware and software were initially intended as tools of modernization. However, as McQuail (1983, p. 44) pointed out, "media can help modernization by introducing western values, but they do so at the cost of a breakdown of traditional values and the loss of authentic local cultures."

Various scholars have studied the international mass communication flow and, although tend to explain it differently, most find it to be one-way flow—from the richer to the poorer nations. Read (1976) looked at U.S. media with a heavy presence overseas, such as the news agencies, television programming, and specific U.S. magazines, and agreed that such media in developing nations "nourish expectations" that cannot be fulfilled (p. 164). He nevertheless argued that other nations themselves have a responsibility to protect their people from foreign media influence if they feel these media are more of a threat than a benefit to their national culture. However, Read believed that modernization, which all nations are trying to achieve, will necessarily have homogenizing effects.

In looking at the cultural industries, Guback and Varis (1982) suggested, "Once foreign influence has become dominant it has been very difficult to introduce and enforce laws designed to stimulate national film and television industries and decrease foreign dependence" (p. 49). Even those nations able to produce some of their own programs follow norms and media practices established by Western nations. As Katz and Wedell (1977) reported from their study of broadcasting in developing nations, "indigenous self-expression, which requires initiative and the confidence to experiment still tends to take second place to the use of standardized forms exported from the metropolitan centers, not just in content but in style" (p. 206).

Hamelink (1983) wrote that the importation of communication technology and transnational advertising are "two of cultural synchronization's vital channels." Similarly, Schiller (1969, p. 107) quoted Time-Life's then-vice president MicKelson who said: "The various underdeveloped countries are having to permit commercials because they can't afford a television system otherwise."

Smythe (1981, p. 13) suggested that "the prime item on the agenda of consciousness industry is producing people motivated to buy the 'new models' of consumer goods and services...." According to Schiller (1969), the American television programs are designed to hold and secure mass audiences, and then advertising takes hold. However, transnational advertising not only sells products, but also "it informs, educates, changes attitudes, and builds images" (Hamelink, 1983, p. 16). According to Hamelink, advertising is the main propaganda arm for the products of the large American conglomerates.

Hedebro (1982) wrote that it may not be just the advertising of products that is important but the promotion of consumerism as well (p. 60). Similarly, Hamelink (1978, p. 6) suggested that "world market and world customer demand an optimal synchronization of cultural values in order for authentic national characteristics not to jeopardize the unity of the transnational system." Although this is done primarily for economic reasons, it nevertheless, demands the cultural synchronization of the world.

Similarly, Sarti (1981, p. 317) stated that the transnational corporations have "undertaken an ideological effort to induce the acceptance of capitalist values in the organization of production and consumption patterns.... In short, to guarantee the reign of a homogeneous capitalist mentality." To support his case, Schiller (1969, p. 106) quoted two very respected mass communication scholars testifying before a congressional committee on the subject of modern communication and foreign policy. First, Ithiel de Sola Pool is quoted as saying "the function that American international communications can serve is to provide people with things for which they are craving but which are not readily available to them." Joseph Klapper is the second scholar, who stated that foreign music "is not likely to have any immediate effect on the audience's political attitude ... but this kind of communication nevertheless provides a sort of entryway of western ideas and western concepts...."

Fisher (1979) believed that this emerging internationalized culture, which is a "composite of western conventions, and increasingly a reflection of contemporary America," is a consequence of a purely economic matter, that is, the attempt of various companies to maximize their profit (p. 16). Fisher further seemed to justify the internationalization of culture as he stated that in many societies this global homogeneity satisfies an "identity–definition function." The new urban middle sectors, he wrote, "are frustrated because their own national culture has not changed enough to meet their own psychological needs" (p. 17). Fisher admitted that, "for the larger part of such societies, however, the onslaught of international culture is a serious threat to the cultural values which have provided integration and meaning to daily life" (p. 18).

No matter whether this process is an invasion or not, or whether it is the result of a conspiracy or simple diffusion, the issue is "essentially how much of the foreign and imported material rubs off on the receivers" (McPhail, 1981, p. 20). He added, "In the 20th Century the mass media system serves to portray a value system that will create a climate favorable to the economic system of the western nations" (p. 24).

If economics is the key to this "invasion," culture may be the means to that end. Smith (1980) stated:

> existing relationships in the field of politics and economics ... will be perpetuated by cultural exports, and that entertainment material will continue to create an awareness of American culture, which contributes to the receiving society's continued economic dependence upon the goods and life-styles of the major donor society ... (i.e.) the flow of media exports acts as a kind of ideological prerequisite for the flow of other material exports. (p. 13)

However, there are those who believe that this "exchange" has a positive influence. Read (1976) for example, agreed that the U.S. media have a dominant position in the world, but argued that they do not overwhelm a single national market. He sees the imbalance in the flow of TV programming between the United States and Europe as an example of the interdependence between the continents. He stated that the Europeans "don't have the resources to produce American quality television programs," whereas the Americans "export to off-set high production costs" (p. 152). Cherry (1971) also did not feel that this imbalance would lead into a kind of global political and cultural homogenization. Nevertheless, many others do fear the cultural and economic domination of smaller nations even in seemingly harmless mass media outlets such as comic books (Dorfman & Mattelart, 1975). Hartman (1978) mainly saw (U.S.) American, middle-class values transmitted via the mass media, values which "are not necessarily consistent with the needs and aspirations of developing countries. Furthermore, the persistent depiction of western locations and life styles as "where it's at" amount to an implicit denigration of local ways and concerns and has an eroding effect on national pride and cultural identity" (p. 2).

CONTEMPORARY APPROACHES TO CULTURAL IMPERIALISM

The preceding views on this issue represent the old paradigm of the cultural imperialism scholarship. Part of the problem with this paradigm is the lack of data beyond simple television import/export statistics. A one-way flow may signal domination, but does not necessarily signal cultural influence. As Tomlinson (1997) pointed out, we have to look beyond the self-evidence of global cultural goods and actually examine whether they have deeper cultural or ideological effects. In a sense, the old paradigm operated on the assumption of hypodermic needle model effects. We know that media effects are more complex than that and are neither direct nor uniform, but could be powerful nonetheless.

The era of globalization and media privatization has complicated this issue even further. For example, is globalization the next phase of cultural imperialism? Certainly, as critics charge, globalization has meant an Americanization of international business, including the Americanization of the cultural industries. At the same time, media privatization has resulted in more American-style entertainment programs, but also greater domestic production of television programming. Furthermore, other regional television producing powers have emerged, such as Brazil and Mexico, although home-produced programs are usually on top of the ratings in most nations.

Various scholars have attempted to study empirically the issue of cultural effects, with varying degrees of success. Elliott (1994) for example, used cultivation analysis to study U.S. television in Mexico, and although he found very little support for the cultivation hypothesis, he concluded that cultural imperialism is not a dead issue in countries with strong national television industries, as U.S. television programs dominate even there.

In a metaanalysis of many of these studies, Elasmar and Hunter (1996) found a weak, positive correlation between exposure to foreign TV and local viewers' knowledge, attitudes, beliefs, values, and behaviors. Specifically, they found that exposure to foreign TV increases the purchase of foreign products, especially clothing and other consumer products, but in a very small way. Similarly, exposure to foreign TV increases the tendency of audience members to hold values similar to those present in the country producing the foreign message, but again, in a very small way. At the same time, they found no relationship between exposure and holding positive attitudes toward the country of export (p. 63).

In a series of studies testing the cultivation hypothesis as it relates to U.S. television in Greece, Zaharopoulos (1996) found that Greek teenagers with a positive attitude toward U.S. music videos tend to have a more positive attitude toward the United States. However, this study found that gender was an intervening variable, as young women were more positive toward the United States and U.S. cultural values, and less negative about U.S. character traits.

Similarly, young Greeks who are heavy viewers of U.S. television programs were found to compare U.S. ethical values and the U.S. family system more favorably (Zaharopoulos, 1997). A similar study found that those Greek adolescents who are more exposed to U.S. television tend to have a more favorable image of the United States. However, this was found to be a complex relationship as an unexpected variable came to intervene—later defined as Greek ethnocentrism. This trait was present in those who watch more Greek TV programs, feel safer in Greece, whose mother has leftist political beliefs, and in primarily males. These have a more negative attitude toward the United States and tend to watch less U.S. television (Zaharopoulos, 1999).

Given all this, the issue becomes to determine the complexity of these relationships, because these relationships cannot be direct and cannot be seen as relationships between single variables. Elasmar and Sim (1997), who similarly found a strong positive correlation between exposure to U.S. media content and preference for U.S. food, saw the examination of these simple relationships as myopic. They pointed out that we need to see them as multivariate relationships.

A major variable in the relationship between exposure and foreign media influence is culture. Sreberny-Mohammadi (1997) pointed out that culture is not the product of cultural industries. And Tomlinson (1991) pointed out that foreign shows in many nations operate at a cultural discount in terms of their popularity with audiences.

Katz and Liebes (1990) used a more qualitative approach to find the meanings that a foreign program, such as *Dallas*, holds for the viewers overseas. They concluded that the program does not promote attitudes and actions that are incompatible with the true interest of the local viewers.

Straubhaar, Duarte, Kahl, Veii, and Goodman (1997) for example, concluded that language, culture and, social class do seem to be significant moderators of television flows. They can both facilitate and provide barriers against internationalizing and globalizing flows of television. Language, humor, ethnicity, lifestyle, and politics can play a role in screening this foreign flow.

CULTURAL IMPERIALISM, CULTIVATION, AND THE GREEK ENVIRONMENT

In a study of foreign mass communication in Greece, Zaharopoulos (1985) found that Greek cultural traits do play a role in mediating the influence of foreign media. Greek language and culture screen out certain cultural influences while encouraging others. Zaharopoulos found that whereas language (even under attack) served as a defense mechanism, competition for social status in Greece promoted cultural change in the form of the adoption of new things, including alien lifestyles. He stated, "advertising uses this Greek character trait to promote its goals, one of which is cultural change" (p. 302). In this participant observation study, advertising was found to be the most important means of promoting foreign lifestyles and cultural values, as "advertising embodies the promotion of cultural values and the promotion of products" (p. 303).

It is no coincidence that advertising agencies were instrumental in sponsoring foreign shows at the onset of Greek television in 1968, and also pushed hard for private television in 1988 (Zaharopoulos & Paraschos, 1993). Zaharopoulos (1985) wrote, "The media ... create an environment in which cultural change is possible. This cultural change results in the acceptability of foreign cultural norms, alien lifestyles and ideologies, and consumer goods which these ideologies produce" (p. 304). At the same time, however, he concluded that cultural synchronization is not absolute.

Greek television has historically carried a good deal of U.S. television programming since its inception in the late 1960s. Up until the late 1980s, when there were only two Greek television channels, they averaged between 38% and 48% in imported programming, most of which came from the United States (Zaharopoulos & Paraschos, 1993). During the 1980s Greek television, still under state monopoly, imported over 40% of all its programs. More importantly, over 70% of its entertainment programs were imported, many of which were on prime time. The introduction of private television in Greece in 1989 revolutionized the market. Initially, imports from the United States were the main source of programming for the new private stations, oftentimes making up over 50% of their total programming (Mavromichali, 1996). Slowly, as the major Greek stations increased their local production, the share of foreign programming per major station decreased. Overall, however, more U.S. programs are imported today as there are more television stations.

Another change is that even Greek shows today are more Americanized in terms of styles and formats. Diversity in content has decreased as private stations are entertainment-oriented (Mavromichali, 1996). Nevertheless, today U.S. programs are rarely broadcast during prime time. At the same time, Greek television has helped introduce to young Greeks their parents' favorite Greek movies from the 1960s, and, through these movies, the Greek music that was popular at that time, which has once again become popular.

Any cultivation study dealing with issues of cultural imperialism must take into account not only media flow, but media effects on culture and the complexity of culture itself. According to Morgan (1990), cultivation is highly culture specific. "The symbolic environment of any culture reveals social and institutional dynamics, and because it expresses social patterns it also cultivates them" (p. 226). When this approach is used to study U.S. television overseas, cultivation predictions cannot be as certain. For example, in an Australian study of over 1,000 students, Hawkins and Pingree (1982) unexpectedly found that watching violent U.S. television programs was more related to conceptions of reality in Australia than the reality of violence in the United States. As such, cultivation was found to hold true even though the violent programs were imported (p. 104).

Later studies of cultivation have criticized the Gerbner studies because they did not look at specific television programs but only total viewing (see Potter, 1993, 1994). Another important issue in this type of research is the perceived realism of television programs (Potter, 1986). For example, those who perceive television as more realistic are more likely to be influenced by its content. Again, one would expect that foreign viewers of U.S. programs would differ with American viewers, because foreign viewers do not have an American experience with which to compare U.S. television content. Elliott and Slater (1980), in a U.S. study, found that frequent viewers of certain programs tend to see them as more realistic, and that those with direct positive experience with the TV content (in this case with the police) perceived programs as less realistic.

A further refinement of traditional cultivation research is the attention to the respondents' motivation to watch. For example, Stilling (1994) found that motivation and exposure to certain genres was a better predictor of television's acculturation effect than simply amount of viewing. Generally, however, Gerbner, Gross, Signorielli, Morgan, and Jackson-Beeck (1979) believed that "heavy television viewers perceive social reality differently from light TV viewers even when other factors are held constant" (p. 193), and this social reality is influenced by the amount of television viewing.

HYPOTHESES AND RESEARCH QUESTIONS

Taking into account the Gerbner studies and their criticisms, as well as the empirical studies of imported media influences, this chapter aims to test the following hypotheses:

1. Heavy television viewers will tend to have a favorable attitude toward foreign consumer goods.
2. Heavy viewers of U.S. television programs will tend to have a favorable attitude toward foreign consumer goods.
3. Heavy viewers of U.S. television will perceive that the ownership of foreign consumer goods elevates people's prestige.
4. Heavy viewers of Greek television programs will tend to believe that foreign cultures present a threat to Greek cultural identity.

Furthermore, this study poses the following research question: What demographic, media consumption patterns, and other socioeconomic variables play a role in how viewers see foreign products and cultures? Of particular interest are such variables as U.S. TV viewing, motivation to watch television, perception of realism of television programs, and specific types of media consumption.

Method

Two Greek senior high schools, or lycea, were chosen for this research. One was in a lower middle-class section of Athens, and the other was in the agricultural town of Amaliada, which has a population of about 17,000, in southwestern Greece. These schools were chosen because they represent the urban/rural dichotomy of Greece, because they represent Greek society without extreme socioeconomic characteristics, and because access to these schools was easier, in terms of cooperating teachers and principals.

A survey questionnaire was designed first in English, using questions like ones used in similar studies around the world, such as Kang and Morgan (1988), but also using questions related to perceived cultural influence. It included Likert-type

4. TELEVISION VIEWING IN GREECE

questions, as well as some open-ended ones. This questionnaire was initially translated in the United States, was later proofread and polished by professional proofreaders in Greece, and then back translated. Following approval of the proposed research by the Greek Ministry of Education and its Pedagogical Institute, which examined the questionnaire, the instrument was administered at the two schools. One teacher at each school was trained to instruct the other teachers on how to administer the questionnaire in their respective classes during that day.

In order to test the hypotheses, participants were split into groups of heavy and light television viewers. Generally those watching television as much as the average student participant were classified as light viewers, while those watching more than the average were classified as heavy viewers.

To answer the research question, a stepwise regression analysis was used to find significant predictor variables. The following independent variables were used: overall TV viewing, frequency of U.S. program viewing, proportion of viewing devoted U.S. and Greek programs, demographic and other socioeconomic characteristics of student and parents, amount of radio listening, frequency of newspaper reading, types of television viewing, specific program viewing, perceived realism of television programs, and motivation to watch.

Results

Of the 508 usable surveys, 255 came from Amaliada, and 253 from Athens. Males make up 40.9% of the sample (208), and females make up 58.5% (297), while three students did not respond to this question. The Greek senior high school is made up of three grades, and students were equally divided between the three: 170 from the 10th grade, 168 from the 11th grade, and 170 from the 12th grade. The students' ages ranged from 15 to 19 years old.

Television and Other Media Consumption. The students, on average, watch 3 hours of television each day, including weekends, although they watch more on weekends than on weekdays. In terms of viewing U.S. television programs, 63.6% of the students said their favorite foreign television shows come from the United States. Furthermore, 18.5% of the respondents reported watching U.S. television programs on a daily basis; 45.4% on a weekly basis; 18.1% on a monthly basis; and 18.1% reported that they rarely or never watch U.S. shows. Overall, respondents reported they spend an average of a little over 3 hours a week watching U.S. programs. Those who watch at least some U.S. programs report that they spend an average 37.5% of their total viewing watching U.S. television shows.

Generally males watch more television than females (199 minutes per day vs. 176 for females)

$$[F(1, 484) = 6.11, p < .014]$$

However, males spend 60% of their TV time watching Greek shows, while females spend 53.7% of their time doing the same

$$[F(1, 434) = 8, p < .005]$$

As expected, males and females also differ in terms of which programs they watch. Males watch more Greek sports programs and *NBA Basketball*, as well as Greek late night talk shows. Females watch Greek sitcoms (*E Men kai E De, Dis Ex' Amartin*), *Beverly Hills 90210, Dr. Quinn: Medicine Woman, Melrose Place*, soap operas like *Loving*, and Greek telenovelas or social dramas (*Telefteo Antio, Lampsi*)

$$[X^2 (30, N = 432) = 126, p < .0001]$$

Beverly Hills 90210 was the most popular program overall, as 8% of all students made an effort to watch it each week.

Generally the students were divided as to whether U.S. programs accurately portray life in the United States. About 38% felt they generally do, 32.6% had no opinion, and 29.4% said U.S. programs generally do not accurately portray life in the United States.

Perceptions of Foreign Goods. To gauge their attitudes and perceptions, students were asked to respond to a series of Likert-type statements. Responding to the statement "I like to buy well-known brands like Nike, Jordache, Benetton, etc.," the students' response, as a group, was in the affirmative (mean = 2.5 out of 5). An analysis of variance indicates that heavy viewers are more positive toward well-known brands than light TV viewers

$$[F(1, 386) = 20.3, p < .0001]$$

This supports hypothesis one.

Similarly, heavy viewers of U.S. television are more positive toward famous brands of clothing than light viewers of U.S. television

$$[F(1, 458) = 7.7, p < .006]$$

Hypothesis two is also supported.

Responding to the statement "I like to wear jeans" the average response was 1.48, meaning most students like to wear jeans. On this issue, heavy viewers of U.S. television, in terms of the percentage of their viewing time devoted to U.S. shows, are more likely to wear jeans

$$[F(1, 495) = 8, p < .006]$$

However, there was no significant difference between light and heavy television viewers overall

$$[F(1, 387) = .24, p > .05]$$

as most young Greeks have accepted the desirability of wearing jeans and the cultural image that accompanies them.

Students were also asked to respond to the statement, "ownership of expensive, foreign products enhance one's prestige" (mean = 3). This reflects a Greek cultural characteristic, which values competition, including that for social status and prestige. The only significant difference here is between heavy and light viewers of Greek programs in terms of the percentage of viewing devoted to Greek shows

$$[F(1, 485) = 8.8, p < .004]$$

Heavy viewers of Greek programs do not feel that ownership of foreign products enhances one's prestige. No significant difference exists between light and heavy viewers overall

$$[F(1, 380) = 2.3, p > .05]$$

Similarly, no significant difference exists between light and heavy viewers of US programs

$$[F(1, 483) = 2.8, p > .05]$$

As such, hypothesis three is rejected.

Cultural Affinity and Identity. Students were asked to respond to the statement "American and European cultures will reduce the uniqueness of Greek cultural identity," and they mostly agreed (mean = 2.7). This study finds a significant difference between light and heavy viewers on this issue. Heavy viewers of television overall are *less* likely to feel Greek cultural identity is endangered

$$[F(1, 380) = 4.5, p < .035]$$

At the same time, however, heavy viewers of US programs are *more* likely to feel that Greek cultural identity is endangered

$$[F(1, 453) = 8, p < .04]$$

No difference was found between light and heavy viewers of Greek shows

$$[F(1, 487) = 1, p > .05]$$

Hypothesis four is rejected.

A regression analysis was used to answer the research question about demographics, media consumption patterns, and other socioeconomic variables that play a role in how viewers see foreign products and cultures. On the issue of perceived threats to Greek cultural identity, significant predictor variables include watching (more) movies on TV, watching (fewer) TV game shows, watching specific shows, having a (bleak) picture of Greece's cultural future, and the student's father's (leftist) politics. These variables account for 21% of the variance (see Table 4.1). It seems that viewing specific television programs and genres plays a role, but so do other variables.

Another variable relates to the statement "it would be better if Greeks had a lifestyle similar to Americans." The respondents generally disagreed (61% generally disagreed; 18% generally agreed). Predictor variables for this are favorable attitude toward U.S. music videos, and the belief that Greek TV is fairly realistic. These two account for 13% of the variance (see Table 4.1).

TABLE 4.1
Significant Predictors of Perception of Foreign Cultural Influence

American and European cultures will decrease the uniqueness of Greek cultural identity				
Significant Predictors	ß	t	p	Direction
Watching movies on TV	−.44	−4.3	< .001	more movies
Watching TV game shows	.23	2.5	< .014	fewer game shows
Not watching certain shows	.23	2.4	< .018	Dr. Quinn, kids, erotic
Greece's cultural future	−.19	−2.0	< .042	bleak
Father's politics	.27	2.8	< .006	leftist
Total adjusted $R^2 = .21$	$F = 6.1$	$p < .001$		
It would be positive if Greeks had a lifestyle similar to Americans				
Feelings about U.S. Music videos	.30	3.1	< .003	favorable
Realism of Greek TV shows	.21	2.1	< .034	more realistic
Total adjusted $R^2 = .13$	$F = 7.9$	$p < .001$		
I know more about the lifestyle in the United States than that of Cyprus				
City of residence	−.24	−2.6	< .01	Athenians
Magazine reading	.20	2.1	< .031	more often
Favorite source of foreign TV	.33	3.5	< .001	United States
Greece's cultural future	−.26	−2.7	< .01	bleak
Total adjusted $R^2 = .23$	$F = 6.8$	$p < .001$		

Another statement was intended to compare what the students know about the lifestyle of United States versus that of Cyprus, which Greeks consider a sister nation. The majority of the students (54.3%) agreed that they know more about the United States than they do about Cyprus. Predictor variables for this include city of residence (Athenians), magazine reading, the United States as the favorite source of foreign TV programs, and having a (bleak) picture of Greece's cultural future. These account for 23% of the variance (see Table 4.1).

The role and desirability of foreign products was explored with three statements: First, students responded to the statement "I like to buy known brand names." Significant predictors for this include (more) overall television viewing, watching (fewer) TV cartoons, and the perception that Greek TV is unrealistic. They account for 12% of the variance (see Table 4.2).

TABLE 4.2
Significant Predictors of Perception of Foreign Products

I like to buy known brand names such as Nike, Jordache, Benetton, etc.				
Significant Predictors	*ß*	*t*	*p*	*Direction*
Total TV viewing	−.31	−3.0	< .003	more viewing
Watching TV cartoons	.23	2.2	< .025	Fewer cartoons
Realism of Greek TV	−.22	−2.2	< .035	unrealistic
Total adjusted $R^2 = .12$	$F = 5.3$	$p < .003$		
I like to wear jeans				
Total TV viewing	.22	2.3	< .023	less viewing
Radio listening	−.30	−3.0	< .003	more radio
Watching TV discussion shows	.24	2.5	< .013	less discussion TV
Mother's education	.20	2.1	< .035	more educated
Total adjusted $R^2 = .20$	$F = 5.5$	$p < .001$		
Ownership of foreign products raises one's prestige				
Reasons for watching TV	.28	2.9	< .004	like the show
Greece's cultural future	−.30	−3.3	< .002	bleak
Student's politics	−.40	−3.2	< .002	right wing
Father's politics	.29	2.2	< .025	left wing
Total adjusted $R^2 = .20$	$F = 7$	$p < .001$		

Second, predictor variables for liking to wear jeans include amount of (less) television viewing, (more) radio listening, watching (less) TV discussions, and having a more educated mother. These account for 20% of the variance.

Third, the belief that ownership of foreign products raises one's prestige is predicted by watching TV because they like the show, having a (bleak) picture of the cultural future of Greece, student's (conservative) politics, and father's (leftist) politics. These account for 20% of the variance. It is interesting to note that students who designate themselves as right of center coincide with the predictor of father's politics to the right of center. This could be a relative difference, but could also indicate a generational gap (see Table 4.2).

Significant predictors of student responses to a favorable comparison of the Greek family system to that of the United States include reading newspapers, watching TV to relax, and perception of U.S. television as unrealistic. These account for 12% of the variance (see Table 4.3).

Significant predictors of student responses to a favorable comparison of Greek ethical values to those of Americans include watching TV comedies, watching (fewer) documentaries, and having friends or relatives in the United States (works negatively toward the strength of U.S. ethics). These account for 18% of the variance (see Table 4.3).

CONCLUSIONS

The issue of foreign media influence over local culture is indeed a very complex one. It is not a simple relationship between two variables, but one that involves a multi-

TABLE 4.3
Significant Predictors of Comparative Values

Significant Predictors	ß	t	p	Direction
The Greek family system is better than that of the United States				
Reading newspapers	.33	3.3	< .002	more frequently
Reason for watching TV	−.20	−2.0	< .05	relax or no reason
Realism of U.S. TV	−.21	−2.1	< .031	unrealistic
Total adjusted $R^2 = .12$	$F = 5.3$	$p < .002$		
Ethical values of Americans are weaker than those of the Greeks				
Watching TV comedies	−.28	−2.9	< .004	more viewing
Watching TV documentaries	.33	3.5	< .001	less viewing
Having friends/relatives in U.S.	.20	2.1	< .036	more likely
Total adjusted $R^2 = .178$	$F = 7.65$	$p < .001$		

plicity of variables and constructs. As such, cultural imperialism scholarship must go beyond simple examinations of media or television flow and domination, and must also examine media effects. However, the concept of culture is such a multifaceted concept that quantitative methodological tools may not be enough to empirically determine foreign influence over local culture.

This study looked at effects in terms of the cultivation hypothesis, and specifically, at the relationship between television exposure and its relationship to the perception of foreign consumer goods; to perceived threat to Greek cultural identity; and to comparative values and lifestyles between the United States and Greece.

Part of the problem as stated, is the limitation of the methods used, which cannot provide us with cause and effect conclusions. Furthermore, we cannot make secure conclusions about U.S. cultural influence by only examining U.S. television, because we cannot control for all other means of transmission of U.S. cultural values and lifestyle. Globalization today is a reality, and it is an impossible task to filter U.S. cultural influence.

Nevertheless, this study finds that television does play a small role in cultivating a view of reality that is U.S.-influenced, but other variables play a larger role. This study finds that heavy viewers of television in general, as well as heavy viewers of U.S. television, tend to have a more favorable attitude toward (foreign) brand-name clothing. In addition, despite the extensive use of jeans by today's youth all over the world, Greek heavy viewers of U.S. television are more likely to wear them than light viewers. On the other hand, heavy viewers of Greek television do not feel that ownership of such consumer goods raise one's prestige.

Similarly, heavy viewers of U.S. television are more likely to feel that Greek cultural identity is threatened. This was unexpected and it does provide a bit of reassurance in that at least these young people are aware of the possibility of this threat. Heavy viewers of television overall, however, are less likely to perceive this threat.

In examining these and other similar relationships, this study looked for predictors of such perceptions. Heavy viewing of U.S. television rarely turns out to be a significant predictor. Favorable attitude toward U.S. music videos is a significant predictor of a desire for Greeks to have a similar lifestyle to that of Americans. Listing the United States as a favorite source of foreign television programs significantly predicts knowing more about the United States than Cyprus. And finally, the perceived realism of U.S. television is a significant predictor of a favorable comparison of the U.S. family system to that of Greece.

Other than the foregoing, most predictor variables are related to type of television viewing, perceived realism of television, the perceived future of Greece, an individual's and his or her parents' politics, reason for watching television, and other media consumption patterns. As such, this study finds elements of cultivation at work. However, the influence over Greek culture (as defined here) seems to be a result of a multiplicity of variables, very few of which relate to U.S. television. Thus, although U.S. television is important to this relationship, other variables are more important.

As such, the old cultural imperialism paradigm seems simplistic and inadequate. There is no doubt that U.S. cultural dispersion is taking place via numerous means, including the mass media. However, changes in media economics as well as cultural evolution allow for almost a selective acceptance of U.S. cultural products and influences. Furthermore, these influences are more related to an individual's sociocultural and political identity than to a mass cultural conversion. This individual identity is related to what one watches on television or feels about Greece, which in turn is related to how one feels about Greek culture or American cultural products.

Obviously this study did not undertake a content analysis to determine the actual amount of American cultural messages. Also, this is a study of adolescents, and the results here cannot necessarily be generalized to the whole population. Future studies need to examine how viewers actually process television entertainment and information, because television influence seems to be related to already held attitudes and perceptions and we do not know precisely how those interact with television viewing. It may be, for example, that those with an affinity toward U.S. culture turn to U.S. programming for gratification, whereas for others, watching U.S. television leads to the acceptability of U.S. cultural goods and ideologies. Indeed, as Katz and Liebes (1990) suggested, these messages may be functional for both "hegemonic senders" and local receivers at the same time.

ACKNOWLEDGMENTS

A Fulbright Scholar Grant made data collection possible.

REFERENCES

Adoni, H., & Mane, S. (1984). Media and the social construction of reality: Toward an integration of theory and research. *Communication Research, 11,* 323–340.

Cherry, C. (1971). *World communication: Threat or promise.* New York: Wiley Interscience.

Dorfman, A., & Mattelart, A. (1975). *How to read Donald Duck: Imperialist ideology in the Disney comic.* New York: International General.

Elasmar, M. G., & Hunter, J. E. (1996). The impact of foreign TV on a domestic audience: A meta-analysis. In B. R. Burleson (Ed.), *Communication yearbook 20* (pp. 47–69). Thousand Oaks, CA: Sage.

Elasmar, M. G., & Sim, K. (1997, April). *Unmasking the myopic effect: Questioning the adequacy of media imperialism theory in explaining the impact of foreign TV.* Paper presented at the conference of the Broadcast Education Association, Las Vegas, NV.

Elliott, L. S. (1994, August). *Comparing cultural influences of U.S. and Mexican television in Mexico.* Paper presented at the conference of the Association for Education in Journalism and Mass Communication, Atlanta, GA.

Elliott, W. R., & Slater, D. (1980). Exposure, experience, and perceived television reality for adolescents. *Journalism Quarterly, 57*(3), 409–414, 431.

Fisher, G. (1979). *American communication in a global society.* Norwood, NJ: Ablex.

Gerbner, G., Gross, L., Eleey, M. F., Jackson-Beeck, M., Jeffries-Fox, S., & Signorielli, N. (1977). TV violence profile No. 8: The highlights. *Journal of Communication, 27*(2), 171–180.

Gerbner, G., Gross, L., Jackson-Beeck, M., Jeffries-Fox, S., & Signorielli, N. (1978). Cultural indicators: Violence profile No. 9. *Journal of Communication, 28*(3), 176–207.

Gerbner, G., Gross, L., Signorielli, N., Morgan, M., & Jackson-Beeck, M. (1979). The demonstration of power: Violence profile No. 10. *Journal of Communication, 29*(3), 177–196.

Guback, T., & Varis, T. (1982). Transnational communication and cultural industries. *Reports and papers on mass communication, No 92.* Paris: UNESCO.

Hamelink, C. (1978). The cultural synchronization of the world. *WACC Journal, 25,* 2–4.

Hamelink, C. (1983). *Cultural autonomy in global communications.* New York: Longman.

Hartman, P. (1978). Cultural identity and media dependency. *WACC Journal, 25,* 2–4.

Hawkins, R. P., & Pingree, S. (1982). Television's influence on social reality. In D. Pearl, L. Bouthilet, & J. Lazar (Eds.), *Television and behavior: Ten years of scientific progress and implications for the eighties* (DHHS Publication No. ADM 82-1196, Vol. 2, pp. 224–247. Washington, DC: U.S. Government Printing Office.

Hawkins, R. P., Pingree, S., & Alter, I. (1987). Searching for cognitive processes in the cultivation effect: Adult and adolescent samples in the United States and Australia. *Human Communication Research, 13*(4), 553–577.

Hedebro, G. (1982). *Communication and social change in developing nations: A critical review.* Ames, IA: Iowa State University.

International Commission for the Study of Communication Problems. (1980). *Many voices, one world.* Paris: UNESCO.

Kang, J. G., & Morgan, M. (1988). Cultural clash: Impact of US television in Korea. *Journalism Quarterly, 65*(2), 431–438.

Katz, E., & Liebes, T. (1990).The export of meaning: Cross-cultural readings of American TV. In P. Larson (Ed.), *Import/Export: International flow of television fiction* (pp. 69–82). Paris: UNESCO.

Katz, E., & Wedell, G. (1977). *Broadcasting in the Third World: Promise and performance.* Cambridge, MA: Harvard University Press.

McPhail, T. L. (1981). *Electronic colonialism.* Beverly Hills, CA: Sage.

McQuail, D. (1983). *Mass communication theory.* London: Sage.

Mavromichali, I. (1996, February). *Media utterances and the identity of the Greek television: Cultural imperialism or cultural synchronization?* Paper presented at the 13th Intercultural and International Communication conference, Miami, FL.

Morgan, M. (1990). International cultivation analysis. In N. Signorielli & M. Morgan (Eds.), *Cultivation analysis: New directions in media effects research* (pp. 225–247). Newbury Park, CA: Sage.

Potter, W. J. (1986, Spring). Perceived reality and the cultivation hypothesis. *Journal of Broadcasting and Electronic Media, 30*(2), 159–174.

Potter, W. J. (1993). Cultivation theory and research: A conceptual critique. *Human Communication Research, 19*(4), 564–601.

Potter, W. J. (1994). Cultivation theory and research: A methodological critique. *Journalism Monographs, 147* (October 1994).

Prosser, M. (1978). *The cultural dialogue.* Boston: Houghton Mifflin.

Read, W. (1976). *America's mass media merchants.* Baltimore: Johns Hopkins University Press.

Sarti, I. (1981). Communication and cultural dependency. In E. G. McAnany, J. Schnitman, & N. Janus (Eds.), *Communication and social structure: Critical studies in mass media research* (pp. 317–334). New York: Praeger.

Schiller, H. I. (1969). *Mass communication and American empire.* New York: Augustus Kelley.

Signorielli, N., & Morgan, M. (Eds.). (1990). *Cultivation analysis: New directions in media effects research.* Newbury Park: Sage.
Smith, A. (1980). *The geopolitics of information: How Western cultures dominate the world.* London: Faber & Faber.
Smythe, D. W. (1981). *Dependency road. Communication, capitalism, consciousness and Canada.* Norwood, NJ: Ablex.
Sreberny-Mohammadi, A. (1997). The many cultural faces of imperialism. In P. Golding & P. Harris (Eds.), *Beyond cultural imperialism: Globalization, communication and the new international order* (pp. 49–68). London: Sage.
Stilling, E. A. (1994, April). *The electronic melting pot hypothesis: The cultivation of acculturation among Hispanics through television viewing.* Paper presented at the Broadcast Education Association convention, Las Vegas, NV.
Straubhaar, J., Duarte, L., Kahl, S., Veii, V., & Goodman, R. (1997, August). *Culture, language, and social class in the globalization of television.* Paper presented at the conference of the Association for Education in Journalism and Mass Communication, Chicago, IL.
Tomlinson, J. (1991). *Cultural imperialism: A critical introduction.* London: Pinter.
Tomlinson, J. (1997). Cultural globalization and cultural imperialism. In A. Mohammadi (Ed.), *International communication and globalization* (pp. 170–190). London: Sage.
Zaharopoulos, T. (1985). *Foreign mass communication in Greece: Its impact on Greek culture and influence on Greek society.* Unpublished doctoral dissertation, Southern Illinois University, Carbondale.
Zaharopoulos, T. (1996, April). *The role of radio, music, and music videos in the perception of the United States by Greek adolescents.* Paper presented at the conference of the Popular Culture Association, San Antonio, TX.
Zaharopoulos, T. (1997, April). *U.S. television and American cultural stereotypes in Greece.* Paper presented at the conference of the Broadcast Education Association, Las Vegas, NV.
Zaharopoulos, T. (1999). Television viewing and the perception of the United States by Greek teenagers. In Y. Kamalipour (Ed.), *Images of the U.S. around the world: A multicultural perspective* (pp. 279–294). Albany: State University of New York Press.
Zaharopoulos, T., & Paraschos, M. (1993). *Mass media in Greece: Power, politics, and privatization.* Westport, CT: Praeger.

CHAPTER

5

The Influence of Television and Media Use on Argentines About Perceptions of the United States

Mary Beadle
John Carroll University

"All international business activity involves communication."
—Martin & Chaney (1992, p. 268)

Cross-cultural business communication has become increasingly important over the past decade and a half. A major factor is the growth of international trade. The combined value of import export trade for the United States grew to over $2,000 billion in 1997, an increase from $900 billion in 1990 (*International Financial Statistics Yearbook*, 2001, p. 1031). One of every six manufacturing jobs is related to exports (Martin & Chaney, 1992, p. 267). Another contributing factor to the increase is international trade agreements like NAFTA and GATT. As Ferraro (1994) reminded us "... a fundamental precondition to any successful international business enterprise is effective communication" (p. 42).

Communication across cultures is difficult because it includes more than language. United States firms have had between 45% to 85% of their expatriate U.S. citizens return early from foreign assignments because of their inability to adapt to a new culture (Martin & Chaney, 1992). Competing successfully in the global marketplace requires study and understanding of the communication systems of other countries. Barriers to intercultural communication include verbal and nonverbal messages, ethnocentrism, lack of empathy, and differences in perception. Perceptions and how they are formed are critical in the understanding of the communication process. To begin to understand how people of different cultures perceive U.S. business professionals, it might be helpful to learn about other people's opinion of U.S. social reality and explore possible influences on perceptions.

The technology that allows the importation and distribution of television signals from around the world, combined with the exportation of U.S. television programming, presents U.S. cultural stereotypes and thus effects communication between cultures. With the increase of business activity between the United States and South America, understanding this factor in business communication is important; knowledge about another culture will help to decide on appropriate communication. Argentina can serve as one example. The Direction of Trade Statistics Yearbook (2001) reports that United States imports from Argentina for 2000 were $3,313 million and exports to Argentina were $4,679 million (p. 478). Like many South American countries, Argentina has low wages, raw materials, large energy reserves, and geographic advantages. Unlike Mexico and Brazil, Argentina has had less direct contact with American business people. However, Argentine television and media has been heavily influenced by U.S. programming from the 1950s. As U.S. markets continue to expand into South America, Argentina provides an illustration of a people whose business communication may be more influenced by exposure to U.S. media than by direct personal contact.

This chapter is a report of a study conducted in Buenos Aires, Argentina in the summer and fall of 1997. The purpose was to discover if there is evidence of influence by U.S. media on the perceptions Argentine business men and women have of U.S. social reality. This is important for two reasons: first, little research of this type has been done with an adult sample; second, there appears to be an increase in business contacts between U.S. businesses and Argentina. If a better understanding of conditions were known, suggestions to improve communication between U.S. business people and their Latin American counterparts could be made. Further, the United States is a major exporter of television and entertainment programs around the world. More research has been called for about the impact of U.S. television and influences such as personal contact and demographic factors on audiences in other countries to further the understanding of relationships between television consumption, use of media, and viewer's perceptions of U.S. social reality.

PERCEPTIONS OF NORTH AMERICANS AND OTHERS

Research in intercultural communication has studied differences in international business communication (Ferraro, 1994; Friday, 1997; Ruch & Crawford, 1991; Stefani, Samovar, & Hellwig, 1997). These studies indicate differences in perception as to how U.S. citizens and foreigners see U.S. communication behavior. In general, people from the United States see themselves as warm, friendly, open, and informal. A U.S. manager values promptness and efficiency and accepts impersonal relationships in business dealings. North Americans are known to be individualistic, assertive, and informal in dress, gestures, and discussion.

Ruch and Crawford (1991) reported that foreigners see U.S. citizens as overly personal and familiar before a proper personal relationship has developed, driven, getting right to the point, slaves to the clock, materialistic, and valuing self over others. In general, they report that Latin American business cultures prefer face to face communication, are conservative and formal, direct and to the point in discussions, but require a sizing-up period. Generally, confrontations are avoided and family matters would be placed above business matters. Communication difficulties between these two cultures may include perceptions that U.S. business men and women would be "pushy" or aggressive, not interested in family, and more interested in pursuing self interests.

Stefani, Samovar, and Hellwig (1997) reported that Latin American negotiators are expressive and spontaneous, share ideas, and interrupt as often as North Americans. Latin American cultures first establish a friendship with those they do business. This means that often a direct "no" is avoided because of the risk of breaking a friendship. Although work on intercultural communication has been the topic of scholarly work for the last three decades (most notably Hall), international business communication is a "nascent field" (Limaye & Victor, 1991, p. 281). A difficulty in the field according to them is lack of empirical research specifically on business communication alone.

TELEVISION AND THE CULTIVATION OF PERCEPTIONS

Initially, for many citizens of South American nations, their impression of the United States may be from U. S. media, particularly television. How are business people portrayed on U.S. television shows? How do American television producers present social stereotypes? A recent study done for the Media Research Center examined 863 network sitcoms, dramas, and TV movies from 1995 to early 1997. Of the 514 criminal characters found during the study period, nearly 30% were business owners or corporate executives. In contrast, less than 10% were career criminals and less than 1% were lawyers (Elber, 1997, p. 1). This study parallels a report on prime time television from 1955 to 1986 that reported businessmen committed 40% of the dramatized murders (Elber, p. 3). Certainly, additional factors such as interpersonal contacts with the United States, exposure to other U.S. media, and the viewer's perception of the degree of reality of television programs are other important considerations to explore the influence of media on perceptions of social reality. Cultivation theory provides a framework to analyze this phenomenon.

Cultivation research focuses on "television as a socializing agent, or a continuing stream of reality" (Rubin, Perse, & Taylor, 1988, p. 107). In this view, television influences the perception of images about the real world. The relationship between images in the media, the amount of television exposure, and the viewer's belief in the reliability and reality of that message is the primary focus of cultivation study (Gerbner, 1990). Although first applied to viewers in the United States, the theory has been used to analyze the effects of television viewing in other cultures with mixed results.

Elasmar and Hunter (1993) used meta-analysis on 27 communication studies to investigate the size of effects of foreign television on domestic audiences. They discovered that the effects found are "very weak and could be due to some other factors that may be influencing the audience to seek and view foreign television programs" (p. 47).

Zaharopoulos (1997) studied the relationship between television viewing of U.S. programs and the perception that Greek high school students have of U.S. cultural values. He found that those students who watch U.S. programs more frequently tend to have more positive perceptions of the character of U.S. citizens. Gender was an important variable with males using more negative value orientations to describe U.S. citizens than females.

Tan, Li, and Simpson (1986) studied Taiwanese and Mexican students, and Tan and Suarchavarat (1988) studied Thai students. Results of these two studies indicated that American television is the major source of social stereotypes about Americans. The amount of television viewing was the most important predictor of American traits.

Weimann (1984) studied Israeli adolescents and undergraduates. His findings indicated both heavy and light viewers overestimated the rates of wealth and income in America. Heavy viewers overestimated to a greater degree than light viewers. Heavy viewers tend to paint a better picture of life in the United States in terms of wealth and standard of living. Also, Hawkins and Pingree (1980) reported Australian children who were heavy viewers held television-like beliefs about the world.

Kang and Morgan (1988) studied the relationship between U.S. programs and the attitudes of college students in Korea. Differences were found between males and females. Females who viewed U.S. television were associated with more liberal attitudes about gender roles and family values. Among males, greater exposure to U.S. television was associated with hostility toward the United States and protectiveness of Korean culture.

Morgan and Shanahan (1992) compared the cultivation effects of television on adolescents in Argentina and Taiwan. Their study found that the U.S. cultivation hypotheses was more predictive of the correlates of television viewing among adolescents in Argentina than in Taiwan. They attribute this difference to more television viewing and more entertainment programming in Argentina than in Taiwan. Morgan and Shanahan (1991) studied the relationship between television and the development of political attitudes in Argentine adolescents. They concluded that heavy television viewers were more likely "to agree that people should obey authority, to approve of limits on freedom of speech, and to think that it is someone's own fault if he or she is poor" (p. 88). A more significant conclusion by these authors may be that cultivation research need not be limited to the United States. Some research has suggested that cultivation is inappropriate outside the United States (Morgan & Shanahan, 1992, p. 176). Morgan and Shanahan suggested that Latin America, in general, and Argentina, in particular, is an appropriate subject for the use of cultivation theory as a legitimate research framework because the structure and programming is based on the U.S. television model (p. 102).

Meta-analysis of studies by Elasmar and Hunter (1993) indicates that the effect of foreign television on domestic viewers is quite weak. Despite the controversy surrounding the use of cultivation theory to study the influence of U.S. media on perceptions of foreign audiences, many studies have been conducted that explore this idea. Further, other findings seem to be consistent in reporting differences between men and women and heavy and light viewers. Heavy viewers tend to have more positive perceptions of U.S. wealth and living conditions. Males often have more negative perceptions than females. Much of the research has focused on adolescent audiences, thus there was a need to explore the influence of U.S. media on perception of U.S. social reality on older audiences. Similarity of Argentina's media system to the U.S. media system and the amount of U.S. media found in Argentina over a long period of time provide an appropriate subject for this research.

ARGENTINA AND MEDIA

Argentina is the eighth largest country in the world, slightly smaller than India. In South America, only Brazil is slightly larger. Nearly 40% of the country's 33 million people live in greater Buenos Aires, and there is considerable political and economic power located in the city. The Argentine economy was returning to a somewhat stable situation after inflation exceeded 50% in the 1970s and early 1980s. However, in 2001, political and economic instability reappeared, which may affect business relationships with U.S. companies.

Argentina is one of the most literate countries in South America and supports a wide variety of books, magazines, and newspapers. The most important media development in the last few years is the end of the government monopoly on electronic media, which has resulted in more variety. As early as 1984, Schement and Rogers described television as the dominant medium. The three major U.S. television networks helped establish the early Argentine television system and supplied programming and financing (Straubhaar & King, 1987). Broadcasting in Argentina has had significant time devoted to imported programs (Antola & Rogers, 1984). Since 1992, the widely adapted use of fiber optic cable in greater Buenos Aires has reinforced the dominance of the television medium and the use of imported television.

Cable television is very prominent and has developed rapidly since the early 1990s. Argentina has the largest cable penetration in Latin America, 51% compared with an overall rate of 12% for the continent (*Cabled Up*, 1997, p. 30). More people have cable television than telephones (Rionda, 1997, p.1). Competing cable systems offer up to 65 channels. Most of the programming is imported from other Latin

American countries and the United States. Fiber optic cable in Buenos Aires and competition between two cable companies (Cablevision-TCI and Video Cable Communication-VCC) has provided the citizens in greater Buenos Aires access to many foreign television programs. Programming from the United States, broadcast almost exclusively in English, include: CNN, MTV, Discovery Channel, Cartoon Network, Worldnet, TNT, ESPN, USA, and Fox. Other imported programs are from Brazil, Chile, Spain, Mexico, Italy, and Germany. For example, VCC provides 47 channels: 10 are U.S., 7 are other foreign services.

In greater Buenos Aires, many AM and FM stations are available. In the Provinces (the area outside greater Buenos Aires), access is somewhat limited for both cable and radio, but does include television programming from around the world. The University of Buenos Aires provides academic courses over a radio network.

In general, the influence of U.S. music and a deejay style of announcing has been an important force in radio formats. More recently, the addition of talk radio follows the U.S. pattern. One of the more recent adaptions is an imitation of David Letterman, host of a late night television program. Letterman's format includes a live band, a background featuring a city skyline, and a popular gimmick, the "Top 10 List." Roberto Pettinato hosts *Duro de Acostar*, which features a talkative bandleader, a city backdrop, and a nightly Top 5 list. According to Ulanovsky the American influence in format development is so strong that "all successful formulas have been adapted and copied from U.S. television" (Ulanovsky, 1997, p. 102). Some of the popular U.S. imports are movies, sitcoms, and drama (*The Simpsons*, *ER*, and *The Nanny*). The cable channels also broadcast imported programs from around the world, including many news shows.

RESEARCH QUESTIONS

A review of the literature on intercultural communication, cultivation studies using foreign audiences, and the history of U.S. media in Argentina indicates the following research questions:

1. Are there differences between males and females in Argentine business settings and their perceptions of U.S. social reality, perceived realism, and media use?
2. Are there differences between heavy (more than 4 hours per day) and light (less than 4 hours per day) viewers of television who work in Argentine business, and in their perceptions of U.S. social reality, perceived realism, and media use?
3. Is perceived realism of television correlated with perceptions of U.S. social reality?
4. Are there differences between those Argentine business people who use U.S. print media and those who do not, in their perceptions of U.S. social reality and perceived realism?

5. Are there differences between those Argentine business people who have personal contact with U.S. citizens and those who do not, in their perceptions of U.S. social reality and perceived realism?
6. Is age, ability to understand English, or education correlated with perceptions of U.S. social reality?

Methodology

In the summer and fall of 1997, the researcher contacted numerous businesses in Buenos Aires to gain their cooperation to participate in this study. Permission was given from 12 companies. These were: Rockwell International, Otis Elevator, Jose Litwin and Associates, Lloyds Bank, Telefonica de Argentina, AT&T, American Express, TGS, Suchard-Kraft Foods, Delphi Corporation (Packard Electric), Buco, and Norte. Also, one federal government office, the ISEG (Institute for Government Economics) and students in a Master's business program at the University of Buenos Aires (this is a program developed for those employed full time) participated. From June through October of 1997 surveys were distributed and collected by the researchers and her assistants. A total of 316 surveys were collected.

An attempt was made to include both American-owned or -related and Argentine-owned businesses. However, gaining cooperation was difficult, despite personal contact with organizations by the researcher. Most of the companies participating in the survey were American-owned or -related. Also, managers were reluctant to have anyone other than management personnel complete the surveys. Secretaries and others who may have contact with U. S. personnel were a small segment of the respondents. Therefore, the results may be limited.

A questionnaire was developed by the researcher based on her previous studies in Argentina and Paraguay (Beadle, 1997, 2001) and on other cultivation studies. The major sections of the questionnaire were: demographic information, exposure and use of U.S. media (television, visual, and print), personal contact with U. S. citizens (face to face, phone, trips to the United States, U.S. friends), belief in the accuracy of television reality, and 18 statements about perceptions of U.S. social reality and qualities of U.S. persons. Eight of the social reality questions were based on a survey developed and used by El-Koussa and Elasmar (1995). These statements asked for estimates of the percentage of U.S. social reality conditions (professions, living conditions, arrest for rapes, and blacks in jail). Answers on were a 5-point scale that ranged from less than 10% (1) to more than 90% (5). Accuracy of perception was based on U.S. census data (Statistical Abstract of the U.S., 1995). The additional perceptual questions were developed by this researcher based on a pilot study in Paraguay completed in 1995, and a similar study with a sample of university students also completed in 1995. Ten statements including both positive and negative qualities about U.S. citizens were answered on a 5-point scale from strongly agree (1) to strongly disagree (5).

Two statements were used to test reliability of perceptions of media reality, which resulted in a Perceived Realism Index (PRI). The two statements were: Television programs present things as they really are; and Foreign television programs present an accurate picture of how people live in foreign countries. These statements were developed by El-Koussa and Elasmar (1995) and based on Rubin (1981). A 5-point scale was used to determine respondents' agreement or disagreement with the statement. The lower the score the stronger the agreement with the statement (1 = strongly agree, 5 = strongly disagree). A test for reliability resulted in an alpha of .71.

A factor analysis with varimax rotations applied to the 18 perceptual statements revealed four underlying variables (see Table 5.1), with factor loadings of .6 or more to load highly enough to be considered part of the scale. These four variables accounted for 49% of the variance. Professions, Factor 1 (alpha = .71), consisted of three statements concerning perceptions of the number of high ranking professions (doctors, lawyers, business owners) in the United States. The lower the score, the lower the estimated percentage of people in professional careers. For example, a 1 indicates an estimate of fewer than 10%; a 5 indicates an estimate of more than 90%. Positive perceptions, Factor 2 (alpha = .65), consisted of four statements concerning positive perceptions of U. S. citizens. (Americans are generally polite, friendly, trustworthy, happy, lead a comfortable life). The lower the score, the more agreement with the statement; for example, 1 = strongly agree, 5 = strongly disagree. Household conditions, Factor 3 (alpha = .65), consisted of three statements concerning household conditions in the United States and included perceptions of the number of two-car families, the number of families earning over $75,000, and the number of houses with air conditioning. The lower the score, the lower the estimated percentage of people in professional careers.

TABLE 5.1
Factors and Factor Loadings of Rotated Factor Matrix

Factor 1 Number of Professionals		Factor 2 Positive Qualities		Factor 3 Household Conditions		Factor 4 Negative Qualities	
Lawyers	.81	Friendly	.79	Air conditioning	.76	U.S. Households with guns	.75
Doctors	.79	Polite	.67	$75,000 salary	.70	U.S. Is a violent culture	.74
Business people	.68	Happy	.64	2 or more cars	.69	Argentine family life better	.61
		Trustworthy	.60				
Alpha = .71		Alpha = .65		Alpha = .65		Alpha = .55	

For example, a 1 indicates an estimate of fewer than 10%; a 5 indicates an estimate of more than 90%. Negative perceptions, Factor 4 (alpha = .55), consisted of three statements related to negative perceptions of U.S. lifestyle, particularly the perceptions that the United States is a violent society and most U.S. citizens own guns. These statements asked for respondents to indicate agreement or disagreement on a 5-point scale; lower scores indicate more agreement (1 = strongly agree, 5 = strongly disagree). The statements were: Argentines are more concerned about their family than North Americans, the U.S. is a violent society, most Americans own and use guns.

Results

Description of the Sample. The total number of surveys returned was 316. Some of the reported numbers may not total 316 and percentages may not total 100% because not all surveys were complete. Males comprised 60.8% of the sample ($N = 192$); females, 35.4% ($N = 112$). Twelve surveys were left blank in this category (3.8%). Seventy-two respondents (22.8%) were younger than 24; 126 (39.9 %) were between the ages of 25 and 35; 74 (23.4%) were between the ages of 36 and 45; 31 (9.8%) were between the ages of 46 and 55; and 11 (3.5%) were over the age of 56. Two surveys had no response (0.6%). The educational level of the sample was fairly high with 42 (13.3%) graduates of high school; 108 (34.2%) having some university education; 115 (36.4%) as graduates of university; 41 or 13% had some postgraduate education. The remaining surveys indicated no response (3%). Some 85% of the sample indicates some understanding of English. Fifteen and a half percent report they do not speak English. However, 48.4% indicate they speak English well or very well. Others indicate they speak English in an average manner (35.8%). Work experience was also extensive, most of the sample has worked for more than 15 years. Ninety-two (29.1%) worked 15 years or less; 72 (22.8%) worked 5 to 10 years; 85 (26.9%) worked 11 to 20 years and 56 (17.7 %) worked more than 20 years. The remaining surveys had no response (3.5%). One hundred and fifty-three respondents (48.4%) report they expect to work with U.S. businesses in the next 5 years. The careers of the respondents reflected their educational level and their age. About one third of the sample report management positions. One hundred and eleven (32%) were managers or middle managers; staff comprised 38.3% ($N = 121$); 19 (6%) indicate a technical job; 28 (8.9%) report a clerical position. Other jobs include civil servants, a photographer, and medical workers. Ninety-six (36.4%) of the respondents were in the banking or financial field; 45 (14.2 %) were in manufacturing; 24 (7.6%) were in energy; 18 (5.7%) were in technology, and 12 (3.8%) were in the computer field. The remaining were in diverse fields such as government, education, and medicine.

Personal contact included phone contact, actual face to face contact, friends in the United States and U.S. travel. Generally, about half the sample had some type of personal contact with U.S. citizens ($N = 160$), although the type of contact varied from person to person and some had more than one type of personal contact. Not quite half the responses (40.2%) indicate friends in the United States; almost 60% indicate they do not have friends in the United States. Almost 40% indicate face to face contact with U.S. citizens; 49.1% indicate no face to face contact; 12% gave no response. Thirty-eight percent indicate phone contact with U.S. citizens; 48.4% indicate no phone contact, and 13.6% gave no response. Forty-two point two percent had traveled to the United States; 55.1% had not traveled to the United States, and 5.2% gave no response.

Media usage included overall use of television, U.S. television, U.S. films, U.S. print media, and the Internet. Almost 90% of the respondents indicate they watch U.S.-made films and almost 90% indicate weekly or less viewing of U.S. films. Almost 40% read U.S. newspapers or magazines. Respondents were asked to indicate the amount of print media use on a scale of 1 (daily) to 4 (less than once per month). About 40% indicate weekly or less reading of U.S. print media.

Overall this sample did not watch a considerable amount of television. As the sample was business professionals who worked in companies in a very cosmopolitan area, Buenos Aires, it is not representative of a general population, and therefore would not be expected to approximate the general population. Many of the companies had some association to U.S. companies, for example Rockwell International, AT&T, and American Express. Almost 30% indicate they watched less than 1 hour per day, 64.2% indicate they watched 1 to 3 hours per day. Heavy viewers made up 6% of the respondents; they watch 4 or more hours per day. However, of those who watch TV, 82% indicate they watch U.S. television. Of those who indicate they watch U.S. television, 48.3% watch weekly; 22.8% watch daily; 3.5% watch monthly; 18.4 % watch less than monthly, and 9.8% gave no response. One purpose of the study was to determine if differences existed between light and heavy television viewers. Unfortunately, only 19 out of the 316 respondents were heavy users of television, so this difference was not determined.

Internet use was also included in media use. About 25% of this sample use the Internet. Overall, the respondents use a variety of U.S. media, but few in the sample could be considered heavy users of *one* media. Respondents also indicate preferences for the country of origin of foreign television shows. Programming from the United States was listed as most preferred (see Table 5.2). Argentina was written in by 30 respondents, even though this is obviously not a source of foreign programming.

Perceptions of Males and Females. Differences between males and females were minimal. Using *t* tests, significant differences ($p < .05$ t-value = .31; $df = 289$) were found between males and females in the Perceived Realism Index (PRI). Males perceived the media to be less realistic than females. However, both perceived the media as somewhat unrealistic. Males watched more U.S. television than females ($p < .05$ t-value = $-.97$; $df = 288$). As Table 5.3 indicates, no other sig-

TABLE 5.2
Preferred Country of Foreign Television Programs

Country	N	(%)
1. United States	184	(58.2%)
2. Argentina	30	(9.5%)
3. British	5	(1.6%)
4. Italian	3	(0.9%)
5. Spanish	7	(2.2%)
6. French	1	(0.3%)
7. German	1	(0.3%)

nificant differences were found between males and females in perceptions of U.S. social reality.

Perceptions of Heavy and Light Television Viewers. This sample consisted of 19 heavy viewers out of 316 respondents. Due to the small number of heavy viewers, statistical analysis of differences between heavy and light viewers were not performed. Correlations were run between reported over all television viewing (light = less than 1 hour per day; medium = 1 to 3 hours per day; heavy = 4 or more hours per day), perceived realism, and the four variables determined by the factor analysis. Further, a series of *t* tests between those that chose to watch a particular medium or television program and those that did not were run to determine any differences in perceptions between users and non-users of a specific type of pro-

TABLE 5.3
T-tests Between Male and Female Respondents
$N = 192(M)\ N = 112(F)$

Variables	t-value	Significance	df
Perceived realism	0.31	$p < .05$	287
U.S. TV Viewing	−0.97	$p < .05$	288
Perceptions of Professions	−3.69	$p > .50$	268
Perceptions of Positive Qualities	−0.55	$p > .50$	277
Perceptions of Household	−2.45	$p > .40$	270
Perceptions of Negative Qualities	−2.09	$p > .50$	283

gram or media source. Although the sample had a very small number of heavy televison users, the percentage of respondents who watch U.S. television was 259 or 82% of the sample. They also use other U.S. media, including print and U.S. sources on the Internet.

Further, the respondents were asked to give their perceptions on the impact of U.S. television in Argentina. As Table 5.4 shows, as a group, these respondents were not particularly concerned about the impact of U.S. media in Argentina. United States media was not seen as threatening or overwhelming local media. In fact as previously stated, it was the respondents' most frequent source of foreign television programs, despite the availability of many other foreign television programs.

Table 5.5 indicates there was one significant correlation ($r = .13$; $p < .05$) between overall TV viewing and the perception of positive qualities in U.S. citizens. This indicates that the fewer the hours of television viewing, the more one agreed with the positive statements about the U.S.; the more one watched televison, the less agreement there was with the positive qualities about U.S. citizens. This finding tends to contradict some previously reported studies related to heavy television viewers that an increase in television viewing results in a more positive picture of the United States. In this sample, there were few heavy television viewers. Also, this was an older and more educated group than those in some of the reported studies and almost half of whom had previous contact with U.S. citizens in a business setting. This probably influenced the perceptions in a different way than previously reported (see section on age).

Despite a lack of heavy viewers and a perception that U.S. media has little importance, correlations between the four variables determined by the factor analysis and the PRI resulted in significant differences with two of the variables: perceptions of positive qualities ($r = .14$; $p < .05$) and household conditions ($r = -.13$; $p < .05$). Those who perceived television to be more realistic and accurate about foreign countries agreed more with the positive factors about the Unites States. In other

TABLE 5.4
Frequencies of Perceptions of the Impact and Amount of U.S. Media in Argentina

Response	N	%
Too much	49	15.5%
Not enough	23	7.3%
Just enough	76	24.1%
Doesn't matter	59	18.7%
Dangerous to Argentine culture	13	4.1%
Dangerous to Argentine values	11	3.5%
Important for the future	38	12.0%

TABLE 5.5
Intercorrelations of Perceived Realism, Amount of Overall TV Viewing, Amount of Overall U.S. Reading and Social Reality Perceptions

Variables	PR	Overall TV Viewing	Overall U.S. Reading
Perceptions of professions	−.08 ($p = .20$)	.08 ($p = .19$)	−.15 ($p < .01$)
Perceptions of positive qualities	.14 ($p < .05$)	.13 ($p < .05$)	−.15 ($p < .01$)
Perceptions of household	−.13 ($p < .05$)	.01 ($p = .83$)	.02 ($p = .80$)
Perceptions of negative qualities	.10 ($p = .07$)	.07 ($p = .21$)	−.05 ($p = .38$)

words, those who believed television to be more accurate also indicated stronger agreement with the positive qualities about U.S. citizens. The negative correlation between the PRI and household conditions means that those who perceived television to be more realistic indicated higher percentages for people in the U.S. who earn more than $75,000/year, have 2 or more cars, and have air conditioning at home. This negative correlation is very interesting because the negative correlation actually indicates a more accurate view of household conditions in the United States if answers are compared to the reality of lifestyle reported in the 1995 U.S. Census Report.

Influence of Specific Media Sources. T tests were run between those who used a specific media such as a newspaper, magazine, Internet, or watched a specific TV program. There was a significant difference between those who watched CNN (t-value = −1.43; $p < .05$; $df = 293$) or read *Newsweek* magazine (t-value = −2.51; $p < .05$; $df = 290$) and those who did not concerning perceptions of negative qualities of U.S. citizens. Those who watched CNN ($N = 176$) or read *Newsweek* ($N = 41$) agreed more with the negative statements about U.S. society. Further analysis indicated that the viewers of CNN and readers of *Newsweek* were essentially the same people; there were only five people who did not use both media. *Newsweek* readers also perceived television as less realistic than those who did not read *Newsweek*.

Two other significant differences were found with program viewers and nonviewers. Those who watched ESPN ($N = 165$; 52.5%) considered the media more realistic than those who did not watch ESPN (t-value = −.18; $p < .05$; $df = 296$). The other program that resulted in significant differences between viewers and nonviewers was *Kung Fu* ($N = 164$; 51.9%). Those who watched *Kung Fu* perceived the media as more realistic than those who did not watch it ($t = −.17$; $p < .01$; $df = 296$).

Perceptions of Those Using Print and Electronic Media. In addition to television, this study was also interested in exploring the relationship between the use of print media and the influence on perceptions of U.S. social reality. Table 5.5 reports two significant correlations between the overall amount of time reading U.S. print material (magazines and newspapers) and social reality variables. Overall, time spent reading U.S. newspapers and magazines was significant and negatively correlated with perceptions about the number of professionals in the U.S. ($r = -.15$; $p < .01$) and the positive qualities of U.S. citizens ($r = -.15$; $p < .01$). Those who read more frequently had lower estimates of the number of professionals in the United States. However, based on U.S. Census Bureau data, these estimates indicate a more accurate perception regarding the number of people employed in professional careers in the United States. The other significant negative correlation indicates that those who read more U.S. print material indicated less agreement with the positive statements about U.S. citizens.

No other significant differences were found between users and non-users of print media or between users and non-users of the Internet.

Perceptions of Those Having Personal Contact with U.S. Citizens. Another influence on the perception of U.S. social reality may be personal contact. To determine if there was a significant relationship between personal contact and perceptual statements, correlations were run with the number of trips to the United States. For items in which a yes (1)/no (0) response was given, *t* tests were run to determine if any differences existed between those who have personal contact and those who do not (phone, face to face, friends in the United States).

Table 5.6 reports the results of *t* tests between those who have had various personal contact with U.S. citizens and those who have not, and the social reality variables and the PRI. Perception of negative qualities was significantly different for those who had face to face interaction and for those who did not (t-value = .35; $p < .01$; $df = 264$). Those who had face to face contact agreed more with the negative statements and showed negatively correlation with perceptions of the number of professionals in the United States (t-value = -2.28; $p < .05$; $df = 249$). Those who had more face to face contact were lower in estimates of the number of professionals and thus were more accurate (based on U.S. Census Bureau data). Those who had face to face contact also perceived the media (PRI) as less real than those who had no personal contact (t-value = $-.60$; $p < .05$; $df = 264$).

Table 5.6 reports the results of *t* tests between those who have phone contact with U.S. citizens and those who do not. Significant differences were found with estimates of professionals (t-value = -1.45; $p < .01$; $df = 245$) and negative qualities (t-value = 1.99; $p < .01$; $df = 258$). Those who had phone contact estimated a lower percentage of professionals, which was more accurate and agreed less with the negative statements about U.S. citizens. Table 5.6 reports the results of *t* tests between those who have friends in the United States and those who do not. The perception of negative qualities was significantly different between those who had friends in the United States and those who did not have friends in the United States (t value =

TABLE 5.6
T-Tests Between Those Who Have Phone Contact, Face to Face Contact, or Friends in the U.S., and Those Who Do Not, and Social Realty Perceptions and PRI

Variables	Phone	Face To Face	Friends
Perceptions of professions	−1.45 ($p < .01$) 245 (*df*)	−2.28 ($p < .05$) 249 (*df*)	−.29 ($p = .37$) 274 (*df*)
Perceptions of positive qualities	−3.67 ($p = .52$) 252 (*df*)	−3.64 ($p = .97$) 256 (*df*)	−1.36 ($p = .60$) 281 (*df*)
Perceptions of households	1.35 ($p = .79$) 249 (*df*)	.84 ($p = .35$) 252 (*df*)	.86 ($p = .58$) 276 (*df*)
Perceptions of negative qualities	1.99 ($p < .01$) 258 (*df*)	1.64 ($p < .01$) 264 (*df*)	.35 ($p < .01$) 289 (*df*)
PRI	.06 ($p = .53$) 259 (*df*)	.60 ($p < .05$) 264 (*df*)	−.07 ($p = .62$) 291 (*df*)

(*df*) = degrees of freedom

.35; $p < .01$; $df = 289$). Those who had friends in the United States perceived Americans less negatively than those who did not.

Influence of Age, Ability to Understand English or Education and Number of Trips to the United States. Three demographic factors were correlated with the four variables determined by the factor analysis and the PRI: age, level of education, and perceived ability to speak English (see Table 5.7). Education ($r = -.27; p < .01$) and age ($r = -.18; p < .01$) were significant and negatively correlated with estimates of the number of people employed in professional careers in the United States. Ability to speak English ($r = .16; p < .05$) was positively correlated with estimates of the number of people employed in professional careers in the United States. Older people had lower estimates of the number of U.S. professionals and were more accurate; those who were more educated had lower estimates of U.S. professions and were more accurate; those who perceived themselves to speak better English were lower in estimates and more accurate.

TABLE 5.7
Intercorrelations of Age, Education, Ability to Speak English, and U.S. Trips and Social Reality Perceptions and PRI

Variables	Age	Education	English	U.S. Trips
Perceptions of professions	−.18 ($p < .01$)	−.27 ($p < .01$)	.16 ($p < .05$)	−.12 ($p < .05$)
Perceptions of positive qualities	−.10 ($p = .08$)	−.13 ($p < .05$)	.03 ($p = .57$)	−.11 ($p = .09$)
Perceptions of household	.04 ($p = .49$)	−.13 ($p < .03$)	−.01 ($p = .93$)	.20 ($p < .01$)
Perceptions of negative qualities	.01 ($p = .83$)	.05 ($p = .37$)	.08 ($p = .17$)	−.15 ($p < .01$)
PRI	−.16 ($p < .01$)	.00 ($p = 1$)	−.06 ($p = .27$)	−.09 ($p = .13$)

The level of education ($r = -.13$; $p < .05$) was significant and negatively correlated with positive qualities. Those who were more educated agreed more with the positive statements about Americans. The level of education ($r = -.13$; $p < .03$) was significant and negatively correlated with household conditions. The more education one had, the lower the perceptions of household items such as air conditioning and number of cars.

Age was significant and negatively correlated with the PRI ($r = -.16$; $p < .01$). The older one was, the more one agreed that television is realistic.

As Table 5.7 reports, the number of trips to the United States was significant and negatively correlated with perceptions about the number of professionals ($r = -.12$; $p < .05$), and negative qualities ($r = -.15$; $p < .01$) and significant and positively correlated with household conditions ($r = .20$; $p < .01$). Those who traveled more often to the United States were lower in their estimates in the number of professionals there and, based on U.S. Census Bureau data, were more accurate. Also, the more trips to the United States the more one agreed with the statements that were negative about U.S. social reality. Those who traveled more to the United States had higher estimates of household conditions such as salary, number of cars, and air conditioning. In other words, the more one traveled, the more accurate they were in estimating professionals and household conditions and the more they agreed with the negative qualities about the United States.

DISCUSSION

The purpose of this study was to explore whether U.S. television specifically and U.S. media generally influences the perception of U.S. social reality on Argentine business men and women. This is an important study because older audiences have not been the subject of research as frequently as university and high school students. Also, if U.S. media is influencing perceptions and thus communications between the United States and Argentina, U.S. businesses could provide improved training and better methods for intercultural business communication based on this knowledge. Better performance may result. Research reports from cultivation studies and intercultural business communication were reviewed and resulted in the development of this survey used for this study.

Based on the findings of the survey, this study showed that male viewers were significantly different than females viewers in only two areas. However, this difference did not result in any significant differences in the perceptions of U.S. social reality. This may be due to a number of other factors: age, education, experience, lack of television, or personal contact. Differences that were found seem to indicate that these additional factors influence perception in some way and suggest a need for further research in this area.

Personal contact seems to be an important influence on perceptions of Argentines. This lends support to the idea than Latin Americans prefer face to face contact. An indication of the importance of personal contact is the tendency to perceive the media as less realistic for those who had had some personal contact with U.S. business people.

Some demographic characteristics were correlated with perceptions. This may indicate experience, education, and sophistication also influence perceptions and is also worthy of further exploration. Because older audiences may not be heavy users of television, this calls into question the use of cultivation as a theoretical framework for the study of media impact in foreign countries with older audiences.

A question first posed by Schement and Rogers in 1984 concerned the effects of different types of programming such as entertainment or news. It is interesting to note that the television shows that did show some differences between viewers and nonviewers were in each of these categories. Viewers of CNN held more negative perceptions of U.S. social reality than those who did not. Those who watched some of the entertainment programming perceived the media to be less real than those who did not watch them. Perhaps this says more about the viewer and their predisposition to choose a U.S. television program for their own reasons rather than U.S. television influencing the viewer. One caution in reading too much into these differences is the lack of heavy television viewers in the sample. However, despite this limitation, differences still resulted. This idea of user choice is also reflected by the readers of *Newsweek*. They may choose to read *Newsweek* because they see television as unrealistic and therefore are making conscious choices about the type of media to use. They are active participants in gathering information about the world.

Two major results of cultivation research are differences in perceptions about social reality between heavy and light users of television and male and female viewers. This study offers little support for these two aspects of cultivation theory in international settings. It does seem to support the idea that the influence of foreign media on domestic audiences is quite weak (Elasmar & Hunter, 1993). However, results also indicate some effect on perceptions resulting from a variety of media exposure, personal contact, and demographic factors. Generally, exposure to U.S. media results in development of a more accurate picture of U.S. living conditions but seems also to result in a less positive perception of a U.S. citizen's personal qualities. The influence of CNN on the development of more negative perceptions about U.S. citizens is interesting. Argentines have a more accurate picture of living conditions, but seem to develop some less positive perceptions about American citizens. Also, it appears that those who watch ESPN and *Kung Fu* are quite aware of the fantasy world of television entertainment.

This study also brings up an interesting research dilemma. Although this group does not watch one media heavily, in total they use a substantial amount of different media. Also, Argentines have been exposed to U.S. media for many years and do not consider it to be that threatening. Perhaps there needs to be a more controlled look at the cumulative effect of using a variety of media over time.

Finally, the results of this study and one completed in Argentina in 1995 by this author using a group of first-year university students (Beadle, 1997), indicate the perception of Argentines about U.S. lifestyle are more complicated than merely exposure to media . As Straubhaar (1999) pointed out, the relationship is not a simple one of effects. Education, family, friends, travel, religion, gender, and age help to determine media choices, which in turn contribute to the development of perceptions and interpretations of media events. The context in which the viewers watch television must be considered in attempting to understand the influence of U.S. media on foreign audiences.

The results of this study indicate that personal contact is important in dispelling inaccurate perceptions about personal qualities of foreigners and may be more influential for adults than exposure to U.S. media. Further research that includes a focus on the cumulative effect of using a variety of U.S. media over time combined with other factors such as education, family, income, religion, and interpersonal contacts is needed. The challenge for this research agenda is to develop a framework that includes all of these variables. One idea that may be helpful is cultural capital. Education, family, travel, religion, and associations help determine media choices. However, media is also an aspect of cultural capital. As Straubhaar (1999) stated, the relationship of media to individual perceptions is not a simple one of effects. Media are sources of ideas about society, but so are other sources, such as travel. It is a complex interaction and one that warrants additional study.

REFERENCES

Antola, L., & Rogers, E. (1984). Television flows in Latin America. *Communication Research, 11*(2), 183–202.

Beadle, M. E. (1997, February). *Television and Argentine perceptions of the United States.* Paper presented at the Conference of the Americas, Mexico City, Mexico.

Beadle, M. (2001). Communication in international business education: Considerations for Latin America. *Journal of Teaching in International Business, 12,* 71–85.

Cabled up in Argentina. (1997, July 21–27). *Variety,* p. 30.

Direction of trade statistics. (1996). Washington, DC: International Monetary Fund, p. 564.

Elasmar, M. G., & Hunter, J. (1993). The impact of foreign TV on a domestic audience: A meta-analysis. *Communication Yearbook, 20,* 47–69.

Elber, L. (1997, June 26). American online. *Associated Press,* pp. 1–4.

El-Koussa, H., & Elasmar, M. (1995, April). *The influences of imported U.S. TV programs on the perception of U.S. social reality among students in Lebanon.* Paper presented at the annual meeting of Broadcast Educators Association, Las Vegas, Nevada.

Ferraro, G. (1994). *The cultural dimension of international business* (2nd ed.). Englewood Cliffs, NJ: Prentice-Hall.

Friday, R. (1997). Contrasts in discussion behaviors of German and American managers. In L. A. Samovar & R. E. Porter (Eds.), *Intercultural communication: A reader* (8th ed., pp. 297–307). Belmont, CA: Wadsworth.

Gerbner, G. (1990). Advancing on the path of righteousness (maybe). In M. Morgan & N. Signorelli (Eds.), *Cultivation analysis* (pp. 249–262). Newbury Park, CA: Sage.

Hawkins, R., & Pingree, S. (1980). Some processes in the cultivation effect. *Communication Research, 7,* 193–226.

International financial statistics yearbook. (1998). Washington, DC: International Monetary Fund, p. 895.

Jornadas de Television por Cable '94. (1994). *Sesiones Academicas ATVC '94* [Brochure]. Buenos Aires, Argentina: Asociacion Argentina de Television por Cable (ATVC).

Kang, J., & Morgan, M. (1988). Culture clash: Impact of U.S. television in Korea. *Journalism Quarterly, 65,* 431–438.

Limaye, M., & Victor, D. (1991). Cross-cultural business communication research: State of the art and hypotheses for the 1990s. *Journal of Business Communication, 28*(3), 277–299.

Martin, J., & Chaney, L. (1992). Determination of content for a collegiate course in intercultural business communication by three delphi panels. *Journal of Business Communication, 29*(3), 267–283.

Morgan, M., & Shanahan, J. (1991). Television and the cultivation of political attitudes in Argentina. *Journal of Communication, 41*(1), 88–103.

Morgan, M., & Shanahan, J. (1992). Comparative cultivation analysis. In F. Korzenny & S. Ting-Toomey (Eds.), *Mass media effects across cultures* (pp. 173–197). Newbury Park, CA: Sage.

Rionda, G. (1997). TV households in Latin America expected to increase from the present 90 mil to 110 mil by the year 2000. *Multichannel News International Supplement, 3*(10), 1.

Rubin, A., Perse, E., & Taylor, D. (1988). A methodological examination of cultivation. *Communication Research, 15,* 107–134.

Rubin, A. (1981). An examination of television viewing motivations. *Communication Research, 8,* 141–165.

Ruch, W. V., & Crawford, M. L. (1991). *Business communication.* New York: Macmillan.

Schement, J., & Rogers, E. (1984). Media flows in Latin America. *Communication Research, 11*(2), 305–320.

Shrum, L. J. (1996). Psychological processes underlying cultivation effects. *Human Communication Research, 22*(4), 482–509.

Statistical Abstract of the U.S. (1995, September). *The national data book.* Washington, DC: U.S. Department of Commerce.

Stefani, L., Samovar, L., & Hellwig, S. (1997). Culture and its impact on negotiation. In L. A. Samovar & R. E. Porter (Eds.), *Intercultural communication : A reader* (8th ed., pp. 307–317). Belmont, CA: Wadsworth.

Straubhaar, J. (1999). *Cultural capital, language, and cultural proximity in the globalization of television.* Paper presented at the annual meeting of Association for Education in Journalism and Mass Communication (AEJMC), New Orleans.

Straubhaar, J., & King, G. (1987). Effects of television on film in Argentina, Brazil, and Mexico. In B. A. Austin (Ed.), *Current research in film: Audiences, economics, and law* (Vol. 3, pp. 52–71). Norwood, NJ: Ablex.

Tan, A., Li, S., & Simpson, C. (1986). American TV and social stereotypes of America in Taiwan and Mexico. *Journalism Quarterly, 63,* 809–814.

Tan, A., & Suarchavarat, K. (1988). American TV and social stereotypes of Americans in Thailand. *Journalism Quarterly, 65,* 648–654.

Ulanovsky, C. (1997). The United States on Argentine radio. In M. Zago (Ed.), *The United States in Argentina* (pp. 99–102). Buenos Aires: Marique Zago.

Weimann, G. (1984). Images of life in America: The impact of American TV in Israel. *International Journal of Intercultural Relations, 8,* 185–197.

Zaharopoulos, T. (1997). U.S. television and American cultural stereotypes in Greece. *World Communication, 26*(1), 30–44.

CHAPTER

6

Choosing National TV: Cultural Capital, Language, and Cultural Proximity in Brazil

Joseph Straubhaar
University of Texas

There are many ways of looking at culture and the globalization of television. This study looks at that aspect of culture that is the individual and collective synthesis of identity in interaction with media, particularly television. In this sense, the movement from traditional local life to modern interaction with mass media has produced identities that are already multilayered with elements that are very local, regional (subnational but larger than the very local), and national (Anderson, 1983). This study argues that television viewers around the world continue to strongly reflect these layers or aspects of identity while many also acquire new layers of identity that are supranational, based on cultural–linguistic "regions," and global. The chapter argues, however, based on an analysis of in-depth interviews in Brazil, that the proportion of people whose identity is deeply globalized is actually quite small, that the traditional layers of identity at the local, regional, and national levels are still the strongest for the large majority of people, with cultural–linguistic region rapidly becoming very important for some cultures.

In a more practical and immediate sense, this chapter uses cultural capital as a concept to sum up a series of identifiable sets of knowledge and disposition that people tend to use when deciding what they want to watch on television. Although a number of studies have focused on the role of language in defining television markets (Wildman & Siwek, 1988), this chapter tries to define and demonstrate a number of the cultural factors that also define television markets, by defining what audiences' cultural identities and cultural capital leads them to prefer. Those are specific things like humor, gender images, dress, style, lifestyle, knowledge about other lifestyles, ethnic types, religion, and values. Cultural groups defined by their differences on these kinds of factors often overlap greatly with language groups. This chapter elaborates the aspects of cultural capital that are most relevant to audience choices about global, cultural–linguistic regional and national television, as well as their ability to make sense of what they watch from such different sources.

Cultural capital, identity, and language tend to favor an audience desire for cultural proximity, which leads audiences to prefer local and national productions over those that are globalized and/or American. However, cultural proximity is itself limited by social class stratification. Groups united by language and/or culture seem to be increasingly fragmented by both economic and cultural capital in the senses defined by Bourdieu (1984). Economic capital (Bourdieu, 1984) gives some people in the economic elite of many countries access to television channels, particularly those delivered by satellite or cable, that the vast majority or the population cannot afford (Porto, 1998). Even more subtly, in most countries, only elites or upper middle classes have the education, employment experiences, travel opportunities, and family backgrounds that give them the cultural capital (Bourdieu, 1984) required to understand and enjoy programs in other languages. In fact, this chapter argues that this also extends beyond language to culture, that the cultural capital required for wanting to watch many kinds of imported programs also tends to be concentrated in middle and upper classes. That is due in large part to the fact that their wealth provides opportunities for education, travel, and personal contact with outsiders. Thus, although cultural capital is separable from economic capital, the former is bounded and constrained by the latter, the economic aspects of social class.

Overall, this chapter further defines and operationalizes in in-depth interviews in Brazil the concept of cultural proximity. Whereas cultural proximity is more of a factor within certain social classes than within others, it is still a factor in media choices for almost all, even the group we will call the global elite. The general dimensions of cultural proximity that tend to extend across social classes will be looked at in terms of cultural affinities, common values (Elasmar & Hunter, 1996), perceived similarities (Iwabuchi, 1997), and perceived relevance (Paterson, 1998). The dimensions of the audience that divide social classes and limit cultural proximity are looked at in terms of cultural capital, building on the manner in which Bourdieu (1984) used the concept to examine social class distinctions in taste within a culture, like France.

GLOBAL TV FLOWS: FROM DEPENDENCY TO REDISCOVERING THE AUDIENCE

During the 1960s and 1970s, many studies pointed out to a one-way flow of television, news, and music from a few First World countries to the rest of the world (Beltran & Fox, 1979; Boyd-Barrett, 1980; Nordenstreng & Varis, 1974). Several theoretical explanations were developed, notably cultural dependency (Hamelink, 1983), dependent development (Evans, 1979), and media imperialism (Lee, 1980).

6. CULTURAL CAPITAL, LANGUAGE, CULTURAL PROXIMITY 79

Both the empirical findings of a one-way flow and the theoretical explanations for it began to be challenged. Although the United States still makes a great deal of money exporting television programming, studies in Latin America (Antola & Rogers, 1984) and Asia (Waterman & Rogers, 1994) observe that national production was increasing in many countries, particularly in prime time. A 20- nation study of television production and importation in 1961, 1971, 1981, and 1991 by Straubhaar, Campbell, Youn, Champagnie, Elasmar, & Castellon (1992) confirmed that almost all but the smallest nations, such as the English-speaking Caribbean, and those that share English as a native language with the United States, such as Canada, seemed to be reducing U.S. imports, producing more national programs, and importing more programs from within cultural– linguistic regions, such as Latin America, or Chinese-speaking Asia. Increasingly, although poor countries still import much of their programming, it no longer primarily comes in a one-way flow from the United States. For example, the Dominican Republic is now more likely to import many genres, such as comedies, variety shows, and news from Mexico, a dominant producer for the Latin American cultural–linguistic market, than from the United States (Straubhaar, 1991b). Mozambique imports about as much entertainment from Brazil, a dominant producer for Portuguese-speaking countries, as from the United States; furthermore, the Brazilian material is much more likely to be in prime time (personal interviews at Radio–TV Mozambique, 1992, 1996, 2002).

This constitutes a much more complex flow. Television programming now flows horizontally from one developing country to another quite frequently. Some programs even flow back to the United States. and Europe. Brazilian television now tends to dominate the prime time programming of its former colonial power, Portugal (Marques de Melo, 1988, 1992). Mexico long dominated the television and radio programming of the Hispanic audience in the United States (Schement, Gonzales, Lum, & Valencia, 1984), although more programming is increasingly created by U.S. Latinos for the unique interests of that population itself. The flow of television is still asymmetric but there is now an interpenetration of cultures, both by migration and by media. Media products like television programs still flow largely from the developed North to the developing South, but increasingly television flows from South to South as well.

One of the factors changing the production of television is the producer–audience interaction over time. Technology becomes cheaper and easier to use over time, enabling more production, more location/out of studio production, cheaper special effects, and overall, much lower production costs (personal interview with L. F. Santoro, 1990). Television and video producers experiment with different genres (as we see later) over time, develop their expertise in genre production, and, perhaps most importantly, gain a sense of what their audiences are most interested in.

For some years in the 1960s and 1970s, many scholars had thought imported programming frequently was more entertaining or more desirable to the audience, anticipating "Wall-to-wall *Dallas*" (Collins, 1986). It does seem that there is still a powerful appeal of exotic, nonlocal programming, particularly in some genres like action–adventure films and programs. Violence still travels very well (Herman & McChesney, 1997). So does sex appeal, as the export of *Baywatch* to over 60 countries demonstrates. However, as Parameswaran (1997) pointed out, more positively, sometimes women or other particular groups can find certain imported genres to be more emancipating or supportive of their particular needs than much locally produced material.

CULTURAL DISCOUNT AND CULTURAL PROXIMITY

However, as more time elapses and television systems develop further, it begins to seem that relevance to local culture may give many kinds of local or national programming an advantage. In a study of television in Brazil, Kottak (1990) observed, "Common to all mass culture successes, no matter what the country, the first requirement is that they fit the existing culture. They must be *preadapted* to their culture by virtue of *cultural appropriateness* [emphases in the original]. If a product is to be a mass culture success, it must be immediately acceptable, understandable, familiar, and conducive to mass participation" (p. 43).

Hoskins and Mirus (1988) have also created a useful concept for examining the attraction of national programming to national audiences, the cultural discount:

> A particular programme rooted in one culture, and thus attractive in that environment, will have a diminished appeal elsewhere as viewers find it difficult to identify with the style, values, beliefs, institutions and behavioural patterns of the material in question. Included in the cultural discount are reductions in appreciation due to dubbing or subtitling.... As a result of the diminished appeal, fewer viewers will watch a foreign programme than a domestic programme of the same type and quality, and hence the value to the broadcasters, equal to the advertising revenue induced if the broadcaster is financed from this source, will be less ... the cultural discount explains why trade is predominantly in entertainment, primarily drama, programming (see Varis, 1985; Chapman, 1987) where the size of this discount is minimized. Informative programming is much more culture specific and hence, particularly for news and public affairs programming, subject to such a large discount that little trade takes place.... (pp. 500–501)

The idea of cultural proximity (Straubhaar, 1991) tries to explain why television production is growing within Latin America and other regions of the world at both the national and regional levels. The argument, building on Pool (1977), is that all other things being equal, audiences will tend to prefer programming that is closest or most proximate to their own culture: national programming if it can be supported by the local economy.

We anticipate that when national production is available, audiences tend to prefer it (driving an increase in national production). This is reflected in an increase over time in the proportion of national productions appearing in prime time, reflecting audiences' primary preferences. Audience data, such as ratings, tend to support this idea in Brazil, Chile, Dominican Republic, Mexico, and Venezuela.

The Brazilian case shows how strong the preference is for national programming. The major channel, TV Globo, produces over 12 hours a day of programming for itself, including over 80% of prime time programming. This kind of production can be achieved when the domestic producers respond to audience interests. Within Brazil, the desire for yet more cultural proximity is also leading toward an expressed desire for increased localization in news and entertainment to express and satisfy regional cultures within Brazil (personal interview with L. F. Santoro, 1990).

A similar desire for the most relevant or similar programs also seems to lead many national audiences to prefer cultural–linguistic regional programming in genres that small countries cannot afford to produce for themselves. The case of the audiences in smaller countries, such as the Dominican Republic, shows clearly a second layer of the search for cultural proximity; a preference first for national material, but when that cannot be filled in certain genres, a tendency to look next to regional Latin American, or in other regions, Arab world, Asian, or African productions, which are relatively more culturally proximate or similar than are those of the United States. The United States continues to have an advantage primarily in genres that even large Third World countries cannot afford to produce, such as feature films, cartoons, and action–adventure series.

Language Defined Markets

In the formation of television markets across national boundaries, almost all studies to date agree on the importance of language in creating television markets. This has been confirmed by economic studies of markets and, as we see later, by studies of individual behavior in several countries as well.

There is a distinct economic advantage for television or film producers who have a large natural language market. "Producers in countries that belong to large natural language markets, have a financial incentive to create larger budget films and programs that generally have greater intrinsic audience appeal, a clear advantage in international competition" (Wildman & Siwek, 1988, p. 68). Scholars such as Read have long pointed out that Hollywood producers had an intrinsic advantage in the size of the United States' market. The size and wealth of the U.S. market permitted producers to cover costs and even make a profit within the national market, permitting them to export programs at whatever price the importer could afford to pay (Read, 1976). A quick examination of the short list of global television exporters shows that most of the countries have large domestic markets: Brazil, Egypt, India, Mexico, and the United States.

However, a number of successful television exporting nations are not so much large as relatively wealthy, compared to other nations of the world. When one considers the export success of France, Great Britain, Hong Kong, and Japan, one can see that there is also a distinct advantage to wealthy natural language markets. Such wealth tends to coincide with either having been a colonial power, like Britain, Japan, or France, or having had a relatively privileged economic position within an empire, like Hong Kong. So, in addition to size of domestic market, the demographics of cultural–linguistic markets are crucial; wealth counts even more than size.

The wealth and size of language markets cumulates across boundaries, as well. The combined wealth of the English-speaking nations (Australia, Canada, Great Britain, the United States) makes it the language of advantage in providing a base for television production and export. As countries group together in cultural–linguistic markets, the combined wealth of the various national audiences will make other cultural–linguistic groupings other than English into very attractive markets. One can already see this logic at work in the growth of Spanish, Chinese, Hindi, and Arabic markets, where combined audiences across national markets are attractive to producers.

Regulatory openness also affects the attractiveness of markets. English and Spanish-speaking cultural–linguistic markets may have developed earlier than some others in part because their governments created fewer barriers to the flow of television programs across borders and into their markets. By contrast, several of the main Chinese-speaking markets remained closed to intraregional imports by national policy until recently, as a multicountry study of television flow from 1962 to 1992 by Straubhaar et al. (1992) shows.

There also may be an advantage to culturally diverse natural language markets. "The variety of populations immersed in the melting pot of the United States gave U.S. producers a kind of microcosm of the developed world's population as a home market ... their invention of a cultural form that is the closest to transnational acceptability of any yet contrived" (Collins, 1990, pp. 214–215).

At the individual audience level, competence, ability to speak or at least understand the language of a broadcast, is an important ingredient in audiences' selection of a program and their enjoyment of it. Language is a critical element of cultural capital (Bourdieu, 1984). However, we might also expect that language competence is more important for some kinds of programs than others, for verbally oriented programs more than visually oriented ones. Because some program genres are more visually oriented, like action–adventure programs that rely on violence and chase scenes, they ought to be less demanding of cultural capital, at least in linguistic terms. In contrast, language-oriented comedies and soap operas probably demand more language competence. So, whereas a person who can't speak English might still be able to enjoy an action movie or a music video, they probably would not enjoy a soap opera or a sitcom, unless it was virtually visual slapstick and not focused on language-based jokes.

Some studies such as those by Wildman or other economists tend to focus on language as the main issue in definition of cultural and linguistic markets. However, if language is most crucial, why are dubbed programs not as popular as local productions? The acceptability of dubbing seems to have been lower historically in large natural language markets, where demand could be effectively expressed for local production and where large production industries grew up to meet that demand for local production. For example, audiences in the United States, Germany, and Brazil all seem to reject dubbed programs in favor of locally produced ones where available (Straubhaar, 1991; Tracey, 1988).

On the other hand, a number of same language markets have clearly developed across national lines: Spanish, Chinese, Arabic, English, French, German, Hindi, Tamil, Malay, Portuguese. Some of these are primarily coincident with geographic regions, like Spanish (Latin America), Chinese (East and Southeast Asia), Arabic (Mid-East), German (Europe), Hindi and Tamil (South Asia), and Malay (Southeast Asia). Some are spread across the globe along former colonial lines, such as English, French, and Portuguese.

Cultural proximity is based to a large degree in language. However, besides language, there are other levels of similarity or proximity, based in cultural elements, per se: dress, ethnic types, gestures, body language, definitions of humor, ideas about story pacing, music traditions, religious elements, and so on. Indian movies are popular in the Arab world for such similarities, Brazilian *telenovelas* (evening serials or soaps) dubbed into Spanish are more popular than *Dallas* or *Dynasty* because of such similarities (Straubhaar, 1991b). Iwabuchi (1997) showed that Taiwanese young people see Japanese television and music as culturally proximate, sharing a sense of "Asian modernity," despite the language difference between Japanese and Chinese.

Culturally Defined Markets

Cultural–linguistic markets are defined by several factors, language, and other aspects of culture. "Audiences share the same or similar languages as well as intertwined histories and overlapping cultural characteristics … shared colonial legacies, independence movements, struggles against foreign hegemony, development challenges and the like have knit together a region where similarities extend beyond the languages spoken" (Wilkinson, 1995, pp. viii, 52).

Although cultural factors tend to be associated with language, they do often span similar cultures with differing languages. That often has to do with shared histories and geographic proximities, like those of Iberia, which unite Spanish and Portuguese cultures in many ways. Although Brazilians speak Portuguese rather than Spanish, they have a great deal in common with Spanish-speaking Latin Americans in terms of underlying culture inherited from Iberia and further developed and hybridized with other cultures in Latin America. So even though a Brazilian television program might have to be dubbed from Portuguese into Spanish, it will otherwise tend to look far more familiar to a Venezuelan than will a program from New York. The same logic is essentially true for Indian programs going into Pakistan, for example, and perhaps even Indian programs going into Saudi Arabia, where there is a long history of cultural contact.

There are a number of aspects of shared history that tend to draw countries together in cultural–linguistic markets. Ethnic groups migrated across areas separated by current political borders. It is common to have groups geographically isolated from their parent populations, like the multiple layers of Chinese, South Asians, and others that maintain their original languages and many aspects of their original cultures while coexisting with the dominant Malay population in Indonesia. There was a great deal of pre-European cultural and language group diffusion. Besides migrations, precolonial empires made conquests and resettled ethnic groups. European empires moved people around even more dramatically. For example, the dominant ethnic face of Latin America is due to the migration of Iberian colonists, who then brought millions of African slaves, who were followed in the 19th and 20th centuries by new waves of Europeans and Asians. Postcolonial relationships were formed when colonial populations also began to move back to the colonial power centers, such as Algerians moving to France or Jamaicans to Great Britain. Former colonies also interact with each other, borrowing elements from their shared roots. For example, shared African roots make it easy for Brazilians to borrow elements of Jamaican reggae to synthesize with their own samba, both variations on African rhythmic and percussive traditions.

Media programmers or marketers can take such commonalties and consciously try to synthesize a cultural–linguistic market out of common elements, glossing over significant differences. For example, broadcasters and marketers in the United States have attempted the construction of a pan-ethnic Hispanic audience in order to create a broader Latino market to economically justify production of programming and generate broader potential sales. Rodriques (1994) remarked that "This conceptualization of ethnicity ignores or submerges structural variables such as race and class, represented in differing U.S. immigration histories." As Rodrigues further noted, this construction of a pan-ethnic Latino audience (submerging racial identities ranging from indigenous, Black, or European to various combinations) has been consciously related to the creation of a broader Latin American market. "Latino panethnicity has been broadened in the construction of panamericanism, the notion that the U.S. Hispanic market is one segment—albeit the wealthiest segment—of a hemispheric market that embraces Spanish speakers in North, Central and South America" (Rodrigues, 1994).

Cultural proximity is an ambivalent factor in the creation of such broad cultural–linguistic markets, however. Whereas Chinese language and cultural heritage may draw together China, Hong Kong, and Taiwan into "Greater China" (Man Chan, 1996) and whereas Spanish language and cultural heritage may do the same in Latin America (Wilkinson, 1995), viewers' preferred level of cultural proximity may be very much more localized. Constituent elements of cultural proximity, such as dress and style, topical and locally relevant humor, familiar stars and actors, familiar ethnic types, familiar values, and issues, all tend to be very localized. For example, a certain idea for an historical soap opera about a famous Chinese judge, Judge Bao, has been produced in several different Chinese language markets. Although Taiwanese audiences did watch and enjoy a Hong Kong production of the story, Taiwanese producers interviewed by the author indicated that a local production was more popular. The Taiwan production pacing was slower (which the audience apparently preferred), the Mandarin idiom more localized, and the national television stars were more familiar. Rodrigues (1994) similarly noted that many of the subgroups of the U.S. Latino or Hispanic audience would really prefer to watch television more specific to their identities as Cuban-American, Mexican-American, or Puerto Rican.

DEFINING CULTURAL PROXIMITY

Cultural proximity builds on cultural capital, but is a separate dimension of identity. Cultural capital, as we see later, focuses on the sources of knowledge that permit people to make choices among media and other sources of information and culture. Cultural proximity is more of a disposition or a tendency toward the use of cultural capital in a certain way. Forms of cultural capital, in terms of what one knows about other countries and cultures, can lead people toward or away from cultural proximity, the tendency to prefer media products from one's own culture or the most similar possible culture.

Education is a principal source of cultural capital (Bourdieu, 1984). As we see later in the case of Brazil, basic education is often very nationally focused, reflecting national languages, nationally authorized and focused textbooks, and nationalized teacher training. However, postsecondary education, as the interviews conducted in this Brazilian case reflect, tends to increase exposure to a more globally focused set of knowledge. Basic education might then accentuate an audience focus on cultural proximity, whereas higher education might open interests to a more global view.

Family is the second principle source of cultural capital for Bourdieu (1984). He found striking differences between families of different social class levels in terms of what knowledge and tastes they stressed. Differences can be seen particularly in family daily life routines and what is stressed in daily cultural consumption. Various families emphasize different levels of culture—some very local, some national, some global. In the Brazilian case, we see a fairly consistent social class stratification along these lines, with lower class families being more locally oriented in their knowledge and habits, working class and middle class families more national, and elites more global. In their media choices, we will find lower class, working class, and lower middle class making more local and national choices, based on cultural proximity, then the upper middle classes and elites.

Families and schools, along with neighborhoods, are primary grounds of another source of cultural capital, personal and group networks. We should particularly highlight peer networks, friendships, and continuing ties with schoolmates. British and American sociological work on television audiences and their choices highlights the importance of such networks (Morley, 1992), as does Latin American research on cultural choice and interpretation, or mediation, by Martín-Barbero (1993).

These personal networks are particularly important in Brazil, which is often characterized as a personalistic society, where status and contacts matter greatly (da Matta, 1983). At one extreme, we see that lower class audiences have very localized networks that stress localized cultural capital and a very localized version of cultural proximity, preferring local music to national music, for example. At another extreme, elites often have family and school networks that are global, leading them to direct personal experience with global friends and contacts, perhaps to minimize cultural proximity, acquire a more globalized sense of personal identity, and pursue what they see as more cosmopolitan or global media choices.

Family income and interests tend to define another key source of cultural capital: travel. If some families never travel beyond their immediate locale, while others get to know more of their nation by travel, then the former will have a more localized cultural capital, while the latter are more nationalized in their knowledge and interests. If some families can afford and have interest in international travel, that creates a globalized form of cultural capital that may, again, minimize national or local cultural proximity and stress more global interests.

Religion is another major source of cultural capital. It often cuts across social class lines in a unique manner, but actual religious practices in daily life tend to vary somewhat with social class, at least in Brazil. Although most people in Brazil are at least nominally Catholic, actual forms of practice vary widely. Furthermore, lower class and working class respondents are increasingly more likely to either be involved with syncretic religions that mix Catholicism with African traditions, such as *candomblé* or *macumba*, or actually change religious practices and join the rapidly growing evangelical Protestant groups. Still, activity in most of these religions tends to reinforce a certain sense of local or national tradition and values, which seems to reinforce a sense of cultural proximity, except perhaps for some of the Protestant groups that maintain very strong ties to U.S. churches.

Nonreligious associations, like unions, professional organizations, neighborhood associations, sports clubs, and hobby and interest groups also provide important inputs to cultural capital. In Latin America, Martín-Barbero (1993) seemed to indicate that most of these associations tend to reinforce localized cultural dispositions and forms of knowledge, which we see confirmed in the Brazilian interviews that follow. However, some fraction of the viewing public are drawn into interpersonal associations that help create national, supranational, or global cultural capital, as when someone joins a national or international professional association. However, such direct global interpersonal interaction presupposes both economic capital or wealth and other forms of cultural capital, such as education and family connections.

These are the major channels of cultural capital: schooling, family practices, family networks, personal networks, travel, religion, groups or associations. These help determine or mediate mass media choices (Martín-Barbero, 1993). However,

6. CULTURAL CAPITAL, LANGUAGE, CULTURAL PROXIMITY

the media themselves are also a source of cultural capital. The relationship is not a simple one of effects, either of media affecting values and ideas, or even of values and ideas from other sources cleanly determining media choices and likewise determining interpretations of media contents. Mass media, like television, are a source of cultural capital. However, other sources of cultural capital also mediate choices for mass media, like television. The interaction is complex.

Together with education, family, networks, travel, and religion, media help form specific types of cultural capital. In particular, these channels of communication all help construct meanings for three other principle bases of cultural capital, ethnicity, age and gender. Although ethnicity, age, and gender consist in some part of physical characteristics, the meaning assigned those characteristics is socially constructed (Maccoby, 1966). The meaning constructed for these characteristics becomes part of the cultural capital used by people in making media choices.

Ethnicity is important in the construction of national or "regional" cultural–linguistic markets. In fact, ethnic identity can be seen as constituting a type of cultural capital. The ethnic make-up of a television program cast affects its visual appeal to an audience. If people can recognize themselves or a familiar or desired ethnic type on screen, that would add to the cultural proximity of a program. Ethnic appeal can come from actual ethnicity or ethnic ideals. Within Brazil, for example, there is divergence among broadcasters over whether to broadcast an ethnic ideal that appeals to the more affluent consumer classes, largely European in ethnicity, or whether to appeal to the larger television audience, which is around half African-Brazilian. The main network, TV Globo, has often been accused of underrepresenting African-Brazilians in both programming and commercials (Leslie, 1991). In an effort to segment the national audience and compete with the dominant national network, two other networks, SBT and Record, are creating interview, "reality," game, and variety show type programming that addresses working and lower classes' sense of identity or cultural capital by using participants who are ethnically more representative of the diversity of the Brazilian audience.

Age is sometimes seen as a crucial differentiating demographic characteristic in the preference for globalized culture, almost a basis of cultural capital in itself. Many observers have noted that younger people tend to be more involved in global or at least transnational cultural patterns than older people. A number of studies have shown that young people tend to have more globalized music tastes, for instance (Robinson, Buck, & Cuthbert, 1991), although young people are also divided by class, education, and so on in these same patterns discussed (Straubhaar & Viscasillas, 1991). Young people in Brazil are very divided by class in terms of their preferences, as we see later.

Gender images and concepts about gender roles are also elements of cultural capital that bear on preferences for cultural proximity or cosmopolitanism. If *Baywatch* shows roles for women that clash strongly with locally or nationally held ideas about how women ought to dress and behave, then those local traditions, reflected in and reinforced by religion, family practices, forms of education, and the like function as forms of cultural capital that will likely lead many people to choose to avoid the program. Those sorts of individual and household choices, cumulated across a culture, especially when articulated and reinforced by leaders, like the Iranian clerics, can result in a violent rejection of imported culture, as during the Iranian Revolution. On the other hand, we know from its export success that many people do like to watch *Baywatch*, so we have to be aware of contradictory and dialectic processes within the audience between cultural proximity and the attraction of foreign cultural products.

Class and age seem to be directly related to general preferences for global, regional, national, or local culture. Gender seems tied to cultural use patterns that are less general, more specific to genre. Gender is a powerful factor in patterns of interest, use, and interpretation of a number of television genres. For example, there is evidence from India and from Greece that women find certain kinds of imported genres to be liberating in the sense that they offer messages that seem to show roles for women beyond those indicated by the local culture. Women in India may read romance novels (Parameswaran, 1997) or women in Greece may watch imported television and find such messages, which draws their interest further toward the imported genres (Zaharopoulos, 1997), and leads them to incorporate some of these messages in their own culture. There is some evidence from at least Brazil and the Dominican Republic that men do tend to prefer some major global cultural genres, such as action films or television series more than women (Straubhaar, 1991a, 1991b).

Gender does tend to work in noticeable patterns with national and regional genres as well. Women watch certain kinds of programming more, such as soap operas in the United States, whereas men tend to watch more sports in most countries. Men and women will also read the messages of national and regional productions differently. In Brazil, both women and men watch telenovelas, for example, but several studies have noted that women tend to pick up more messages about alternative women's roles and tend to interpret them in a more emancipating manner (Vink, 1988).

We can identify a number of more specific elements of cultural capital that can tend to favor an audience disposition toward cultural proximity. These tend to be acquired from sources of cultural capital mentioned earlier: schools, family, family networks, travel, and mass media themselves.

A discussion on defining and operationalizing cultural proximity was held at a conference organized in Taiwan by Georgette Wang in 1998. Dr. Eddie Kuo suggested several factors related to cultural affinities and Professor Koichi Iwabuchi noted the importance of perceived similarities. Another set of factors could be termed perceived cultural relevance (Paterson, 1998). A last set of defining factors focuses on images and values. Although these are often treated as effects of both domestic and cross-cultural television on audiences (Elasmar & Hunter, 1996), interviews for this study suggest that they also operate as aspects or considerations within viewing choices by audiences.

Cultural affinities create forms of of cultural capital that inform cultural proximity. Such affinities could be seen in very specific factors such as linguistic commonalities, shared religious histories, gender roles, moral values, common aspirations, common histories with colonialism, shared art forms, shared music forms, similar forms of dress, character types and stereotypes, and ideas about genre, storytelling, and pacing. Perceived cultural similarities also might include ethnic types, gender types (discussed earlier), dress, style, gestures, body language, and lifestyle. Perceived cultural relevance seems to include news and discussion topics, definitions of humor, familiar stars and actors, and audience knowledge about other lifestyles. Images and values include perceptions of other countries and peoples, opinions or evaluations of them, and values about marriage, family relationships, importance of material goods, work, and where and how to live.

These specific kinds or forms of cultural capital add up. By interviewing audience members about what their knowledge and dispositions are in these terms, one can get a sense of whether they are relatively localized or globalized in their approach to media choices. By looking at a television program, listing its qualities or characteristics in these terms, one can get a sense of how well that program might correspond with audience interests. If imported television programming for the United States or other "cosmopolitan" production centers is too different from audience expectations based on these very specific elements of cultural capital, then prospective viewers are very like to apply what Hoskins and Mirus (1988) called a cultural discount and avoid them. On the other hand, because programming created within a culture will probably correspond reasonably well with its audience expectations, we could expect them to apply a sense of cultural proximity and prefer that programming.

CULTURAL "SHAREABILITY" VERSUS CULTURAL PROXIMITY

Theorization and research about cultural proximity must take note of the fact that many programs have successfully crossed cultural and linguistic borders for decades, to the point of being described as a one-way flow from the United States in the early 1970s (Nordenstreng & Varis, 1974). American programming has been successfully exported to most countries and, increasingly, Japan, Mexico, Brazil, and Hong Kong are exporting television programs well beyond markets defined by either language or culture. Although this chapter argues that cultural proximity is a strong factor in most people's media choices, it is clearly contradicted or contravened by other factors, such as the appeal of the exotic (vs. the familiar), of "cosmopolitan" cultures (vs. local cultures), and of certain almost universal themes and archetypes (vs. locally-specific themes and types).

A specific, useful concept that to some degree opposes the notion of cultural proximity is cultural shareability, advanced by Singhal, Svenkrud, and Rogers (Singhal, Obregon, & Rogers, 1994). They noted that successfully exported television programs often share a language, such as the simplified export-oriented Spanish of *Simplemente María*, a Peruvian telenovela popular throughout much of Latin America (Singhal et al., 1994).

In a later work on the globally marketed Japanese television soap opera *Oshin*, Singhal and Udornpim (1997) attributed part of that series' cultural shareability to its use of cultural archetypes that span across a number of cultures. They built on Jung's description of archetypes as independent of mediation, existing in individuals worldwide (p. 174). For *Oshin*'s broad cross-cultural appeal, they cited the universal archetype of "self-seeking individuation," of self-determination, endurance, and strength. They also noted an archetype of the main character as a "disobedient female," a woman who defies oppressive social constraints. Third, they noted an archetype of "heroic struggle" and resistance against enemies, poverty, and misfortune until the heroine ultimately succeeded. We might add a fourth archetype common to soap operas in many cultures: upward mobility by the individual or family from poverty to material success.

So cultural proximity as a force in media choices exists in a dynamic tension with other motives and attractions. Cultural proximity is also limited by three other factors. First, there are material and structural limits at the production level on many cultures' ability to produce media products to meet the potential demand that cultural proximity might generate. Second, there are structural barriers of income or economic capital at the individual reception level that keep many people from getting access to media, particularly new channels like satellite TV or the Internet (Mosco, 1996). Third, there are less tangible barriers of cultural capital, as discussed earlier, at the individual level, which keep people from choosing or understanding some kinds of media, particularly those in other languages or that presume an in-depth knowledge of other cultures.

Continuing Limits of Asymmetrical Interdependence on Media Production

Many would-be producers of television programming are constrained by economic realities. The continuing results of conditions of dependency, such as low income resources, lack of industrial infrastructure, lack of support by weak governments, inappropriate models for production, and lack of trained personnel, keep a number of poorer countries from developing much local or national production, even if their audiences might prefer more national programs. This is particularly true for the smallest and poorest of nations, such as the English-speaking Caribbean (Brown, 1987).

However, many countries, like the Dominican Republic or Mozambique, which have extremely limited industrialization, do produce significant cultural goods, particularly music, but also television. Rather than classic, almost complete dependency, most countries find themselves in a complex, asymmetrical interdependence. This is particularly true in cultural industries, first, because cultural industries are less capital intensive than others. Technology costs for radio and television production, in particular, unlike film, have been falling significantly in the 1980s and 1990s, accelerated by the current wave of digitization that permits complex mixing, effects, and sound work via personal computers. Second, because the "raw materials" of cultural production are found almost everywhere in local music, political talk, humor, and dramatic situations. Third, relatedly, because most people seem to like local productions better in most genres, particularly in music and television, due to cultural proximity. So these factors do impel production, both at the national level in the most affordable genres, such as talk shows, news, live music, and live variety, and in the larger producers for cultural–linguistic regions, in more expensive genres such as soap opera, situation comedies, dramas, and action–adventure (Straubhaar et al., 1992).

Cultural Proximity Modified by Class

Dependency theorists argued that elites and middle classes would tend to be internationalized in their tastes, attentions, and loyalties (Chilcote, 1984; Dos Santos, 1973; Salinas & Paldan, 1979). This chapter examines what has been happening with elite audiences, particularly as they come to have access to the new cable and satellite television services, which offer a new set of global and regional channels. As a working proposition, in line with dependency theory, these elites do in fact seem to be more internationalized in their television use than do lower middle classes, working classes, and the poor.

There is another assumption hidden in theorizations by Dos Santos and Cardoso, that elite notions, tastes, and interests would be passed down in a hegemonic process to the masses of the audience. One problem with this is the assumed passivity of the developing nations' mass audiences. Both behavioral science researchers, such as the uses and gratifications school (Blumler & Katz, 1974), and cultural studies researchers, such as Morley (1980), have consistently rejected the view of the audience as a passive entity. Fejes (1981) and Ang (1996), in reassessing the legacy of critical theory, including international dependency theory, remarked that political economy-based theories did often lose sight of the audience and its actual behavior. However, as Ang noted, it is also too easy to speak glibly of an active audience without considering the political economic context. As noted earlier, national poverty still radically limits the production abilities of many nations. Furthermore, the spread of patterns of commercial television, for example, does limit audience options to the commercially successful formulas, even when locally produced, and does tend to present a strong set of messages driving consumer behavior (Oliveira, 1993).

Economic Capital and the Limits on Individual and Household Television Technology Access

Primarily, this chapter is concerned with how language, cultural proximity, and cultural capital tend to affect what audiences do with television once they have access to it. However, it is very important to continue to recognize that billions of people are limited in their access to television, particularly the newer television technologies, because they cannot afford access to them.

In 1978, the McBride report noted that much of the world's population did not have access to many of the dominant communications technologies, including television (McBride Commission, 1980). Since that time, access to broadcast television has rapidly accelerated in many of the world's larger developing countries. In Brazil and Mexico, almost 90% of all the population have access, greatly increased since the 1970s. China has increased access to television even faster, from only 3 million television sets in 1979 to 230 million sets in 200 million TV households by 1992 (Karp, January 27, 1994). This is largely because a television set has emerged as the number one consumer purchase for much of the world's population, including much of the world's poor. However, in the poorest African countries, such as Mozambique, broadcasters estimate that under one quarter of the population has access to television (from interviews by author with several Southern Africa broadcasters).

The economic capital aspect of social class is the most exclusive with the newest television technologies. Monthly fees for cable television tend to be in the U.S. $20 to $30 range even in developing countries. When median monthly incomes are often still in the U.S. $100 to $200 range for much of the population in countries like Brazil, then access to cable or pay television is simply blocked by lack of economic capital, so that less than 5% of the audience has cable or satellite television as of 1997, whereas almost 75% of homes in increasingly middle-class Taiwan have cable. In most developing countries, cable television is a middle-class or even upper-middle class technology that excludes most of the population. To date, direct broadcast satellite technologies (DBS) tend to be even more expensive, including the initial cost of the satellite dish.

When economic class/capital gives access to new television technologies, that permits privileged audiences a far more globalized form of media consumption. The new television technologies nearly always emphasize global, usually American content, at least at first. The supply of films on videocassette in most countries is still dominated by Hollywood productions, although that may be changing in Asia, where Indian and Hong Kong productions are very popular and widely available on video. The initial offerings of most of the current transnational DBS channels and cable channels also tended to emphasize the existing American, British, or Japanese satellite/cable channels, although one reason cable is so popular in Taiwan is that there are a large number of domestic channels as well as channels from Hong Kong, China, and Japan within the cultural–linguistic region.

Cultural Capital and Limits on Individual Preferences for Global Television

However, building on Bourdieu, we might point out that media access obtained by virtue of economic capital and the cultural capital involved in selecting media contents are not necessarily equivalent. Some of the early critiques that new media

6. CULTURAL CAPITAL, LANGUAGE, CULTURAL PROXIMITY

technologies would unleash a new wave of cultural imperialism contained a degree of technological determinism that seems questionable. Early critiques by Mattelart and Schmucler (1985) and others seemed to imply that all those who had increased access to foreign culture via new media would want to watch that imported culture.

This chapter argues that people in "national" television audiences are divided even more by cultural capital than they are by economic capital. Cultural capital can be very exclusive. "Access to these, not imagined but virtual communities, to these neo-worlds constituted by the 'iconic-symbolic' and 'graphic/dictive' flows is exclusive. It is based on the power and ability to decode (and encode) the signals in the flows. Such decoding/encoding ability depends on the possession of particular, virtual-community-specific types of cultural capital" (Featherstone & Lash, 1995, p. 11).

BRAZILIAN CASE STUDY

To examine cultural capital formation and its relation to television choices, the author conducted a series of in-depth interviews over a 10-year period, 1989 to 1998, in Brazil. Almost 120 baseline interviews were conducted in São Paulo in 1989 to 1990 by the author and students working with him. They were structured but in-depth interviews on media habits and social class identity across a stratified sample based on age, class, and gender profiles from the 1988 Brazilian census update (PENAD). Subsequent in-depth interviews were conducted in São Paulo, with working class, lower middle class, middle class, upper middle class, and upper class people. Interviews were also conducted in Salvador and Ilheus, Bahia, with the same kinds of classes, plus urban and rural poor. These last two cities also provided an opportunity to focus on African-Brazilians, compared to those in São Paulo, who are disproportionately more likely to be of European origin. Another 110 interviews were conducted from 1991 to 1998, making a total of 228 people interviewed. About 35 were reinterviewed at least once over the years.

There is some disagreement among Brazilian audience and market researchers about definition of social classes, particularly about the size of the elite and upper middle class, who are the most avidly sought consumers. This chapter begins with definitions based on Brazilian market research, particularly the ABIPEME social classification system,[1] that focuses on education and major acquisitions, like cars and appliances, that demonstrate purchasing power. This chapter also focuses on characteristics, like travel, occupation, family background and connections, type and quality of formal education, and language education; and on media access, like

---

[1]In Brazil, the weight of cultural capital in determining one's social class standing seems to be clear in the index adopted by the association of audience and market survey agencies ABA/ABIPEME. This weighted point criteria balances the education of the head of the family with the possession of several key icons of acquisitive power to classify social classes in five hierarchical groups, from A to E. Illustratively, having a college degree is worth far more points than completing only the elementary school or owning any home appliance.

Internet, satellite/cable television, print media, that relate to theoretical constructs about globalization that are important to the study.

By ABIPEME definitions, commonly used as a shorthand for class status even in Brazilian media, the elite, Class A, are roughly 3% to 5% of Brazilian society. The upper middle, Class B, is roughly the next 8% to 10%. The middle class, C, are about 15% to 20%. The working class, D, are about 25% to 35%, and the poor, Class E, are 30% to 50%, depending on the region of the country and fluctuating levels of poverty and employment. This chapter uses this rough five-category system and tends to confirm its proportions, but adds a number of factors about media access.

In this chapter, the elite respondents are defined as those who have at least $2,500 a month in income, have all major consumer appliances, and a nice car. Although some of the older elite are self-made and uneducated, the younger members almost all have university education. In terms most relevant to globalization of media and culture, they have access to international travel, to learning foreign languages, to satellite and cable television, to computers and the Internet, and to all print media, often including foreign language media. The most distinguishing thing about them, from these interviews, is that they have direct, unmediated personal access to global culture via travel, work, education, and other direct experiences. They also tended to aspire to a lifestyle defined in global terms by both media and direct experience, like travel to the United States or Europe. This is the group that is potentially truly globalized, although many of the elite do not use their potential global access and have primarily national mediated and personal cultural and informational experience.

The upper middle class tends to have most of the same characteristics, but lacks some of the economic capital that would provide access to frequent international travel and to the kind of private primary and secondary schooling that permits the elite to get into the best universities, including education abroad. Upper middle class people do not have the same access to global interpersonal connections so their access to global information and culture tends to be mediated via mass media and Brazilian schooling. This group does tend to aspire to achieve more direct global experience by travel, education, and so on. They also aspire at least somewhat to a lifestyle defined in part by global media images received at home via television and movies, and are more likely to pursue global media content within Brazil on radio, television, and film.

The middle class in Brazil is largely defined in national terms. The working definition that emerged from the interviews was that middle class meant a car, a telephone, a respectable dwelling (defined in fairly local terms), a few major appliances, like a refrigerator, and good prospects for at least a high school education, with hopes of university. Middle class people were nationally rather than globally focused in media consumption. Their material aspirations seem to be formed primarily by the dominant national media, such as television advertising, lifestyle images from telenovelas, variety shows, and, to lesser degree, by international music and foreign movies that are shown after 10 p.m. on television, although many middle class people don't typically stay up for those. Their experience of the global is almost entirely filtered through Brazilian media, although some middle class people are willing to spend scarce resources for international media, like pay-TV. Within Brazilian media, they are more likely to have access to print media, which carry more global content, as well as television and radio.

The lower middle class and working class are defined in terms of having decent housing (as defined locally), a fairly steady income and employment, and usually some education. They aspire to the national middle class lifestyle, largely as defined by telenovelas, especially a better house, a car, a telephone, more appliances, and maybe a vacation. Their global images are formed almost exclusively by television and music, as print media are mostly priced out of their reach. They often do not realize that brands they aspire to are global—things are framed almost exclusively within a national context for them.

The poor earn little, often well under U.S. $100 a month, or less than the minimum wage. They can afford little consumption, although most who have a fixed dwelling also have a television. Most have a dirt floor, few have refrigerators or stoves. They aspire to the necessities of life, defined in local terms in style of food, clothing, and so on. Few have anything beyond 4 years of primary education. Media access is either radio, which almost all have, or television: around 50% or so of rural dwellers have a TV, compared to 80% or more of the urban poor. Their media consumption tends to be local, provincial/regional, or national. They express little interest in foreign or global content.

Culture and Media Commonalities Across Class Boundaries

Despite the notable differences in class and in media access across classes, a striking amount of national cultural capital is common across classes in Brazil. This common cultural capital is almost all based in either basic schooling or broadcast media, particularly television. More specifically, an enormous amount of this common culture comes from telenovelas, popular music, carnival, and sports, particularly soccer. This replicates findings from Kottak's (1990) mammoth study in the mid-1980s of television and culture in Brazil in six coordinated but geographically dispersed ethnographic field studies. Kottak found that there was a mass, democratizing common knowledge across social classes at his sites, represented in telenovelas, soccer, and carnival. The latter two are both directly experienced but also commonly experienced in terms of national television. He noted the existence of common "codes ... well within the spectator's intellectual, verbal and psychological repertoire" (p. 43).

A base in terms of popularly held notions about Brazilian history and identity does seem to come from primary schooling, but most common culture seems to rely on broadcast media experience, rather than direct experience. Direct experience in Brazil is often still very localized, particularly for the working class and poor, in terms of local climate, local ethnic tradition, local cooking, local music, and local groups and their leadership.

The existence of this broad common national cultural capital base in Brazil is relatively new. Brazilian cultural had traditionally been very regionalized. Even the national popularity of soccer and carnival has grown slowly in the 20th century, impelled first by radio and then television, along with the slow growth in penetration of primary education (Milanesi, 1978). The achievement of the current degree of common national cultural capital and identity represents a substantial achievement of one of the main development goals set first by developmentalist regimes in the late 1950s and most specifically by the military regimes from 1964 to 1985 (Mattos, 1982). The military specifically saw the achievement of a consumer culture and a common national identity via national television as one of their main national security goals (Mattos, 1982, 1990). To achieve this, they poured a great deal of money into television, particularly one main commercial network, TV Globo (Straubhaar, 1984). Kottak (1990) noted that by 1985 TV Globo had indeed achieved this position as a primary source of cultural capital. "The cultural reason that Globo is such a powerful force in contemporary Brazil is its appeal across regions, classes and other social boundaries.... Because Globo offers quality programming, its appeal even extends to upper class people" (p. 44).

This common cultural capital is very largely national. The programs that almost everyone watches on television are telenovelas, some sports (soccer, basketball, and volleyball), reality shows, talk shows, music shows, and variety shows. The music that almost everyone is familiar with from the radio tends to be mostly from several national genres, with a limited amount of foreign rock and pop, mostly a few international songs that are included on telenovela soundtracks. There are some common consumer aspirations, focused on a few things that almost everyone consumes, such as clothes, sandals, beer, and soft drinks. Most of these, except Coke, are national brands, as the broad common level of consumption and aspiration throughout Brazil seldom even reaches the range of the kinds of products that most global manufacturers wish to manufacture. Other than Coca-Cola, most global firms don't try to make the kinds of things that poor people can afford. Even Levis remain out of most people's grasp. The average poor Brazilian wears rubber thong sandals, a T-shirt, and shorts. They like Coke but don't get to drink it that often; they are more likely to drink juice or local alcohol.

This predominance of national cultural capital tends to reinforce a high level of nationally shared interest in cultural proximity across the various class layers of the Brazilian audience. Even the elite watch telenovelas, listen to national music, and pay attention to national issues in news and talk shows.

Some Broadly Shared Globalization via Television

On the other hand, media exposure has produced some degree of globalization in almost all Brazilians. Very few have no global layer at all to their identity or cultural capital. At the simplest level, people are aware that there is an outside world, an America, a Japan, although "foreignness" is relative. More than one Northeastern

6. CULTURAL CAPITAL, LANGUAGE, CULTURAL PROXIMITY

Brazilian interviewee thought Japan was down by São Paulo someplace and didn't realize that people speak languages other than Portuguese, because everything on television is in Portuguese and the dubbing isn't always obvious to people. Almost all people are aware of a few international figures (Kennedy, Hitler, Princess Diana—depending on the generation of the interviewee), a few brands (like Coke), a few stars, movies, and music groups (although many people recognize Beatles' tunes without knowing who they were or where they were from).

But these globalized symbols are also mostly localized in the minds of most people as they become part of the broad common Brazilian cultural capital. For example, for critics, Coke remains the apogee of globalization. It probably is, but it has been successfully de-Americanized in the process. Its meaning for local people has been woven into the fabric of their culture. Coke represents a new, global kind of consumption, but its meaning has also been hybridized. Many people do not think of it as American. One student of the author interviewed a São Paulo man in 1994 who worked at a Coca-Cola bottling plant, but did not realize that it was an "American" product. He argued vehemently that it was Brazilian. This is probably a mark of success for Coke's global marketing that localizes it in Brazil by putting Brazilian national soccer shirts on polar bears holding Coke bottles and soccer balls. The polar bears are themselves a global symbol of cold that has been hybridized into tropical Brazil, where a selling point for both beer and soft drinks is that they are sold very cold (*"bem geladinha"*). Global symbols like these are interpreted in a local context and through hybridization (Canclini, 1995), eventually becoming part of the local context, changing and globalizing that context.

This minimum globalization that almost all Brazilians have is almost entirely as result of media exposure, particularly radio, television, and movies on television. Interviews by both the author and students working with the author show that few Brazilians outside the upper middle and upper classes have any direct, unmediated contact with foreigners or with "global" culture. In contrast, interviews in the Dominican Republic in 1987 to 1988 showed that almost everyone knew someone who has been in the United States to work or live, so Dominicans participate much more in the diasporic or migrant approach to globalization, emphasized by scholars like Bhahba (1994). In contrast, due to its geographic distance to the United States and its more self-contained economy, the vast majority of Brazilians participate only in mediated and very limited globalization, acquiring very little global cultural capital.

Cultural Capital of Poor Brazilians

Many rural and extremely poor urban Brazilians are only beginning to acquire cultural capital via media and schooling. Many are still relying very heavily on traditional oral cultures that tend to be very localized, so many poor Brazilians are only somewhat inserted into the national cultural context. As noted previously, however, even most poor Brazilians are coming into increasing contact with radio and television. Whereas radio is still often a localizing force in terms of music, news, and particularly talk, television is very much a nationalizing force in the lives of poor people.

The vast majority of what little global influence reaches poor people does so through television. In rural areas, access to television varies with electrification, proximity to or coverage by broadcast television signals, access to satellite dishes, and economical capital, or income. The very poorest 10% or so are not geographically stable, migrating to look for land or work. Increasingly, those who are stable on land or have a permanent urban dwelling have access to television. Recent migrants to urbanized areas acquire television very quickly before almost anything else. Rural dwellers are working hard to acquire television. For example, in the Cajueiro land reform community settled about 10 years ago (1988) near Una and Ilheus, Bahia, less than a third of the 55 settled families had television as of 1998, although people could watch a solar-powered set in the settlement school sometimes.

Rural dwellers are increasingly likely to share in the minimum common Brazilian national and global cultural capital described earlier. Writing of the mid-1980s, Kottak (1990) noted that "rural Brazilians' knowledge of the contemporary world … is certainly greater now than it was before television. By the mid-1980s, as a direct result of exposure to television, villagers had become much more world wise" (p. 134). Kottak and others observed that almost all of what rural and poor people in Brazil learn from television and radio is nationally focused. People in this study and in Kottak's spoke of national soccer, characters and themes on telenovelas, awareness of a few national political issues, and a general sense of what Brazilians have in common. Kottak noted that one of the primary impacts of television in Brazil has been to make previously isolated people feel comfortable with other Brazilians and with being Brazilian. Kottak gave the example of one very shy rural woman who remained very isolated even within her new village until her family got television. With television, and more regular social opportunities, she gradually became more outgoing and socially integrated (pp. 133–134).

The results of both Kottak's study and the present one show that television tends to add a number of national factors to the cultural capital of rural Brazilians. They become aware of Brazilian city life, as portrayed in the telenovelas, but the actual motivation to migrate to the city has much more to do with interpersonal contacts with migrants, particularly among their own families. They become aware of new ideas about race and gender roles, which tend to change locally held definitions and stereotypes. Kottak (1990) considered this process a powerful and largely positive liberalization of attitudes. They become aware of national holidays, foods, sports, and music, which gradually begin to supplement traditional local activities and consumption. They do also tend to receive a very minimal global awareness as described previously.

Interestingly enough, whereas relatively little global influence reaches rural Brazilians via television, other aspects of globalization can sometimes reach them more directly, if still in relatively small numbers. Rural dwellers do interact with aspects of the global economy in terms of who they work for, where they sell their crops, and what

6. CULTURAL CAPITAL, LANGUAGE, CULTURAL PROXIMITY 99

they aspire to buy. Because of global nongovernmental organization (NGO) concerns over issues like land reform, forest preservation, and sustainable agriculture, rural dwellers have increasing likelihood of direct contact with other Brazilians who are working for or with global NGOs. For example, rural organizations in Brazil, such as the *Movimento dos Sem Terra* (Movement of the Landless), have formed to obtain or defend land for landless or recently settled small farmers. The Cajueiro land reform settlement of formerly landless farmers is affiliated with that national organization and several local ones. Discussions in 1994, 1996, and 1998 with several Cajueiro community members showed that their knowledge and cultural capital was largely traditional, but they had been very much affected by several kinds of direct contact with both the landless movement and ecologically oriented Brazilian NGOs funded by Conservation International and the World Wildlife Fund. They had learned how to organize cooperative work groups and had begun to build co-op facilities to improve their access to fertilizer, crop processing, basic education, and medical aid. They had also become aware of the ideas of sustainable agriculture to preserve the rather fragile soils of their land and of preservation of some of the tropical forest that remained on the land they had seized to settle.

The poorest of the urban poor tend to have more contact with media, but theirs is often limited to watching television with neighbors or in public places. Like rural people, those without permanent dwellings are least drawn into media contact with either the national or the global. Interviews in 1989 and in 1994 with dwelling-less people in São Paulo showed that most of their cultural capital was based on interpersonal contacts within an oral culture context. Most are migrants to the city from rural areas and small towns. Much of their cultural capital is an adaptation of rural traditions to the city, but as they get drawn into urban social life and media use, their cultural capital becomes a hybrid of rural tradition and national urban culture. For example, the traditional music that rural migrants brought with them from the Northeast of Brazil to the major cities of the Southeast, like São Paulo, has been transformed into various hybrids that add electronic instruments, urban images and themes, and industrial production and marketing, to rural tunes, stories, and images. According to interviews, this kind of hybrid is welcomed by the migrants because it helps them adjust to life in the city while preserving a memory of the (oral) culture they grew up with.

Luiz Roberto Alves has studied the effort of migrants to São Paulo's industrial suburbs to maintain the memory of their original rural cultures. In a 1992 interview with the author, he observed that migrants tend to use hybrid media that maintain rural elements, but even more importantly, the migrants form interpretive communities of interpersonal communication that help them interpret national mass media in ways that help them create hybrid identities that bridge the urban and rural, the new national televised culture and the old oral, local culture. Interviews from 1989 to 1998 in São Paulo reflect that poor and working class people tend to make television viewing choices that are somewhat different from the national majority. They do tend to watch the dominant popular culture in TV Globo's telenovelas, but frequently they turn away from TV Globo to watch other channels that target programs more directly at this very substantial number of urban poor, working poor, working class, and lower middle class people. Two networks target variety and talk shows at the rural and urban working class and poor. SBT (Sistema Brasileira de Televisão, owned by longtime salesman and variety show host Silvio Santos) aims its variety shows, game shows, talk shows, telenovelas, and music specifically at this segment of the population (Mira, 1990), as a strategy of segmented competition with TV Globo, which tends to dominate the general mass audience. More recently, the Record Network has re-targeted the same kind of working class and poor audience with sensationalist talk/interview programs modeled on Jerry Springer and the like in the United States. These kinds of programs are often denounced by Brazilian critics as tasteless, coarse, even grotesque, but as Sodre (1972) noted in early work on variety shows, such shows do revive and incorporate both the styles and content of traditional Brazil oral culture and rural folklore. Further, as current critics, like Esther Hamburger of the *Folha de São Paulo*, often note, these shows raise issue of genuine concern to the urban poor and working class, airing grievances about roads, health conditions, medical care, and crime, as well as revealing sensational sexual scandals and provoking fistfights among participants. Hamburger (April 12, 1998) noted that one of the most sensationalist shows, *Ratinho*, (Little Mouse) on TV Record, actually beat TV Globo in the ratings one evening when Globo showed an imported series, *ER* instead of a telenovela in late prime time. She observed that although *ER* was a very high quality import, *Ratinho* was arguably much more relevant to people's lives and much more within their areas of interest and awareness.

Interviews with urban poor reflect a cultural capital that is a transition from the kind of local and traditional rural cultural capital just described to the national televised common cultural capital described earlier. Their cultural capital tends to focus on increasing awareness of urban issues, of city and national leaders, of urban transport and working conditions, of working class consumer aspirations (particularly in food, clothes, and basic household products), of national ethnic and religious images, of new urban gender roles, of less traditional sexual behavior and imagery, and a slightly greater knowledge of global culture than they had before coming to the city. Although much of this comes from national television, interviews show that the urban poor rely mostly on oral communication with the people and groups they know for essential cultural capital for adjusting to city life.

Working Class Cultural Capital

Not unlike the urban poor, from which they mostly come, working class people in Brazil have cultural capital that is mostly focused on the local and the regional, to lesser degree on the national, and fairly little on the international or global. Interviews in São Paulo and Salvador, Bahia for this study show that the interpersonal sources of working class cultural capital are focused and based on the extended

6. CULTURAL CAPITAL, LANGUAGE, CULTURAL PROXIMITY 101

family, the neighborhood, groups of friends of the same age and gender, the workplace and union, and, most of all, the immediate nuclear family and the home. Jacks (1995) talked about the importance of the home and of daily life as the crux of people's reception and understanding of television in Brazil. Whereas this was true of most of those interviewed for this study, it seemed particularly key for working class people who are working hard to establish and maintain a stable residence and home environment, aware of the danger of slipping back into the urban poor and maybe even into homelessness. Interviews from 1989 to 1992 evidenced a particularly strong sense of anxiety about this. The church, either Catholic or Protestant, is important for some, but not all, as an additional source of cultural capital.

Media sources, particularly radio and television, are very important for most working class people as a primary source of cultural capital. Among those interviewed, almost all global and cultural–linguistic "regional" cultural capital comes to working class or poor people via media, or to a lesser degree, formal schooling. Working class schooling is often limited, however, to 4 to 6 years of primary school, which limits schooling's role in cultural capital formation. However, working class parents and youth, with a certain amount of stability in the city, tend to start focusing more on the school as a source of educational capital for upward mobility.

Working class people, based on a locally or nationally oriented store of cultural capital, tend to make media choices that reinforce what is familiar or culturally proximate to them. Working class people are much more likely to listen to radio stations that play only national or local music genres, such as samba, forró (Northeastern dance music), Axé (samba plus reggae), or Musica Popular Brasileiro (MPB—Brazilian pop music), whereas upper middle or upper class interviewees were more likely to listen to stations that played either U.S./European pop music or a mixture of imported and Brazilian music.

Working class print media exposure is much more limited and much more largely national than is the print media usage of the upper middle and upper class. Working class people mostly read magazines and newspapers, rather than books, a trend noted across Latin America by Martin-Barbero (1993). The books read by working class interviewees tended to be either national popular literature or popular U.S./European genre novels in translation.

Working class Brazilians travel between cities by bus while the upper middle class and upper class tend to go by airplane. It is revealing therefore to compare what is in a large bookstore or newsstand in a São Paulo bus station with what is in an equivalent shop in the São Paulo airport. The bus station shop has more magazines, comics, and cheaply printed chapterbooks and pamphlets than books, although the book section is of a respectable size. Aside from the comics, many of which are Disney, Marvel, and DC translations, and the translated novels, almost everything else is national in origin. At the airport, the same national newspapers, magazines, and books are available, as are the translated comics and novels. The selection in the latter two is different with a more affluent audience, with more expensive book editions and more H.Q. or "high quality" comics translations. What is most noticeable is much more foreign literature in translation and a significant number of foreign language books, magazines, and newspapers aimed at both international travelers and those Brazilians with elite cultural capital such as sufficient foreign language skills to read comfortably for pleasure in another language.

Middle Class Cultural Capital

Working class Brazilians aspire to be middle class, at least lower middle class. That typically means a nicer dwelling, a car, more appliances, a telephone, and more and better education, aiming at completed secondary or maybe even university education. To the interviewees, it also implies a less blue collar occupation, different neighborhoods, paying for private schools, and adherence to what is seen as a more conventional set of values and mores.

An image of what it is to be middle class seems to be one of the main items of cultural capital that interviewees acquire from watching television, particularly the telenovelas. Although census statistics tend to indicate that mobility from working class or lower to the middle class is fairly low in real life in Brazil, this is very much the stuff of which telenovela plots are made, according to reviewers like Artur da Távola (1984). Reviewing an ostensibly Americanized telenovela with discos, called *Dancin' Days*, in the late 1970s, da Távola observed that it, like most novelas, was really about how to become middle class. The defining moment for him came not in the disco scenes, but when one of the characters asked his wife if she would like a refrigerator and she burst into tears of joy (cited in Straubhar, 1982). Interviewees agree. They think telenovelas mostly focus on romance, getting ahead in life (upward mobility—"*subir na vida*"), and the urban middle class. Aside from consumer items, like refrigerators, the Brazilian cultural capital understanding or perception of "middle class" seems to focus on education, family stability, a better and more varied diet, greater leisure options, better housing, and a sense of security, according to interviewees, both in the middle class and beneath it.

The cultural capital of those actually in the middle class still largely comes from television. Middle class television choices are somewhat different, tending to disdain the working class-oriented variety shows of SBT and focus much more on the telenovela-oriented contents of TV Globo. Middle class cultural capital is much more heavily supplemented beyond television, however, by education, print media use, personal contacts, and organizations like churches, clubs, and networks of friends from school. Several newspaper critics and this study's interviewees noted that one of the key differences between working class and middle class is that the latter has more nonmediated options for information, entertainment, and leisure ("Televisão, a triste lazer dos paulistanos," March 1977).

Middle class Brazilians are somewhat more globalized than are the working class in the kinds of media choices they make. Middle class interviewees are much more likely to stay up after 10 p.m. so they can watch the American movies that are typically shown then on several channels. That expresses cultural capital already acquired through schooling and media, but it also reinforces a more globalized

6. CULTURAL CAPITAL, LANGUAGE, CULTURAL PROXIMITY

cultural capital. Movies in the cinema houses have become very expensive, so even middle class people go to them fairly infrequently. But between late movies on television and rented movies on video, feature films seem to be an important source of American and global cultural capital for a fair number of middle class Brazilians, whereas American or other imported movies do not seem particularly important to working class or poor Brazilians, who are much more likely to prefer the national programs broadcast on television. However, even middle class or upper middle class Brazilians usually prefer prime time telenovelas to watching movies on video, even when they have the VCR sometimes gathering dust on a shelf. Although some middle class Brazilians do have satellite dishes and/or cable connections, those interviewed for this study were more likely to be using them to get a good quality signal for TV Globo than to buy pay-TV packages that would deliver dozens of extra channels in English.

Upper Middle and Upper Class Cultural Capital

A greater degree of globalization, both in media choices and in direct personal experience, is perhaps the main thing that divided upper middle class and upper class interviewees from those in the middle class and working class. The upper class are characterized by a number of globalized attributes: language skills, particularly in English; higher education, with either study abroad or aspirations to do so; international travel, particularly to the United States and Europe; occupations that lend themselves to contact with people in the United States and Europe, or, increasingly, Asia; interest in U.S. and European lifestyles; knowledge of those lifestyles; identification with European standards of beauty, including ethnicity; and detailed knowledge of both high culture and popular culture in the United States and Europe. Upper class Brazilians are often divided in whether their global cultural capital is linked to Europe or to the United States, particularly for those who have been at least partially educated abroad, and who have learned English versus another of the European languages.

The upper middle class interviewees tend to aspire to all of this direct experience with the global. Their actual experience with global culture is likely to be more heavily mediated, however. Most upper middle class Brazilians have eventually made a trip to Miami and/or Disney World, but they have otherwise traveled far less than the elite. Upper middle class global cultural capital tends to be more focused on the United States and less on Europe, perhaps because physical access to the United States is cheaper, study of English as a foreign language is more prevalent, and because U.S. culture is much more widely available in mediated forms. Upper middle class interviewees seemed to be the most likely to watch American movies on video or to make use of the movie channels on pay-TV packages for satellite dishes or cable TV.

Language skill is one sharp dividing line between the upper class elite, and the upper middle classes. Comments by interviewees indicate that real skill in English, sufficient to watch and enjoy CNN, for example, is largely limited to the upper class.

Middle class people find language a major barrier to access to globalized information. So do many in the upper middle class, but many of them have set a serious goal to acquire better English as a tool to bridge into elite-level media access to more global sources. English and access to information through it are seen by many in the upper middle class as a crucial tool to be acquired. However, for most of them it also remains a crucial barrier that ultimately tends to reinforce their use of national media, particularly the telenovelas, music shows, variety shows, and so on, that are part of the broad national cultural capital.

Brazilian MTV provides an interesting case of globalization aimed at the upper, upper middle, and some of the middle class in Brazil. MTV Brazil is a joint venture between MTV and the large publisher Editor Abril. It plays 70% to 80% U.S. and European rock and pop music videos, but only targets the upper 20% to 30% of the population, in terms of class status and buying power, according to interviews in 1994 and 1998 with MTV Brazil research and marketing staff members. That is because their advertisers target the more affluent and the more globalized among Brazilian youth in terms of consumer preferences. They also target this group because it has the most interest in the U.S. and European music that MTV has to offer. The target is reached. A 1997 MARPLAN audience study of eight major urban markets in Brazil shows that 22% of MTV's audience tends to be in class A (upper class), 44% in class B (upper middle class), 28% in class C middle class), 6% in class D (working class) and none in class E (the poor) (*MTV Brazil*, 1997).

These middle, upper middle, and upper class youths have the cultural capital base that leads them away from a strictly national cultural capital and in a more globalized direction. They have a more elite education, which often includes serious study of English. They are more likely to have traveled abroad, or to know people there. They are more likely to be aware of American and European brands, due in part to MTV's own role in their cultural capital. They are more likely to be aware of American stars, lifestyles, and images, again partially due to MTV, as well as to movies at both cinema and video. However, even these more upper class youth still usually like Brazilian music, particularly that which incorporates rock, like Brazilian urban rock; reggae, like Axé; rap, funk, and other global elements. Some Brazilian music is part of the broad cultural capital shared across class lines that was discussed earlier.

CONCLUSION

Language, cultural capital, and cultural proximity do seem to be significant moderators of television flows between countries. Although the original cultural imperialism paradigm did not seem to anticipate this, it does seem that language, culture, and class can either facilitate or bar the internationalizing and globalizing flows of television.

Dependency theorists did anticipate the internationalization of the bourgeoisie (Chilcote, 1984; Dos Santos, 1973). This study finds that both economic capital and cultural capital do encourage the elite and upper middle classes of Brazil to watch

6. CULTURAL CAPITAL, LANGUAGE, CULTURAL PROXIMITY

more imported programming, particularly U.S. television programs and feature films. Even when countries in regions like Latin America begin to produce much or even most of their own programming, economic capital still gives privileged classes a continued greater access to foreign programming, first through VCRs and now, increasingly, through cable and satellite TV. This was strongly demonstrated in the interviews in Brazil, where the top 5% to 10% of the population have much more globalized media access.

Cultural capital reinforces the use of this access to imported media and TV programming by giving elites and upper middle classes the ability to understand and enjoy programming imported from outside their cultural–linguistic region. This kind of cultural capital is clearest with language ability, which has been emphasized in economic studies (Hoskins & Mirus, 1988; Wildman & Siwek, 1988), but also includes education, travel abroad, familiarity with the ways of life of other countries, education abroad, work with international companies, and the kind of family life that is produced by and reinforces these kinds of advantages. This study found that nonmediated cultural capital from direct contact with global culture and people was decisive in making Brazilian elites far more globalized than the rest of the Brazilian population.

What media imperialism theorists did not anticipate was the growth of national and regional (cultural–linguistic) television producers, protected and encouraged within national and cultural–linguistic television markets, it seems, by elements of cultural capital that seem to provide natural barriers against interest in many types of imported programming, when national or regional alternatives are available. These are causes of what Hoskins and Mirus (1988) called the "cultural discount" that many audiences apply against imported programming. These aspects of cultural capital seem to include lack of language ability, which is particularly important in the early phases of television technologies and in less developed markets where dubbing is not yet extensively used. When VCRs first hit many markets, imported films were not yet dubbed or even subtitled—particularly when they were pirated copies (Boyd, Straubhaar, & Lent, 1989). In the initial introductions of cable and satellite television, as in the Dominican Republic in the 1980s when signals were taken straight from U.S. distribution satellites, or as in the early-to- mid-1990s in Brazil, where local pay-TV services often carried undubbed U.S. and European channels, language capital was also still crucial for watching the new undubbed channels.

Language is not the only significant aspect of cultural capital that favors national and cultural–linguistic market producers. The interviews cited previously have shown the importance of national references in humor, national or regional/local ethnic types, national or regional/local historical references, local or national political references, unfamiliarity with ways of life outside the nation or cultural–linguistic region, preference for known national or regional stars, and familiar scenery and locales. Another, which is touched on in the Brazilian study, is familiarity with national and regional genres, which even if they have U.S. or European roots, have taken on a life and trajectory of their own within the nation or region. In these Brazilian interviews, there is a distinct preference for the national form of the telenovela. Some of the people interviewed were aware of the Argentine and Mexican telenovelas, but none preferred them to national production. Since national production can fill prime time on several stations now, there is little motivation to watch imports.

To some degree, these attractions of national or culturally and linguistically similar forms of television programming can be summed up in the concept of cultural proximity. Audiences do seem to prefer that culture that is closest to their accumulated tastes, corresponding to their cultural capital. For the broad audience, consisting of lower middle, working, and poor classes, that tends to translate into a preference for national production. Outside of large countries like Brazil, where national production does not fill prime time, that translates into a strong secondary preference for productions from within the cultural–linguistic market to which the medium belongs. However, both economic capital access to new technologies and cultural capital familiarity with cosmopolitan, developed world cultures seem to be leading elites and upper middle classes away from national and cultural–linguistic market television genres and productions. That was reflected in Brazil. Although even elites still listen to Brazilian music and watch quite a bit of Brazilian television, they are strongly drawn to more globalized sources of culture and information.

One might speculate that as more national economies become globalized and as economic growth in many countries leads to a growth in middle classes, their acquisition of greater economic and cultural capital will tend to lead to a steadily larger proportion of many nations' populations viewing more U.S. and European programming. In-depth interviews by the author in both Brazil and the Dominican Republic, however, suggest that this effect will tend to be only partial, however. In both those countries, groups across the cultural capital spectrum all watch national television productions. What seems more likely, from what was suggested in the in-depth interviews, was that those with increased economic and cultural capital begin to have more multilayered identities. In Brazil, for example, elites still seem to identify heavily with Brazilian culture and like what they perceive as the best of Brazilian mass culture, including television and even *telenovelas*. They do, however, come to have other layers of taste for things and cultural products from U.S. and European cultures.

Within a seeming globalization, there seems more of a potential for uneven, multilayered cultural productions, flow or sales, and consumption, a type of asymmterical interdependence among various producing and importing television markets. On the production, sale and flow side, there is an asymmetrical interdependence in which Brazil imports more culture from the United States than it sells to the United States, but may compete quite successfully with U.S. cultural exports to other countries in Latin America, other Portuguese-speaking countries, or even the world market for historical soap opera, in which, incidentally, Brazil has successfully sold programs to over 100 countries (Marques de Melo, 1988, 1992). On the consumption side, there is a sort of uneven balance between the draw of cultural proximity among most of the audience and the draw toward other global offerings available to those members of middle and upper classes with cultural and economic capital.

ACKNOWLEDGMENT

An earlier version of this chapter was published as "Culture, Language and Social Class in the Globalization of Television," in Wang, et al., (Eds.), *The New Communication Landscape*. London: Routledge.

REFERENCES

Anderson, B. (1983). *Imagined communities: Reflections on the origin and spread of nationalism*. New York: Verso.
Ang, I. (1996). *Living room wars: Rethinking media audiences for a post-modern world*. New York: Routledge.
Antola, A., & Rogers, E. M. (1984). Television flows in Latin America. *Communication Research, 2*(11), 183–202.
Beltran, L. R., & Fox, E. (1979). Latin America and the United States: Flaws in the free flow of information. In K. Nordenstreng & H. I. Schilles (Eds.), *National sovereignty and international communications* (pp. 33–64). Norwood, NJ: Ablex.
Bhahba, H. (1994). *The location of culture*. New York: Routledge.
Blumler, J., & Katz, E. (1974). *Sage annual review of communication research* (Vol. 3). Beverly Hills, CA: Sage.
Bourdieu, P. (1984). *Distinction: A social critique of the judgment of taste*. Cambridge, MA: Harvard University Press.
Boyd, D. A., Straubhaar, J. D., & Lent, J. (1989). *The videocassette recorder in the Third World*. New York: Longman.
Boyd-Barret, O. (1980). *The international news agencies*. Beverly Hills: Sage.
Brown, A. (1987). *TV programming trends in the Anglophone Caribbean: the 1980s. Caribbean. Occasional Paper No. 2*. Institute of Mass Communication, University of the West Indies, Kingston, Jamaic
Canclini, N. G., (1998). *Hybrid cultures: strategies for entering and leaving modernity*. Minneapolis: University of Minnesota Press.
Chilcote, R. H. (1984). *Theories of development and underdevelopment*. Boulder, CO: Westview Press.
Collins, R. (1986, May–August). Wall-to-wall Dallas? The U.S.-U.K. trade in television. *Screen, ??,* 66–77.
da Matta, R. (1983). *Carnivais, malandros e heróis* [Carnivals, rounders and heroes] (4th ed.). Rio de Janeiro, Brazil: Zahar Editores.
da Távola, A. (1984). *Comunicação e mito* [Communication and myth]. Rio de Janeiro, Brazil: Editora Nova Fronteira.
dos Santos, T. (1973). *Concepto de clases sociales* [Concepts of social classes]. Santiago de Chile: Pransa Latinoamericana.
Elasmar, M. (1996). The impact of foreign TV on a domestic audience: A meta analysis. *Communication Yearbook, 20*, pp. 47–69.
Elasmar, M. & Hunter, J. (1996). The impact of foreign TV upon a domestic audiernce: A meta analysis. *Communication Yearbook. 80*, 47-69.

Evans, P. (1979). *Dependent development: The alliance of multinational, state and local capital in Brazil.* Princeton: Princeton University Press.
Featherstone, M., & Lash, S. (1995). An introduction. In M. Featherstone, S. Lash, & R. Robertson (Eds.), *Global modernities.* Thousand Oaks, CA: Sage.
Fejes, F. (1981). Media imperialism: An assessment. *Media, Culture and Society, 3*(3), 281–289.
Hamelink, C. J. (1983). *Cultural autonomy in global communications.* New York: Longman.
Herman E., & McChesney, R. (1997). *The global media: The new missionaries of global capitalism.* Washington, DC: Cassell.
Hoskins, C., & Mirus, R. (1988). Reasons for the U.S. dominance of the international trade in television programs. *Media, Culture and Society, 4*(10), 499–515.
Iwabuchi, K. (1997). The sweet scent of Asian modernity: The Japanese presence in the Asian audiovisual market. Paper presented at the Fifth International Symposium on Film, Television and Video—Media Globalization, the Asia-Pacific Region, FuJen University, Taipei, Taiwan, May 1997.
Jacks, N. (1995). Pesquisa de recepção e cultura regional [Research on reception and regional culture]. In M. Wilton (Ed.), *Sujeito, o lado oculto do receptor* [The subject, the hidden side of the receiver] (pp. 151–168). São Paulo: Editora Brasiliense.
Karp, J. (1994, January 27). Cast of thousands. *Far Eastern Economic Review,* pp. 46–53.
Kottak, K. (1990). *Prime time society.* Belmont: Wadsworth.
Lee, C. C. (1980). *Media imperialism reconsidered.* Beverly Hills, CA: Sage.
Leslie, M. (1991). Illusion and reality on commercial television: A comparison of Brazil and the U.S. Paper presented at International Communication Association, May 23-27. Chicago:
Maccoby, E. E. (1966). *The development of sex differences.* Stanford, CA: Stanford University Press.
Man Chan, J. (1996). Television in greater China: Structure, exports and market formation. In J. Sinclair, E. Jacka, & S. Cunningham (Eds.), *Peripheral vision: New patterns in global television* (pp. ??). New York: Oxford University Press.
McBride Commission. (1980). *One world, many voices.* Paris: UNESCO.
Marques de Melo, J. (1988). *As telenovelas da Globo: Produção e Exportação* [The telenovelas of TV Guide: Production and export]. São Paulo: Summus.
Marques de Melo, J. (1992). *Brazil's role as a television exporter within the Latin American regional market.* Paper presented at the International Communication Association, Miami, May 1992.
Martín-Barbero, J. (1993). *Communication, culture and hegemony: From the media to the mediations.* Newbury Park, CA: Sage.
Mattelart, A., & Schmucler, H. (1985). *Communication and information technologies: Freedom of choice for Latin America?* (D. Bruxton, Trans.). Norwood, NJ: Ablex. Originally published 1983 as *American Latina en la encrucijado telematica.* Buenos Aires: Pardos.
Mattos, S. (1982) The Brazilian military and television. Unpublished master's thesis, University of Texas, Austin.
Mattos, S. A. (1990). *Un perfil da TV Brasileira (40 anos de histórias 1950–1990)* [A profile of Brazilian TV: 40 years of history]. Salvador (Brazil): Associação Brasileira de Agências de Propaganda [Brazilian Association of Advertising Agencies].
Milanesi, L. A. (1978). *O Paraiso via EMBRATEL.* Rio de Janeiro: Editora Paz e Terra.
Mira, M. C. (1990). Modernização e gosto popular—Uma história do sistema Brasileiro de televisão [Modernization and popular taste—a history of the Brazilian television system]. Unpublished master's thesis, Catholic University of São Paulo (PUC).

6. CULTURAL CAPITAL, LANGUAGE, CULTURAL PROXIMITY 109

Morley, D. (1980). *The nationwide audience: Structure and decoding.* London: British Film Institute.
Morley, D. (1992). *Television, audiences and cultural spaces.* New York: Routledge.
Mosco, V. (1996). *The political economy of communication: Rethinking and renewal.* Thousand Oaks, CA: Sage.
MTV Brazil. (1977). *Perfil da penetração* MTV [Profile of MTV penetration]. Mimeo.
Nordenstreng, K., & Varis, T. (1974). *Television traffic—A one-way street.* Reports and Papers on Mass Communication. Paris: UNESCO.
Oliveira, O. S. (1993). Brazilian soaps outshine Hollywood: Is cultural imperialism fading out? In K. Nordenstreng & H. Schiller (Eds.), *Beyond national sovereignty: International communication in the 1990s* (pp. 116–131). Norwood, NJ: Ablex.
Parameswaran, R. (1997). Colonial interventions and the postcolonial situation in India. *Gazette, 59*(1), 21–41.
Paterson, C. (1998). *Panel on cultural proximity and cultural relevance.* Presented at the International Communication Association, Jerusalem, July 1998.
Pool, I. de S. (1977, Spring). The changing flow of television. *Journal of Communications,* 139–149.
Porto, M. (1998). *Novas Tecnologias e Política no Brasil: A Globalização em uma Sociedade Periférica e Desigual* [New technologies and politics in Brazil: The globalization of an unequal peripheral society]. Paper presented at the Latin American Studies Association, Chicago, September 1998.
Read, W. H. (1976). *America's mass media merchants.* Baltimore, MA: Johns Hopkins University Press.
Robinson, D., Buck, E., & Cuthbert, M. (1991). *Music at the margins—Popular music and global cultural diversity.* Newbury Park, CA: Sage.
Rodrigues, A. (1999). Creating an audience and remapping a nation: Brief history of U.S. Spanish language broadcasting, 1930–1980. *Quarterly Review of Film and Video,* 357–374.
Rodrigues, A. (1994). *Latino panethnicity and panamericanism: The imagined audience of the Noticiero Univision.* Paper presented at the International Communication Association, at Albuquerque, NM, May 1994.
Salinas, R., & Paldan, L. (1979). Culture in the process of dependent development: Theoretical perspectives. In K. Nordenstreng & H. I. Schiller (Eds.), *National sovereignty and international communiations* (pp. 82–98). Norwood, NJ: Ablex.
Schement, J., Gonzales, I., Lum, P., & Valencia, R. (1984). The international flow of television programs. *Communication Research, 11*(2), 163–182.
Singhal, A., Obregon, R., & Rogers, E. (1994). Reconstructing the story of *Simplemente María,* the most popular *telenovela* in Latin America of all time. *Gazette, 54,* 1–15.
Singhal, A., & Udornpim, K. (1997). Cultural shareability, archetypes and television soaps: 'Oshindrome' in Thailand. *Gazette, 59*(3), 171–188.
Sodre, M. (1972). *A comunicação do grotesco* [The communication of the grotesque]. Rio de Janeiro: Le Ditora Uozos.
Straubhaar, J. (1984). The decline of American influence on Brazilian television. *Communication Research, 11*(2), 221–240.
Straubhaar, J. (1991a). Beyond media imperialism: Asymmetrical interdependence and cultural proximity. *Critical Studies in Mass Communication,* 8.
Straubhaar, J., Campbell, C., Youn, S.-M., Champagnie, K., Elasmar, M., & Castellon, L. (1992). *The emergence of a Latin American market for television programs.* Paper presented at the International Communication Association, Miami.
Straubhaar, J., & Viscasillas, G. (1991b). Class, genre and the regionalization of the television market in Latin America. *Journal of Communication, 41*(1), 53–69.

Televisão, triste lazer dos Paulistanos [The sad leisure of those in São Paulo]. (1977, March 11). *O Estado de São Paulo* (newspaper).

Tracey, M. (1988). *Popular culture and the economics of global television.* InterMedia.

Vink, N. (1988). *The telenovela and emancipation—A study on TV and social change in Brazil.* Amsterdam: Royal Tropical Institute.

Wallerstein, I. (1990). Culture as the ideological battleground of the modern world system. *Theory and Culture, 7,* 31–56.

Waterman, D., & Rogers, E. (1994). The economics of television program production and trade in Far East Asia. *Journal of Communication, 44*(3), 89–111.

Wildman, S., & Siwek, S. (1988). *International trade in films and television programs.* Cambridge, MA: Ballinger.

Wilkinson, K. (1995) *Where culture, language and communication converge: The Latin-American cultural linguistic market.* Unpublished doctoral dissertation, University of Texas, Austin.

Zaharopoulos, D. (1997, April). *U.S. television and American cultural stereotypes in Greece.* Paper presented at the conference of the Broadcast Education Association, Las Vegas, NV.

CHAPTER

7

Cultural Proximity On the Air in Ecuador: National, Regional Television Outperforms Imported U.S. Programming

Linda Lee Davis
University of Kansas

Ecuador exports hats, oil, and bananas, but when it comes to television programming, Ecuador imports—about twice as much as it produces. When UNESCO sponsored studies of worldwide sources of programming in the 1970s and 1980s, Ecuador, New Zealand, and Iceland topped the list for importing the largest percentage of television programming. In 1983, 66% of Ecuadorian television came from outside the country (Varis, 1984, p. 146). This 1995 case study of a successful Ecuadorian network, Ecuavisa, confirms the same high level of imported programming 12 years later. Predictably, the United States leads the list of programming sources, as it does in so many countries around the world (Varis, 1984, p. 150).

During the 1970s, a debate about the role of U.S. television abroad began within the United Nations. Third World officials and some scholars, beginning with Herbert Schiller, took the view that the dominance of U.S. programming in developing nations constituted media-delivered "cultural imperialism," which should be restricted.[1] The international debate took place under various related theory areas: "... dependence as related to imported media, media imperialism, international media

---

[1] The notion of cultural imperialism emerged in the late 1960s with the work of Schiller and expanded in the 1970s with the contributions from Wells, Nordenstreng, Varis, Somavia, Beltran and others. Proponents of this theory held that U.S. Television dominated third world markets, constituted a form of colonialism, destroyed cultural heritage and autonomy and needed to be limited. On the other side, some advocates from developed   (*continued on next page*)

and sovereignty, and the international flow of information," as Elasmar and Hunter (1997, p. 47) explained. "Although each of these topics can be studied distinctly, they all share a common concern about messages crossing between countries. This concern is based on the tacit assumption that imported messages have negative impacts on audiences in the importing countries" (p. 47). One theorist, Goonasekara (1987), stated that "in the face of this media invasion, the indigenous cultures of the Third World disintegrate consistently and without resistance" (p. 11).

A more likely scenario involving imported television programming than that predicted by Goonasekara can be found in what Joseph Straubhaar calls "cultural proximity" or people's active preference for programming closest to their own culture. Building on the work of Pool and Fiske, Straubhaar (1991) expanded the work of reception analysis with his proposal "that audiences make an active choice to view international or regional or national television programs, a choice that favors the latter two when they are available, based on a search for cultural relevance or proximity" (p. 39).

The purpose of this chapter is to examine the relative roles of local, regional and U.S. television programming in a country importing most of its television programming. Social critics who would disapprove of the plethora of U.S. programming abroad might disapprove of the many U.S. titles on the Ecuavisa schedule, but "counting studies," which simply total up programming hours and countries of origin, present a false impression by failing to consider an even more significant piece of information, the size of the audience. A program placed on the schedule at 8 a.m. cannot possibly generate the same number of viewers as a program placed on the schedule at 8 in prime time.

With this pivotal difference in dayparts in mind, this case study analyzes programming not solely by "hours" but by program rankings and by daypart placement, with primetime as the prime test of popularity. In this way, one can meaningfully compare the relative importance of local, regional, and U.S. programs to Ecuavisa audiences.

BACKGROUND

This study focuses on the successful, two-station, Ecuadorian network owned by Xavier Alvarado Roca of Guayaquil. TV stations in Ecuador are family-owned, and the eight television families often have one station in Quito, in the Andes, and another in Guayaquil, on the Pacific coast. Although two ranges of the Andes divide Ecuador, microwave transmitters provide the country with nearly blanket coverage

---

[1](*continued*) nations argued that information flow among countries should be free and open. Throughout the 1970s and into the 1980s, the often heated debate continued in United Nations forums, especially UNESCO. The issue led to the 1980 McBride Report calling for a New World Information Order and contributed to the mid-1980s U.S. withdrawal from UNESCO (summarized in Wert 6-15; Dominick, Sherman, Copeland 252-53; Stevenson 35-54, 75-94).

7. ON THE AIR IN ECUADOR 113

of Ecuavisa's signal. "For a relatively poor country, Ecuador has a well-developed and sophisticated broadcasting system," observed Jon Vanden Heuvel and Everette E. Dennis in their report on Latin America for the Freedom Forum Media Studies Center at Columbia University (1995).

> Four hundred and two radio stations and 26 televisions stations serve a population of more than 10 million—a high ratio of broadcast outlets by any standard. Four national networks, all of them privately owned (as in other Latin American countries, public television is undeveloped in Ecuador) cover the country. Both television and radio broadcasters bemoan the fact that the broadcasting market is so crowded, saying that the government gave out frequencies with little regard for whether broadcast outlets would be economically viable. (Vanden Heuvel & Dennis, 1995, p. 94)

A local broadcaster is quoted on the profit picture: "There's enough advertising to keep us afloat, but not enough to make big profits" (Vanden Heuvel & Dennis, 1995, p. 94).

Among Ecuadorian television owners, only Alvarado programs his two stations separately, giving Ecuavisa "network" status in a Colorado-sized country.[2] Ecuador provides an unusual example of the role of broadcasting within a Latin American country because the country has two large and important cities. So often in small Latin American countries, the capital city dominates—politically, commercially, culturally, and, therefore, from a media standpoint as well. In Costa Rica, for example, all roads lead to San José. Not so in Ecuador.

"The rivalry between the *sierra*, the grandees of Quito, who represented the country's traditional, landed elites, and the *costa*, the merchant class of Guayaquil, which was more liberal and bourgeois in outlook, characterized 19th-century Ecuadorian politics," Vanden Huevel and Dennis reported (1995, p. 87). The cultural divide remains today, with the *costeños*, the fun-loving beach dwellers in the larger, commercial capital of Guayaquil, and the *sierra* people who live at 9,300 feet in the Andes in the conservative, artistic, political, and cultural capital of Quito.

Method

Because of the cultural divide between the two main cities of Ecuador, Ecuavisa programs somewhat differently in Quito and Guayaquil, and the popularity of programs aired in both markets varies, sometimes greatly, from one city to another. This 1995 case study is based on an analysis of 2 weeks of programming on both stations, and it takes into account Ecuavisa's separation in programming and program ratings for its stations in Quito and Guayaquil. The study investigates Ecuavisa's separate programming as further evidence of "cultural proximity" (Straubhaar, 1991, p. 39), and it takes the theory from its previous national focus to the local

---

[2]Interview, Pancho Arosemena, national general manager of Ecuavisa, Guayaquil, 15 July 1995.

level. The study begins with the traditional "hours count" and then sorts those hours into more significant groupings.

Hours of programming may be one way to characterize television programming, but not all program time slots are created equal. The audience is certainly larger at 8 p.m. than at 2 a.m. Most "counting studies" in international television research fail to answer an important question—Who is watching? Some studies on international programming have tried to measure "audience hours" by multiplying broadcast hours by ratings (Schement & Rogers, 1984, p. 310). But variable and/or unreliable local ratings services have often made it difficult or impossible to determine ratings (In *Buenos Aires*, 1993).

Nielsen figures should have been available in Ecuador during the time of the case study sample, but a local scandal delayed the implementation of the more reliable ratings system. Ecuavisa's Pancho Arosemena, national general manager and nephew of Xavier Alvarado, was part of a group of media executives that invited Nielsen to compete for Ecuador's ratings business.[3] The Nielsen ratings were to begin in March of 1995, but when employees of rival ratings firm CIDEM infiltrated Nielsen locally and began soliciting bribes, Nielsen was forced to reorganize and delay service until fall.[4] Without Nielsen numbers, the key to understanding local television tastes is to focus on prime time, when the biggest audience is watching. Although prime time is not clearly defined in Ecuador, it is calculated in this study as 7 p.m. to 11 p.m.

Research Question

What is the difference between the absolute number of hours of programming from a given source and the size of the audience that programming can generate? And what does that difference tell us about the relative importance of sources of programming? Does the fact that a smaller, poorer nation can supply only a portion of its own television hours mean that such domestic television product has only limited importance? Does the fact that the United States is the primary supplier of television hours in that country mean that U.S. programming is the most watched and most important programming on the network?

What is the role of regional programming? Does programming from Venezuela or Mexico offer audience drawing power more like programming from the significantly different culture of the United States, or do audiences find it more like Ecuadorian programming? Does the role of regional programming on Ecuavisa offer evidence of Straubhaar's (1991) view of cultural proximity? And can the differences in programming between Quito and Guayaquil be seen as cultural proximity at the local level? These questions fueled the investigation of Ecuavisa network in Ecuador.

---

[3]Interview, Pancho Arosemena, 24 July 1995.
[4]Interview, Pancho Arosemena, 24 July 1995.

7. ON THE AIR IN ECUADOR

FINDINGS AND DISCUSSION

Viewers Prefer "National Production," Then Latin American Programs

If one counts hours alone, as Varis–UNESCO studies do, most Ecuavisa programming is imported, as one would expect, and one third of the total programming comes from the United States. Another one third of the programming hours comes from Ecuavisa itself, and other Latin American countries fill a little more than one quarter of its schedule (see Fig. 7.1).

However, a study of audience rankings instead of hours demonstrates a reversal in the order of relative importance of the programming sources. Ecuavisa's own "national production" is the most important programming to the local audience. Other Latin American programming plays a much more pivotal role for Ecuadorian viewers than U.S. programs. American programming may dominate the hours of a schedule, but it does not dominate the ratings. Using ratings, U.S. programming drops to third in importance on the list of three. This case study indicates that local and regional programs dominate prime time and earn the best ratings. This finding of the importance of either local or Latin American programming in Ecuador is evidence of what Straubhaar (1991) calls "cultural proximity" or people's active preference for programming closest to their own culture.

Ecuavisa Close to United States as Source of Total Hours

Broadcasters can either make or buy programming; either way is expensive (Dominick, Sherman, & Copeland, 1996, pp. 392–393). A small country such as Ec-

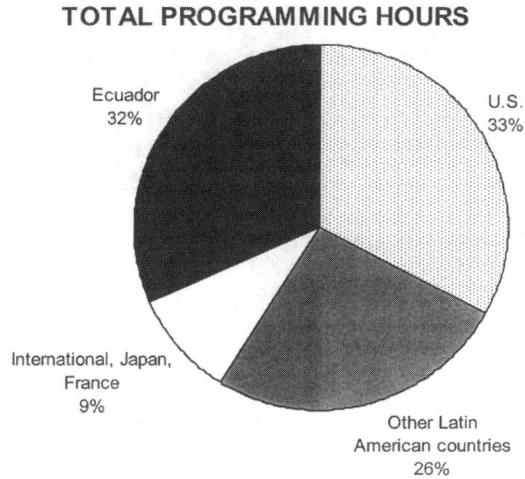

FIG. 7.1.

uador does not enjoy the economies of scale in television production that the United States does. Anyone familiar with Third World broadcasting would expect to see American series such as *Star Trek* or *Un Hogar Casi Perfecto* (*Full House*) and Hollywood movies on the Ecuavisa schedule. Varis' 1983 study of programming in 69 countries showed U.S. programming to be ubiquitous: "In some regions, such as Latin America, the United States is the source of as much as three-quarters of the imported materials" (Varis, 1984, p. 151).

According to this 1995 case study, Ecuavisa imports U.S. programming without letting it dominate the schedule. About one third of Ecuavisa's total programming schedule does come from the United States. However, Ecuador runs a very close second to the United States as a programming source. The third largest source of programming at Ecuavisa includes the three traditional Latin American TV producing powers, Argentina, Brazil, and Mexico, along with Venezuela and Colombia, which are more recent additions to the list (Paterson, 1995, pp. 104–106) (see Table 7.1).

Already, the Ecuavisa example underscores a major development that communications scholars began to notice in the mid-1980s—an "increase in regional exchange" (Varis, 1984, p. 151). At that time, Tapio Varis found this trend most pronounced in the Middle East and less pronounced in Latin America, where "the figure for interregional imports is around ten percent" (p. 151). A decade later, this case study finds the amount of regional programming to be much higher—more than one quarter of the Ecuavisa schedule is regional.

"Low costs and widespread availability have also encouraged increased imports from other Latin American countries," according to a study of programming in the Dominican Republic by Straubhaar and Viscasillas (1991). "Interviews with programmers and advertisers in Santo Domingo in 1987 and 1988 suggest that productions from other Latin American countries are usually cheaper than U.S. programs

TABLE 7.1
Ecuavisa Sources Of Total Programming Hours

Country of Origin	Hours[a]	Percentage	Rank
From United States	184	33	1
From Ecuador	178	32	2
From other Latin American countries	147	26	3
From Internationals	37	6	
From Japan	11	2	
From France	4	1	
Total, all sources	561	100	

[a] over 2 weeks, both channels

and sometimes cheaper than Dominican programs. From within Latin America, telenovelas from Mexico, Venezuela, Brazil, Argentina, and Puerto Rico are the most prominent imports" (p. 57). Programs from almost the same list of contributors are on the air in Ecuador as well.

Some scholars trace a decline in U.S. imports directly to the increase in regional production (Berwanger, 1995, pp. 317–318; Schement & Rogers, 1984). "The rise of TV Globo (of Brazil) and Televisa (of Mexico) as powerful multinational corporations then led to a sharp decrease in imported U.S. television series in Latin America," wrote Schement and Rogers in 1984 (p. 313). In this 1995 study, Ecuavisa's Latin American or regional programming plus the network's original production combine to create 58% of the Ecuavisa schedule. The U.S. contributes one third of total hours, with the remaining 9% of the total programming originating in Europe and Asia or from an international news service.

Prime Time Brings Most Viewers to the Set

In the study's 2-week time frame, the number one source of prime time programming on Ecuavisa was "other Latin American countries." Those prime time hours came from Venezuela, Brazil, and Mexico, in order of contribution. By 1995, these regional producers were contributing more than one fourth of Ecuavisa's total broadcast hours, and their programs were well placed on the schedule. The percentage of prime time hours from the Latin American powers increased to 39% of Ecuavisa's prime time schedule (see Table 7.2).

The United States was not far behind as a prime time source. But the combination of Ecuadorian with other Latin American programming accounts for 62% of the prime time schedule during this case study. The percentage of U.S. hours seen in prime time, 38%, is only slightly higher than the one-third U.S. contribution to total hours. This finding updates information from "media flow" studies of the 1980s. For example, in 1983 when Varis studied imported programming around the world, he found little difference between use of imports in prime time and total

TABLE 7.2
Prime Time On Ecuavisa: Program Sources

Country of Origin	Hours[a]	Percentage	Rank
From other Latin American countries	44	39	1
From United States	43	38	2
From Ecuador	25	23	3
Total	112	100	

[a] over 2 weeks, both channels
International, France, and Japan = 0 hours in prime time.

time, except in Latin America, "where foreign programming tends to dominate more in prime time" (Varis, 1984, p. 147).

By 1995, only 12 years after Varis' study, prime time at Ecuavisa was mostly programmed with local and regional productions, according to this case study. The opportunity to see homegrown, rather than imported, television takes on special significance in Latin America. "For much of Latin America, television is the dominant medium," reported Vanden Heuvel and Dennis (1995, p. 11). "For instance, in Brazil, the number of televisions surpasses the number of refrigerators" (Vanden Heuvel & Dennis, 1995, p. 15). Jean Franco (1994) asserted that in Latin America, television is now the "massive culture industry" among "new audiences for whom print culture has lost its luster" (p. 17). A closer look at that Latin American programming opens a window on Ecuadorian culture (see Figs. 7.2 and 7.3).

Prime Time on Ecuavisa Differs from the United States

Prime time content differs in Ecuador and the United States. An ABC or NBC devotes prime time mainly to series programming, but not so at Ecuavisa, where series programming rarely appears in prime time. Typically, weekday prime time in Quito and Guayaquil, on Ecuavisa and its competitors, begins with a distinctive Latin American programming form—the telenovela (see Fig. 7.4).

Telenovelas, called "novelas" for short, are a unique form of the daytime drama or "soap opera." The Latin American version of a soap opera is characterized by its varied audience—even men and children watch (Antola & Rogers, 1984, p.

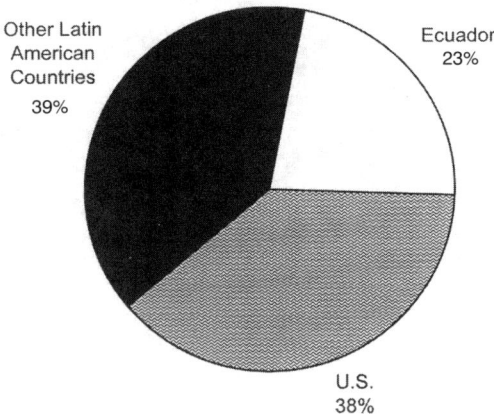

FIG. 7.2.

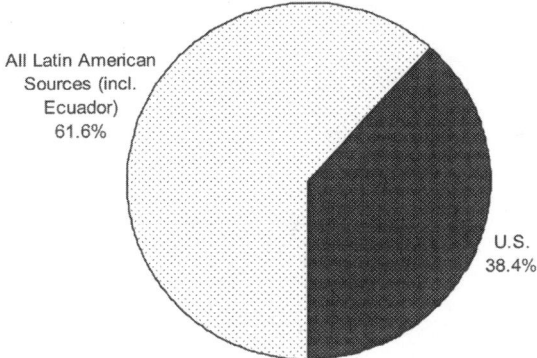

FIG. 7.3.

194)—and by its brevity (Paterson, 1995, p. 104). A novela characteristically lasts 120 to 150 episodes.[5] Ecuavisa executives cannot understand the endlessness of North American soaps. Nor do North American soaps travel south well. "One of the other channels tried *General Hospital*," said Ecuavisa vice president Leonardo Ponce. "It went very badly. If the soap opera goes on too long, the people get tired of it. The American novelas go on for years—how horrible!"[6]

Scholars have tracked the success of novelas (Alleyne, 1995, pp. 47–48; Paterson, 1995, pp. 104–106; Reeves, 1993, pp. 191–197). "Television systems in Latin America, especially in Mexico and Brazil, perfected the telenovela as a genre that has become extremely popular with Latin American audiences," according to Schement and Rogers (1984, p. 313). "This distinctive television product is broadcast at prime-time and secures very high audience ratings. Televisa (Mexico) and TV Globo (Brazil) used the telenovela as their vehicle to replace imported U.S. programming throughout Latin America" (p. 313). Antola and Rogers (1984) found Latin American interest in U.S. programs waning compared to domestic or regional programs, especially novelas (pp. 194, 200).

Telenovelas, News Anchor Prime Time on Ecuavisa

Of the large block of Ecuavisa programming coming from the Latin American producers during this case study, almost 80% of the programming is telenovelas. The

---

[5]Interview, Carla Patiño, former programming chief, Ecuavisa's Channel 8 in Quito, current public relations officer, Quito, 12 July 1995.

[6]Interview, Leonardo Ponce, public relations director and vice-president of Ecuabisa, Quito, 20 July 1995.

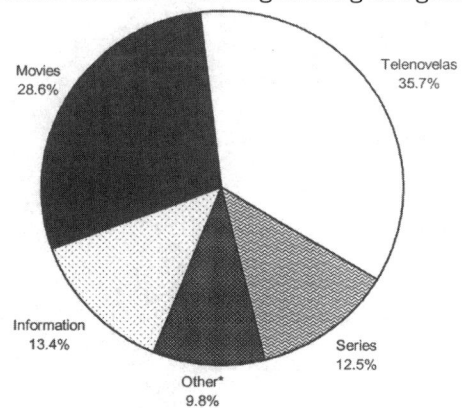

FIG. 7.4.

importance of the novela in Latin American life cannot be overemphasized. Prime time scheduling is one clue; the ability to preempt soccer on the TV schedule is further evidence.[7] Gabriel García Márquez, who is the best-selling author in Latin America, admits that the average telenovela in his native Colombia alone "reaches a public much vaster than the combined readership of all his novels," according to Jean Franco (1994, p. 19), so the Nobel laureate writes for television. "'The medium is the true mass dissemination of one's ideas,'" Franco quoted him, "'and it has to be used.'" *The Wall Street Journal* provides global evidence of the power of novelas in a May, 1996 story about Mexico's media giant, Televisa: "Televisa licenses its melodramas, which star Mexican casts, to more than 100 countries. Its emotion-packed stories are especially popular in Turkey, China and India" (Torres & Millman, 1996, p. A14; see Fig. 7.5).

Klagsbrunn described novelas as "striving after love, social prestige, riches and power" (Berwanger, 1995, p. 319). A political theme is less common than the three usual topics: "sex, sex, and more sex" (Marcus, 1993, p. 15). However, in the 1990s, a new breed of politically charged novelas arrived in Venezuela, Colombia, and Brazil. Each country has produced at least one hard-hitting novela on the once-taboo theme of government corruption. The Venezuelan "soap-with-an-attitude" (Marcus, 1993, pp. 15–16) tracked the daily news and draws half the population to the set. It also drew threats of censorship from Congress and may have inspired the middle class to turn against former president Carlos Andrés Pérez.

---

[7]Interview, Pol Herrmann, Quito native, Lawrence, KS, 9 Aug. 1996.

[8]Interview, Leonardo Ponce, 20 July 1995.

7. ON THE AIR IN ECUADOR 121

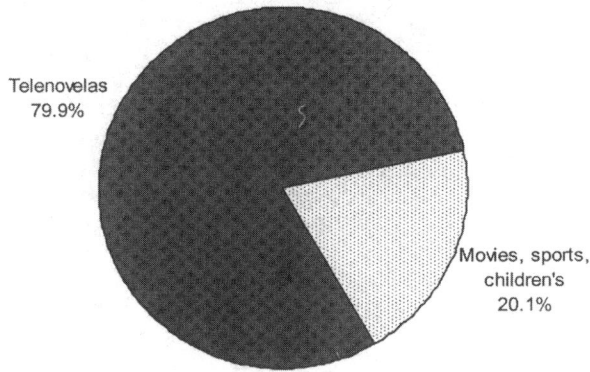

FIG. 7.5.

At Ecuavisa, novelas at 7 and 8:30 p.m. anchor prime time, and the evening news airs between novelas. News airs at 8 p.m. for cultural reasons. After the second prime time novela, U.S. programming finally appears. During the week, Ecuavisa typically programs American movies at 9:30 p.m. Prime time at Ecuavisa derives primarily from novelas, movies, and news, in that order.

Top-Rated Shows: Latin American is Better, Ecuadorian is Best

The final month under the old, pre-Nielsen system at Ecuavisa was May, 1995, when top 10 program ratings at each station were available through IPSA Group Latin America. Those rankings provide a comparative sense of the popularity of various programs. Ecuavisa executives say programming tastes always vary between audiences in Guayaquil and Quito. But a few trends emerge from the combined list.

Sixteen of the top 20 programs in both cities are Latin American. Mexico scored two top 20 programs in Guayaquil with its widely exported novela *Marimar*. Argentina's novela *Celeste Siempre Celeste* also proved popular in Guayaquil. Quito viewers favored Ecuadorian information and comedy, while adding programs from Venezuela and Argentina to their list. Ecuavisa's quality news makes it a top-rated staple at both stations. The fact that programs rank differently in Quito and Guayaquil provides evidence of cultural proximity at an extremely local level (see Table 7.3).

American programs break into the top 10 at both stations, but they rank only in the bottom half of the top 10 in both cities. In Quito, the most popular U.S. programs during the case study were *Kun Fu* (*Kung Fu*), ranking sixth, and the series *Superman*, ranking eighth. In Guayaquil, a U.S. movie and *Un Hogar Casi Perfecto* (*Full House*) ranked 9th and 10th. Overall, the comparative ratings of programs

TABLE 7.3
Combined Top 20—Country of Origin in Both Guayaquil and Quito

Country of Origin	Number of Programs in Top 20
Ecuador	9 programs
Argentina	4 programs
United States	4 programs
Mexico	2 programs
Venezuela	1 program

20 programs total

from all sources in both markets show the popularity and importance of Latin American, especially Ecuadorian, programming among Ecuavisa viewers (see Fig. 7.6).

In this regard, Ecuavisa viewers track preferences noted among six larger Latin American producing countries studied by Antola and Rogers in the 1980s. In Argentina, Brazil, Chile, Mexico, Peru and Venezuela, Antola and Rogers (1984) found a "general trend" among viewers "(1) for locally produced programs, followed by (2) imports from another Latin American country, and (3) last, imported programs from the United States" (p. 188). Antola and Rogers found a similar ratings pattern: "Most of the top ten television programs in audience ratings for a sample week... are locally produced" (p. 188). Entertainment trade magazine *Variety* also noted the success of local programs in March, 1993: "The cornerstone of Ar-

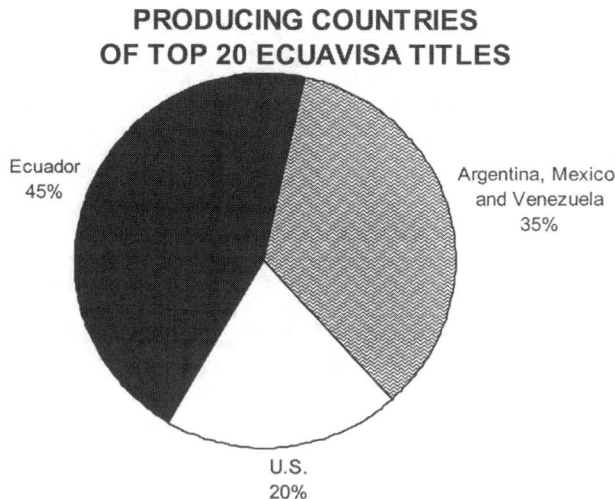

FIG. 7.6.

gentine programming continues to be locally produced shows, which outrate almost all Yank imports" (*Locals Outrank*, 1993).

In Latin American countries with strong local production, such as Brazil and Mexico, some popular American exports fail (Tracey, 1985, p. 34). *Dallas* never ranked above 69th in Brazilian ratings, and it could not break into the top 100 shows in Mexico. "It is simply untrue to say that imported television programs, from the U.S. or other metropolitan countries, always have a dominant presence within an indigenous television culture. Certainly they do not always attract larger audiences than homemade programs, nor do they always threaten national production" (Tracey, 1985, p. 34).

"National Production" in News and Entertainment

"National production" is the term used in the Third World for original programming. In the United States, programs produced by local stations are "almost always news and public affairs programs" (Smith, 1985, p. 211); so too is news the common form of "national production" in Latin America.[8] Ecuador's vibrant media environment is also blessed with a history of press freedom. "Among Latin American countries Ecuador has a reputation for having one of the most open media environments. There is virtually no direct government censorship" (Vanden Heuvel & Dennis, 1995, p. 88). Given the open environment, the relatively low expense of this type of production, and the high level of audience response, it is no wonder that news and information programming makes up most of Ecuavisa's national production. Two thirds of Ecuavisa's national production hours consist of news and information, according to this case study. But what makes Ecuavisa unique in Ecuador is its commitment to innovative entertainment programming (see Fig. 7.7).

Within Ecuador, only Ecuavisa produces Ecuadorian original dramatic series and miniseries, Ecuadorian telenovelas, and the country's first and only situation comedy, all under the guidance of Xavier Alvarado. Ecuavisa programming practices distinguish the network, not only in Ecuador, but also compared to other small-country broadcast systems in Latin America. For its original programming, Ecuavisa serves as an example to countries larger and richer than Ecuador. As Straubhaar and Viscasillas (1991) pointed out in their study of television in the Dominican Republic:

> ... television as a cultural industry in Latin American has undergone considerable change. Some have doubted that small nations could develop strong cultural industries particularly in the relatively expensive medium of television. But in the Dominican Republic (population 6,500,000), which has limited resources for production, there is a significant audience for television.... (p. 55)

In the 1980s, national production seemed to be on the rise in the Dominican Republic in genres including "talk shows (on both politics and society), news panel discussions, live music and various combinations of these" (Straubhaar &

---

[8]Interview, Leonardo Ponce, 20 July 1995.

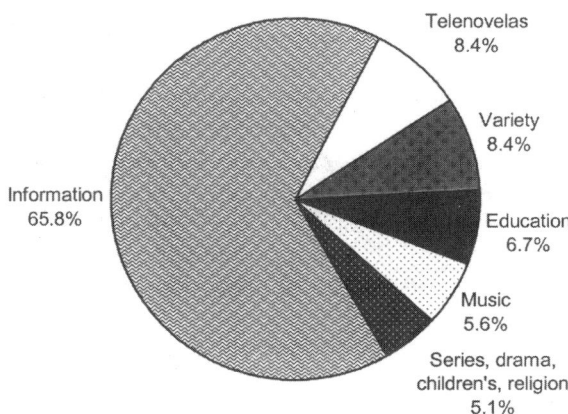

FIG. 7.7.

Viscasillas, 1991, p. 57). Those programs seem to be in the low to middle expense range, but not in the higher range of national production as is the comedy or drama that Ecuavisa owner Alvarado encourages.

Alvarado is a small-country, South American multimedia mogul, the Ecuadorian equivalent of Rupert Murdoch in scope. Unlike Murdoch, Xavier Alvarado has based his broadcasting business on quality news. Ecuavisa produced the vast majority of prime time, information programming aired during the case study. Many of those hours came from Ecuavisa's nationally recognized, prime time news program, *Televistazo*, anchored by Alfonso Espinoza since the network began in 1968.

News—The "First Priority" at Ecuavisa

Ecuavisa's emphasis on news reflects the values of Xavier Alvarado Roca, according to Ecuavisa vice president Leonardo Ponce. "We have the best audience on a national level," Ponce said. "It's objective news, serious news—the first priority of Xavier."[9] Alvarado received an award from The TV Institute in Ecuador to recognize his contribution to the development of television in Ecuador. Ecuavisa reporters have been awarded national prizes for quality news and community service.[10]

Covering the news may be easier in Ecuador than in some other Latin American countries. In a region known for government channels (Gargúrevich & Fox, 1988, pp. 59–61; Katz & Wedell, 1977, p. 47; Schement & Rogers, 1984, p. 307) and government influence on private channels (Franco, 1994, p. 20; Prada, 1988, p. 167),

---

[9]Interview, Leonardo Ponce, 20 July 1995.
[10]Interview, Carla Patiño, Kansas City, MO, 2 Nov. 1996.

Ecuador holds unusual status as one country that has never had a government-operated station[11] (Katz & Wedell, 1977, p. 254; "Latin American TV," 1993). Along with the tradition of private broadcasting comes the tradition of a free press in Ecuador, except during a period of military rule in the 1970s (Alisky, 1981, pp. 11, 23, 152, 228). "We have press freedom here," said former Quito station manager Gabriel Colombo. "You can say practically anything you want. For example, we broke a story about a former Cuban intelligence agent who said most of the leftist parties (in Ecuador) received money from Fidel. We had a few people very upset, but we did it."[12]

A democratic political environment can affect more than news programming, according to Ecuavisa's Leonardo Ponce. "Once Peru had very good soap operas, like *Simplemente María*," Ponce said. The Quito executive said Peru's changeover to military rule in the 1970s and the subsequent crackdown on broadcasting eventually dispersed talent and diminished programming[13] (Alisky, 1981, pp. 76–78; Katz & Wedell, 1977, pp. 31–32; Stevenson, 1988, pp. 88–89).

Original Drama and Comedy—A Small Country Rarity

In addition to producing quality news, Ecuavisa produces more local programming, and more expensive local programming, than any other broadcast operation in the country. "The other channels have national production but in game shows, cooking, these kinds of programs that are easy to do, inexpensive, without quality," said Leonardo Ponce. "We try to make good programs with good quality. The other channels don't make this effort."[14]

Not only is Ecuavisa unique within Ecuador; the scope of the network's original production makes Ecuador unusual compared to all but the six largest countries in Latin America (Antola & Rogers, 1984, p. 188). If one of the biggest advantages of the case study is finding out what you least expected (Wimmer & Dominick, 1991, p. 45), the surprise of this case study was discovering thriving original production in such a small, poor country. Only Bolivia had smaller per capita earnings among South American countries in the mid-1990s. Bolivia also has a smaller population and local television so limited as to be called a "national irresponsibility" (Prada, 1988, p. 170). "Some communities (in Bolivia) receive only foreign television," Prada wrote (1998, p. 169).

In all of Latin America, only Guatemala fairly compares to Ecuador, with similar technical development, a population almost equal to Ecuador's, and per capita

---

[11]Interview, Alfonso Espinoza, Ecuavisa news vice-president and news anchor, Quito, 20 July 1995.

[12]Interview, Gabriel Colombo, former general manager of Ecuavisa's Channel 8 in Quito, Quito, 19 July 1995.

[13]Interview, Leonardo Ponce, 20 July 1995.

[14]Interview, Leonardo Ponce, 20 July 1995.

earnings only a little higher. "It has been confirmed that in Guatemala television is the medium with the least impact; moreover, Guatemala television is the most deficient in the Central American region." (International Idea, 2002) National production in Guatemala is almost exclusively news. The only entertainment programs ever produced in the country were created and aired by the military channel. The output was a few telenovelas with more social message than plot.[15]

Ecuavisa production alone puts Ecuador in a class by itself considering its low per capita gross domestic product of $1,100 (in 1992) and its population of 11 million. A mid-1980s study of three small Central American countries, Panama, Costa Rica, and El Salvador, found limited local viewing options. "Clearly the trends toward local production and regional exchange documented in the larger Latin American countries have not reached these three small countries. They still import 80% to 90% of their programming, most of it—two thirds to three quarters of all imports—from the United States. Only Mexico is visible as a significant supplier" (Wert & Stevenson, 1988, p. 183). In her unpublished thesis, Wert (1985) wrote: "Evidence suggests that the trend toward a more balanced flow is not present yet in countries with small television industries and that changes in the television flow of these countries are not likely to occur in the near future".

The Country's Only Comedy

By the mid-1990s, Ecuavisa was making changes. For almost 4 years, Ecuavisa had been producing the situation comedy called *Dejémonos de Vainas* (*Let It Be*). *Dejémonos* is shot at a real house in a village just outside the capital city and is full of such local "Quiteño" humor that it does not even air on the Guayaquil channel. Quito producer Gonzalo Ponce, who oversees *Dejémonos*, said the comedy about a journalist's family succeeds because Quito viewers recognize the characters from everyday life and say, "That's us."[16] Imagine how much more an Ecuadorian audience can identify with *Dejémonos* than with the usual imported series—a U.S. sitcom with a U.S. setting. In the January 1996 Nielsens, *Dejémonos*, the country's first and only comedy, ranked as the number one show in Quito.[17]

Building National Identity Through Television

Producer Gonzalo Ponce sees television as a way to build cultural identity in a country he finds lacking it. "There is no self-esteem in Ecuador as a country," Ponce said. "There is no national identity. We don't believe in us as we should, and we don't see the future. And that is terrible." Ponce says he seizes every opportunity to showcase

---

[15]Interview, Duamar Antonio Armira, Guatemala native, Lawrence, KS, 13 Sept., 1996.

[16]Interview, Gonzalo Ponce, Eucavisa executive producer, Quito, 18 July 1995.

[17]Interview, Gonzalo Ponce, 18 July 1995.

7. ON THE AIR IN ECUADOR 127

local actors in series and local musicians in music specials. "For self-esteem, it's important to have television," Ponce said.[18]

Part of the challenge of creating original programming in a small country is having only a small local talent pool to draw on. One hallmark of the Latin American television powers, like Mexico or Argentina, is that these broadcasting industries built on existing film (Alisky, 1981, p. 133; Reeves, 1993, pp. 21–22) or theater traditions.[19] Ecuador has neither. Ecuavisa's programming is now the catalyst for a growing creative community in Ecuador. "We are forming a good group of actors with international appeal," Leonardo Ponce said. "In the future, we will be able to compete with Colombia and Venezuela. But now, it's a lot of work."[20]

Producer Gonzalo Ponce reported the intense interest *Dejémonos* has created among the local acting community. "When we started producing *Dejémonos* all my actor friends said, 'This is not theater.' They never even wanted to work with us," Ponce said. "Now all of them want to work with us. If you are not on TV you are nothing now. It's interesting. We are changing the habits of the people."[21]

National Production is "Hard, Expensive"

Xavier Alvarado Roca's willingness to underwrite national production offers a refreshing alternative to a common view of Latin American broadcast systems as cookie-cutter, profit-motive, U.S. imitators. "U.S.-style commercial television broadcasting has been adopted through Latin America: most television systems are privately-owned, commercially-operated, and mainly geared to providing entertainment programming to attract the largest possible audience (which is sold to advertisers)" (Schement & Rogers, 1984, p. 306).

In the summer of 1995, Ecuavisa was also making a special effort in national production by producing its third telenovela, *Maria Soledad*, to air nationally. The show was produced in Guayaquil for about $5,000 an episode, without considering studio overhead.[22] Because Ecuavisa can buy new novelas from Latin American producers for between $300 to $1,500 an hour,[23] local production costs much more than simply buying regional production. No one at Ecuavisa expected *Maria Soledad* to break even, and expectations included only a limited after-market, perhaps small-market sales in Bolivia and Central America.[24] Vanden Heuval and Dennis (1995) stated that Ecuavisa is one of three Ecuadorian networks which "all turn

---

[18]Interview, Gonzalo Ponce, 18 July 1995.

[19]Interview, Gonzalo Ponce, 18 July 1995.

[20]Interview, Leonardo Ponce, 20 July 1995.

[21]Interview, Gonzalo Ponce, 18 July 1995.

[22]Interview, Enrique Arosemena, former producer at Guayaquil studio, Guayaquil, 24 July 1995.

[23]Interview, Gabriel Colombo, 19 July 1995.

[24]Interview, Enrique Arosemena, 24 July 1995.

a profit," but insiders say it's a good thing Alvarado also has the country's most successful newsmagazine, *Vistazo*, among other publications (pp. 94–95).

By the fall of 1996, Ecuavisa had moved into production of a television movie, *Siete Lunas y Siete Serpientes* (*Seven Moons and Seven Serpents*). The newest Ecuavisa drama has received favorable local press reviews and has become the first Ecuavisa program to earn international recognition. At the 1996 meeting of the Mercado Iberoamericano de la Industria, the drama received an honorable mention. But back home, programming recognition is elusive. Two well-known, long-standing Quito programs, *Pasado y Confeso*, a docudrama, and the comedy *Dejémonos* "have been recognized by viewers and TV reporters as favorites," said public relations officer Carla Patiño (personal communication, September 17, 1996), "but they have not received any national awards because there are none to give."[25]

Leonardo Ponce said of original productions:

> It's very hard, very expensive. We try to sell programs, but the competition with other countries like Venezuela or Colombia is very hard because they have much more experience than us. Xavier Alvarado in the matter is very convinced that we have to make that effort, otherwise we will always just buy from everywhere. He's very conscious of that," said Ponce. "National programming is good for the image and good for the ratings. Sometimes you don't always pay your costs. But it's as though we are in the process of putting in the seeds."[26]

CONCLUSION

The United States is the major source of television imports the world over (Varis, 1984, p. 150), and U.S. programs were evident on the Ecuavisa schedule during the case study. The president of a competing Ecuadorian network describes the U.S. advantage: "The U.S. is the TV capital of the world" (Vanden Heuvel & Dennis, 1995, p. 98). Ecuavisa owner Alvarado pointed out whereas the U.S. programs perform less well than they used to,[27] they have a role to play at his network. Quito executive Carla Patiño, who used to buy programming for the Quito station, saw the mix of U.S., regional, and local programming as a good way to meet audience demand. "We'll increase our productions, but I don't think we'll live without American programming," Patiño said (personal communication, September 17, 1996) of Ecuavisa's multiple sources of programing. "We are used to that. We like it. The movies—we'll always import that. We'll never have just local production. Our production is not as good. It will be a long time before we have two or three novelas at once. We struggle with one."[28]

---

[25]Interview, Carla Patiño, 21 July 1995.

[26]Interview, Leonardo Ponce, 20 July 1995.

[27]Interview, Xavier Alvarado, Ecuavisa owner, Guayaquil, 24 July 1995.

7. ON THE AIR IN ECUADOR

"... The assumption of a one-way flow of culture, central to the early cultural imperialist school, was obviously more plausible in an era when even the largest Third World countries relied heavily on programming imported from developed countries, particularly the US, than it is today, when domestic or regionally produced programming dominates in many countries," according to scholar Daniel C. Hallin, writing in the mid-90s (p. 154). Now with the development of huge Latin American transnational media corporations, such as Mexico's Televisa, the flow of programming is different from the patterns of decades ago. "Developments of this sort ...," wrote Hallin, "have in recent years forced a rethinking of the classic literature on broadcasting in the Third World" (1998, p. 153).

The old cultural imperialism model presented a simple vision of U.S. television programming arriving with assumed ill-effect on legions of mesmerized viewers. A newer view, expressed by Celeste Olalquiaga (1992), is one of "an unprecedented degree of reciprocal appropriation and mutual transformation whereby cultural change can no longer be said to be a matter of simple vertical imposition or ransacking, but is rather an intricate horizontal movement of exchange" (p. 76). Straubhaar's (1991) view is that "... we must look at how media are received by the audience as part of cultures and subcultures that resist change" (p. 39). The more recent focus on reception analysis has shifted energy to the useful goal of finding out how audiences really respond to program offerings, whether intercontinental, interregional, or local.

Ecuador's Ecuavisa offers the example of a Latin American television network that imports programming from the United States and the region in greater quantity than it produces. But its viewers reverse the order of importance of that programming. In Ecuador, Ecuadorian television programming is most important, demonstrating the strength of cultural proximity in television. This case study of Ecuavisa finds cultural proximity operating in Ecuador at the local market level, with the highest rated programs reflecting the cultural divide between Quito and Guayaquil. Most smaller Latin American countries have plenty to choose from in the way of American programs and Latin American novelas. What emerges from this case study is the quantity, quality, and impact of national production envisioned by one Ecuadorian media baron and created by one committed network, even in a media-saturated, small-market, Third World environment.

The economies of television production, the size of the country, the limited talent pool, and the inexperience in producing and marketing make the production of Ecuadorian television programming all the more difficult. Against the odds, Ecuavisa provides local viewers news about themselves, dramas about themselves, and the first and only Ecuadorian comedy. Viewers in Quito and Guayaquil can tune in Ecuavisa, and, about one fourth of the time, witness the mundane miracle called "national production." And watch it they do.

REFERENCES

Alisky, M. (1981). *Latin American media: Guidance and censorship.* Ames: Iowa State University Press.
Alleyne, M. D. (1995). *International power and international communication.* New York: St. Martin's.
Antola, L., & Rogers, E. M. (1984). Television flows in Latin America. *Communication Research, 11*(2), 183–202.
Berwanger, D. (1995). The Third World. In A. Smith (Ed.), *Television: An international history* (pp. 317–319). Oxford: Oxford University Press.
Dominick, J. R., Sherman, B. L., & Copeland, G. A. (1996). *Broadcasting/Cable and beyond.* New York: McGraw-Hill.
Elasmar, M. G., & Hunter, J. E. (1997). The impact of foreign TV on a domestic audience: A meta-analysis. In B. R. Burleson & A. W. Kunkel (Eds.), *International Communication Association Communication Yearbook 20* (p. 47). Thousand Oaks, CA: Sage.
Franco, J. (1994). What's left of the intelligentsia? The uncertain future of the printed word. *NACLA Report on the Americas 28*(2), 16–21.
Gargúrevich, J., & Fox, E. (1988). Revolution and the press in Peru. In E. Fox (Ed.), *Media and politics in Latin America: The struggle for democracy* (pp. 56–66). London: Sage.
Goonasekara, A. (1987). The influence of television on cultural values—with special reference to Third World countries. *Media Asia, 14,* 7–12.
Hallin, D. C. (1998). Broadcasting in the Third World: From national development to civil society. In T. Ljebes & J. Curran (Eds.), *Media, Ritual, and Identity* (pp. 153–167). New York: Routledge.
In Buenos Aires, there's room for 2 to be numero uno. (1993, March 29). *Variety,* p. 68.
International Idea Institute for Democracy and Electoral Assistance. (2002, April 22). *The challenge of the media in Guatemala.* Retrieved from http://www.idea.int/publications/Guatemala/engguat-9media.html.
Katz, E., & Wedell, G. (1977). *Broadcasting in the Third World: Promise and performance.* Cambridge, MA: Harvard University Press.
Latin American TV at a glance. (1993, March 29). *Variety,* p. 44.
Locals outrank the Yanks. (1993, March 29). *Variety,* p. 48.
Marcus, D. (1993, September). How a soap opera shatters taboos—and politicians. *IPI (International Press Institute) Report,* 15–16.
Olalquiaga, C. (1992). *Megalopolis: Contemporary cultural sensibilities.* Minneapolis: University of Minnesota Press.
Paterson, R. (1995). Drama and entertainment. In A. Smith (Ed.), *Television: An international history* (pp. 104–106). Oxford: Oxford University Press.
Prada, R. R. (1988). Bolivian television: When reality surpasses fiction. In E. Fox (Ed.), *Media and politics in Latin America: The struggle for democracy* (pp. 164–170). London: Sage.
Reeves, G. (1993). *Communications and the "Third World."* London: Routledge.
Schement, J. R., & Rogers, E. M. (1984). Media flows in Latin America. *Communication Research, 11*(2), 194–200, 305–319.
Smith, M. (1985). *Radio, TV & cable.* New York: CBS College.
Straubhaar, J. D. (1991). Beyond media imperialism: Assymetrical interdependence and cultural proximity. *Critical Studies in Mass Communication 8,* 39–59.
Straubhaar, J. D., & Viscasillas, G. (1991, Winter). Class, genre, and the regionalization of television programming in the Dominican Republic. *Journal of Communication, 41*(1), 53–69.

Stevenson, R. L. (1988). *Communication, development, and the Third World: The global politics of information.* White Plains, NY: Longman.
Torres, C., & Millman, J. (1996, May 30). Televisa seeks to get big part in global play. *Wall Street Journal,* p. A14.
Tracey, M. (1985). The poisoned chalice? International television and the idea of dominance. *Daedalus, Journal of the American Academy of Arts and Sciences, 114*(4), 17–54.
Vanden Heuvel, J., & Dennis, E. E. (1995). *Changing patterns: Latin America's vital media.* New York: The Freedom Forum Media Studies Center at Columbia University.
Varis, T. (1984). The International flow of television programs. *Journal of Communications, 34*(1), 143–152.
Wert, M. C. (1985). *The flow of television in Panama, Costa Rica and El Salvador.* Unpublished master's thesis, University of North Carolina, Chapel Hill.
Wert, M. C., & Stevenson, R. L. (1988). Global television flow to Latin American countries. *Journalism Quarterly, 65*(1), 182–185.
Wimmer, R. D., & Dominick, J. R. (1991). Mass media research. In *The world almanac and book of facts* (1995 ed., p. 45). New York: World Almanac Books.

CHAPTER

8

A Meta-Analysis of Crossborder Effect Studies

Michael G. Elasmar
Boston University
John E. Hunter
Michigan State University

The impact of crossborder communication has long been of special interest to international communication scholars and policy makers. In this chapter the authors use meta-analytic procedures to investigate the size of the effects of crossborder television. The results of this study reveal that, overall, crossborder TV has very weak effects on viewers. This result contradicts cultural imperialism critics, who contend that foreign television has strong and negative impacts on viewers. The effects of foreign TV are usually assumed to be from TV to the audience members. This chapter, however, raises the possibility that the effects found are not only very weak, but could be due to some other factors that may be influencing the audience to seek and view foreign TV programs.

International communication as a topic of study encompasses many issues that have been vigorously debated over the years. Chief among these issues are dependency as related to imported media, media imperialism, international media and sovereignty, and the international flow of information. Although each of these topics can be studied distinctly, they all share a common concern about messages crossing between countries. This concern is based on the tacit assumption that imported messages have negative impacts on audiences in the importing countries.

Although large bodies of literature have been written about various aspects of international communication, few authors have directly addressed the issue of crossborder TV impact. The majority of those who have addressed this topic directly have approached it from a theoretical, conjectural, or speculative perspective.

Unfortunately, many of the papers they have produced can be characterized as tirades or diatribes. Among the most emotional of these have been works expressing fear that local populations will be contaminated by exposure to immoral and exploitative foreigners.

In this chapter we investigate the topic of the crossborder impact of TV using a more objective and less normative approach. We propose to use meta-analytic procedures to analyze the current body of literature about crossborder TV. The general research question of this endeavor is, What are the empirical findings on the effects of crossborder TV?[1] More specific research questions include the following: What is the average effect size of crossborder TV across studies? What does the size of the average effect of crossborder TV mean to international communication scholars?

The outcomes of this study should be practically useful for those engaging in international communication policy debates. However, the analyses reported here also have theoretical implications. Crossborder TV exposes domestic audience members to individuals from distant lands depicted in television program content. In many cases, such mediated encounters may be the only contact domestic audience members will ever have with these imported characters. The imported characters are often from different societies, cultures, traditions, and nations. Thus, any effects stemming from exposure to such characters are of interest to researchers studying the social psychology of intergroup relations, intercultural communications, and international relations.

Although it is not within the scope of this chapter to provide a comprehensive review of qualitative essays that have been written about the impact of crossborder TV, in the following section we highlight the key arguments concerning this topic.

CONCEPTUALIZING THE IMPACT OF FOREIGN TV

During the past few decades, the presence of foreign programs in domestic television schedules has been seen by most observers as a source of national ills. Other observers, however, contend that the impact of such a presence is either negligible or unknown.

Foreign TV: A Source of National Ills

Lee (1980) summarizes the various concerns expressed about imported TV programs as follows: (a) The programs will make products manufactured in cities intensely attractive and encourage their consumption; (b) in many locales, audience members will be greatly frustrated because they cannot obtain or afford most of what these TV programs depict; and (c) the values embodied in these programs will

---

[1] This study is an extension and update of earlier work by Elasmar (1991, 1993), Elasmar and Straubhaar (1993), and Elasmar, Hunter, and Straubhaar (1995).

influence the value structures of audience members. This last concern is the basis of one of the most intense accusations against imported TV: It is an instrument of cultural imperialism (Schiller, 1969). Cultural imperialism (CI) is said to be "a verifiable process of social influence by which a nation imposes on other countries its set of beliefs, values, knowledge and behavioral norms as well as its overall style of life" (Beltran, 1978a, p. 184). According to Goonasekara (1987), cultural imperialism is an effect stemming from the documented flow of television programs from Western countries into Third World television schedules. Advocates of CI theory claim that in "the face of this media invasion, the indigenous cultures of the Third World disintegrate consistently and without resistance" (Goonasekara, 1987, p.11). Hadad (1978) argues that industrialized countries use international television as a tool to extend their domestic commercial activities. He contends that "the best way to achieve this goal is by launching a 'cultural invasion' of developing nations" (p. 19). This fear of domination has even influenced how some observers perceive the importation into Latin America of *Sesame Street*, a U.S. educational program for children. Goldsen and Bibliowicz (1976) contend that *Plaza Sesamo*, the Spanish-language version of the series, will "lay down an important part of the cultural scaffolding that Latin American children will build on. [It will] expose the continent's children to a massive cultural assault whose consequences are incalculable" (p. 125). Herbert Schiller (1991), the main proponent behind the idea of cultural imperialism in the 1960s, still believes that "the global preeminence of American cultural products is being not only maintained but extended to new locales" (p. 22).

Foreign TV: Limited or Unknown Effects

In contrast to those who view foreign TV as a source of cultural domination are those who contend that it has either negligible or unknown effects. For instance, Tracey (1985) asserts that those who support the notion that foreign TV is a source of cultural domination "have tended to study company reports, rather than the realities of individual lives" (p. 45). Taking the individual viewer into consideration, Browne, as early as 1967, explained the hurdles that prevent foreign TV from having a controlled impact on individuals in a domestic setting:

> Experience should have already taught us that there is no universal visual language, any more than there is universal spoken or written language ... [which means that] if one picture is indeed worth a thousand words, those words will not mean the same thing to everyone. (p. 206)

According to Salwen (1991), foreign TV cannot be viewed as a direct cause of individuals' losing their indigenous cultures: "At the very least, factors inherent within cultures ... account for different responses to foreign media messages" (p. 36). Salwen, Tracey, and Browne all base their arguments on the notion of audience activity. That is, they contend that individual audience members are not passive receivers of television messages; rather, audiences actively choose among the many available messages. The concept of audience activity contradicts the thinking of those who believe that audiences exposed to foreign TV are helpless victims influenced by ruthless message designers—the notion that the audience is composed of active receivers does not convince whose who fear cultural imperialism. Schiller (1991), for example, believes that "much of the current work on audience reception comes uncomfortably close to being apologetics for present-day structures of cultural control" (p. 25).

Aside from those who point out the difficulties foreign TV has in achieving effects, there are those who assert that we just don't know enough about the topic to make as assessment. Tracey (1985) notes that "we have barely begun to scratch the surface of understanding the function and consequence of TV as an international cultural process" (p. 50), and Lee (1980) observes that "research on the likely influences of alien televison programs on the decline of traditional cultures and arts is inconclusive" (p. 103).

Some researhers have assessed the effects of foreign TV after carrying out narrative reviews of the existing literature. Yaple and Korzenny (1989), for example, assert that the studies conducted so far "have concluded that media effects across national cultural groups are detectable but relatively small in magnitude, and that ... the environment, cultural situation, and context affect selectivity and the interpretation of content" (p. 313). After a similar narrative review of the literature, Hur (1982) concludes that "exposure to American television and film content by local populations has few cognitive and attitudinal effects, much less behavioral effects" (p. 546).

So far, researchers assessing the impact of foreign TV have done so in one of two ways: (a) by following a set of arguments heavily grounded in political ideology or (b) by carrying out a narrative literature review of selected studies. We propose to use a more objective methodology—meta-analysis—to assess the entire body of quantitative studies about the topic.

STUDY EXPECTATIONS

The various views held regarding the effect of foreign TV enable us to develop expectations about the results of our study. Concerning the concept that foreign TV programs embody a tool of cultural imperialism, we expect the following:

- The results of our meta-analysis will reveal that foreign television programs have strong effects on the domestic audience members who view them.

Concerning the concept that messages are received differently by various audience members, we expect the following:

- The results of our meta-analysis will reveal that the effects of foreign TV differ across audience types (age groups and other demographic factors).

In the following sections, we describe the methods used to locate and then analyze the studies, detail the findings of this endeavor, and present a discussion of the results and their implications.

METHOD

For purposes of this study, we define a *television impact* as any detected variation in an individual at the cognitive, attitudinal, affective, cultural, or behavioral level of analysis that is assumed to be attributed to foreign television consumption.[2] A *foreign* television program is defined as one that is (a) produced in a country different from that in which it is shown, regardless of how it arrived in the latter country (videotape, cable, importation, crossborder TV transmission, direct broadcast satellite), and (b) primarily designed for consumption by the audience of the country in which it was produced.[3] These first two criteria were established in order to distinguish the studies relevant to our research questions. Thus, not included in our analysis are international comparative investigations of domestic television effects (e.g., comparative cultivation studies) and research covering the impact of a message designed in Country A especially to influence the audience of Country B (i.e., propaganda and/or persuasion).

In addition, only empirical studies exploring the impact of a given Country A's television programs on individuals in Country B were selected.[4] In the case that not all hypotheses or relationships satisfied this requirement, only the hypotheses or relationships that did were summarized. Both published and unpublished manuscripts, recent or dated, were sought, and electronic database and manual index searches were conducted to generate potential study leads.[5] In addition, letters were sent to numerous research institutions around the United States asking for unpublished manuscripts about the topic.[6] Copies of all studies identified were then gathered, read, and summarized.

---

[2]The findings of studies conducted about the impact of foreign TV on consumer behavior, for example, would yield information about the likely economic impact of foreign TV on local versus imported products.

[3]The term *foreign TV* encompasses the term *crossborder TV*, as any television signal that is transmitted from Country A to Country B is foreign to Country B. We use the term *foreign TV* here because it also encompasses television content that arrives in Country B from Country A through channels other than direct transmission, such as program importation or home video release. Because the effect of interest to this study is that of the TV program's origin, regardless of its mode of transmission, we use the term *foreign TV*.

[4]The term *empirical* in this context is defined as systematic observations based upon the method of science (as opposed to the other methods of knowing identified by Kerlinger, 1986) and utilizing statistical analytic methods.

[5]Database searches were performed using the Dialog information services. Databases searched were ERIC, PsycINFO, and Sociological Abstracts. The following indexes were searched manually: *Current Contents in the Social and Behavioral Sciences, Psychological Abstracts*, and *Sociological Abstracts*.

[6]Letters were sent to mass communication departments known to conduct research on international communication during 1991. We are grateful to Professor Joseph Straubhaar of Brigham Young University, who helped carry out these contacts. In addition, from 1991 to 1994, the first author contacted researchers specializing in international communication at various professional conferences and asked for leads on unpublished studies about the topic at hand.

The Study Codebook

In order to describe the studies in a systematic manner, we developed a codebook to fit the specific needs of the analysis. Variables coded include year of study, year of publication, author's (or authors') country of affiliation, department of origin, study type, type of publication, study location, primary theory, sample type, and method. After all studies were coded, the data were entered into a computer and statistical software was used to generate descriptive statistics.

Quantification of Results

Meta-analysis is a general procedure for analyzing results across studies. In order to be useful, a study had to report results in some quantitative form. To enable comparison and synthesis of results across studies, the statistical report had to have the property that it could be recoded into a measure of the size of the effect. Only those studies with useful data are included in the meta-analysis portion of this report.

For our report, we coded the size of the effect as the correlation between foreign TV exposure and the dependent variable. Methods for computing correlations from various kinds of statistical reports are available in most textbooks on meta-analysis, such as that by Hunter and Schmidt (1990). Hunter and Schmidt also provide formulas for converting results from correlations into other measures of the size of the effect. The data transformation task was difficult with this particular group of studies because there was so much diversity in the methods of reporting findings.

The following coding rules were adopted for the effects on beliefs, behaviors, and knowledge: A correlation was coded as positive if exposure to imported TV led to an increase in an individual's beliefs, behaviors, or knowledge, regardless of whether these beliefs, behaviors, or knowledge would be regarded as positive or negative from a normative point of view. This was done because it is very hard to reach agreement on which beliefs, behaviors, or knowledge can be normatively considered positive or negative. For example, buying American products is a behavior that may be considered normatively positive by some and normatively negative by others. If a study reported that increases in U.S. TV consumption led to increases in the purchase of American products, we coded the correlation as positive in the meta-analysis, regardless of whether such buying behavior is considered normatively positive or negative. For attitudes, however, a correlation was coded as positive when exposure to foreign TV resulted in a positive attitude toward the country originating the program and as negative when it resulted in a negative attitude toward the originating country. It was fairly simple to distinguish between positive and negative attitudes based upon the wording of the attitude items. For example, a statement such as "I like the United States" expresses a positive attitude toward the United States. Thus, a positive correlation between scores on this item and scores on a U.S. TV exposure measure was coded as positive in the meta-analysis.

Meta-analysis can correct the effects of sampling error and other methodological imperfections and can determine the extent to which study results differ by more than sampling error. This is discussed in meta-analysis under the rubric of "heterogeneity." This is best done by estimating the standard deviation of the population values across studies. It is also possible to use a statistical significance test for homogeneity, though these tests sometimes do not work very well if the number of studies is small. The specific computational formulas used in our report are those of Hunter and Schmidt (1990).

RESULTS

The comprehensive search for literature spanned a time frame beginning with works published in 1960 and ending in January 1995 and located numerous articles addressing the topic of crossborder TV effects.[7] After a careful examination of the content of these articles, it was determined that the majority took a mostly critical approach to the topic at hand (examples include Beltran, 1978a, 1978b; Day, 1975; Dizard, 1965; Goldsen & Bibliowicz, 1976; Tracey, 1985). There were also numerous others that fit the caregory of international comparative TV effects (examples include Bouwman & Stappers, 1982; Hedinson & Windahl, 1982; Morgan & Shanahan, 1992; Straubhaar et al., 1992).

As the literature was being collected, sorted, and categorized, it became clear that quantitative studies examining the effects of foreign television on individuals are rare. After reading all articles obtained ($n = 177$), we found a total of 36 manuscripts to fit the basic criteria set at the start of this endeavor. Figure 8.1 shows the number of studies conducted by year. Few studies were published before 1970, but more studies have been published in recent years. In the 1960s there were 2, in the 1970s there were 5, and in the 1980s there were 18. Based upon this linear trend, we can project that a total of 28 studies will be done during the decade of the 1990s. The majority of the studies (55.6%) were published in academic journals.[8] Convention papers make up 22.2% of the total.

Many of the studies were not theory driven. In fact, 25% did not identify a primary theory from which hypotheses were formulated. The largest number of the investigations that were theory based relied on Gerbner's cultivation theory (recently reviewed by Morgan & Signorielli, 1990). Other theories informing the studies were as follows: cultural imperialism (11.1%), acculturation (6.7%), socialization (5.6%), dependency (5.6%), modernization (2.8%), and social learning (2.8%).

---

[7]Whereas conference papers, theses, and dissertations were obtained through a multimethod search, our finding published articles depended on whether they were included in a database by early January 1995.

[8]The possibility of bias toward significant findings is present in journal articles because journals tend to select for publication studies with effects over those without any effects. In this investigation we attempted to counter this possibility of bias by collecting unpublished studies, including master's theses and conference papers, that had not been subjected to a selection process that favors studies finding effects over those that do not.

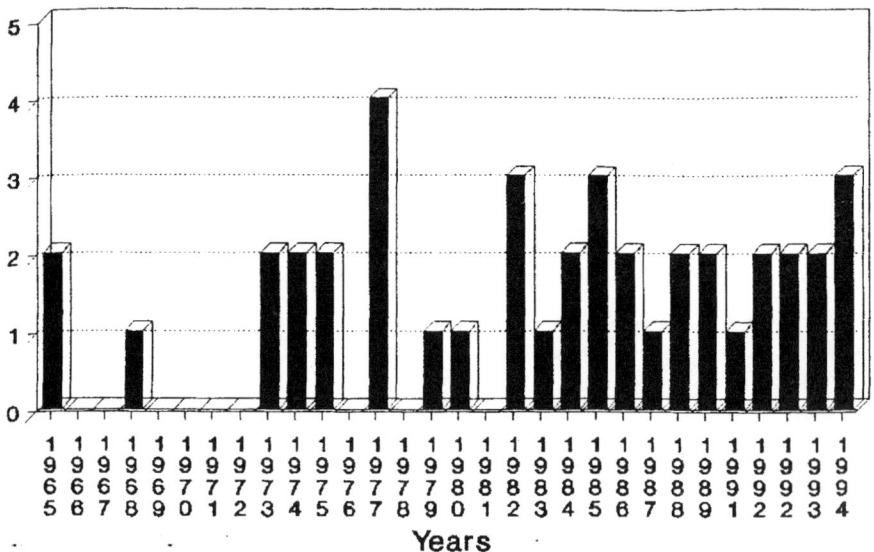

FIG. 8.1. Foreign TV impact studies: Number of studies conducted by year.

Most investigators relied on a group-distributed but self-administered survey method to collect data about individuals. Some researchers preferred to conduct door-to-door personal interviews by themselves (e.g., Oliveira, 1986) or with a few trained assistants (e.g., Veii, 1988) or by hiring a marketing firm (e.g., Skinner, 1984). Those studies that used the personal interview method accounted for 27.8% of the total, whereas those that used a mail survey accounted for 2.8%. Another 2.8% used a combination of methods. Of the 36 studies, 34 (94.4%) used a cross-sectional design, which means that the data were collected at only one point in time. The remaining 2 studies attempted to observe the effects of foreign TV on individuals over several years.

Countries Studied

The studies report results collected in 21 different countries or territories. Table 8.1 lists those countries and the number of studies for each. The number of instances is larger than the number of studies because some studies gathered data in more than one country.

Origin of Country of Content

The country of origin of the foreign television content analyzed in these studies was typically the United States ($n = 28$). The second most investigated foreign TV impact concerned programs of Canadian origin ($n = 6$). The impact of Mexican TV was investigated in a single study, and one of the research reports did not specify the

TABLE 8.1
Locations of crossborder TV Impact Studies

Location	n
Australia	1
Belize	2
Native Canada	4
Nonnative Canada	5
China	3
Denmark	1
Finland	1
Iceland	2
India	1
Israel	1
Japan	3
Korea	4
Lebanon	1
Mexico	1
Namibia	1
Norway	1
Philippines	1
Russia	1
Sweden	1
Taiwan	3
Thailand	1
Trinidad	1
United States nonnative	2
Venezuela	1

origin of the foreign TV programming but merely indicated that it was not domestic (Zhao, 1989).

Classification of Audience Members

The majority of the studies (58.3%) focused upon the effects of foreign TV on students.[9] 22.2% focused upon the general population. That there were only 8 general population studies conducted on this topic in 27 years is surprising. A few investigations looked at the impact of foreign TV on professionals (5.6%), and some even combined students and members of the general public in their samples (13.9%).

Because audiences differ in terms of sophistication, it is possible that the effects of foreign TV are different for different audiences. We coded each study as to audience so that we could check for such results.

Measurement of the Independent Variable

Ideally, each study should measure the exact extent to which each audience member is exposed to foreign TV. The studies varied in the quality of this measurement. Out of a total of 36 studies, 9 (25%) had no direct measure of the individuals' consumption of foreign TV. Instead, some investigators ($n = 7$) simply measured individuals' consumption of television in general (e.g., Werner, 1981), whereas others ($n = 2$) did not bother to assess even that variable (e.g., Tate & Trach, 1980). The former group of studies assumed that, because foreign programming was carried on a domestic TV station, an estimate of television exposure would yield an estimate of exposure to foreign programming. The latter studies assumed that if a leaning toward the United States on the part of audience members was detected, this indicated the impact of American TV programs present in the domestic TV broadcast schedule. The studies that did not clearly measure individuals' consumption of imported TV are not included in the meta-analysis section of this chapter.

The best of the 36 studies were the 27 investigations that did provide some measure of individual consumption of foreign TV. The researchers, however, differed in their measurement of foreign TV exposure and varied in their concern with content specificity. Some investigators measured exposure by assessing individuals' watching particular foreign TV genres, such as comedy, crime, or drama, on a domestic network (e.g., Pingree & Hawkins, 1981). Others measured exposure as the number of hours tuned in to a particular foreign TV network received domestically, regardless of the genres that individuals watched (e.g., Kang & Morgan, 1988). Still others measured exposure as the frequency of watching specific foreign TV programs (not genres) on a domestic network (e.g., Tan & Suarchavarat, 1988). Given

---

[9]This may limit the generalizability of the findings, as students may or may not be representative of the population at large.

the small number of studies at hand, we decided to consider all independent measures as being approximation of one another and best available estimates of foreign TV consumption.

Measures of the Dependent Variable

The researchers differed in how they assessed influence or impact. That is, they differed in both the number and the quality of their measurement of the dependent variables. After a qualitative assessment of the items, we coded the different dependent variables into five categories. The coding was carried out according to the following criteria.

Knowledge. The dependent variable assesses factual knowledge or information, such as the name of the U.S. president. Here a respondent's answer is contrasted with the true answer. The scoring choice is binary: 1 for true, 0 for false for each response. A correlation was coded positive if an increase in foreign TV consumption was associated with an increase in an individual's knowledge about the foreign country.

Beliefs. The dependent variable taps perceptions(s) or opinion(s), such as the perceptions of how wealthy Americans are. The variable here does not assess an individual's affect toward the topic but merely his or her perception or opinion. Here a person is asked what he or she thinks about a topic/object/place. In contrast to knowledge, beliefs are subjective. The researcher cannot assess them using a true/false scheme. Instead, researchers typically estimate the level of a respondent's agreement with the subjective belief in question. A correlation was coded positive if an increase in foreign TV consumption was associated with an increase in the level of beliefs about the foreign country, regardless of the normative evaluation of such beliefs.

Attitudinal. The dependent variable taps an affective belief, such as whether a person likes the United States. Here a person is asked how he or she feels toward a topic/object/place. Attitudes are distinguished from beliefs because whereas a person may strongly agree with a belief statement such as "Americans are wealthy," that person may hold a negative attitude toward Americans and may respond that he or she "doesn't like Americans at all." A correlation was coded as positive if an increase in foreign TV consumption was associated with a more positive attitude toward the foreign country.

Behavioral. The dependent variable assesses an individual's past action, such as past purchasing behavior. A correlation was coded positive if an increase in foreign TV consumption was associated with an increase in the purchasing of foreign goods.

Value. Values are beliefs that are known to be commonly held by a large proportion of a population. A belief is considered a value in Society A if that belief is known to be traditionally held by most individuals in Society A. Although societies may hold many values in common, this study considers to be of interest those values that differ between Society A and Society B. A difference exists when the value is present in Society A and not present in Society B. A difference also exists when a value is present in both Societies A and B but the views of individuals in Society A about the value in question are known to differ from the views of individuals in Society B. The dependent variable here typically assesses the respondent's position on particular issues that have been identified by the author of the study as different in the country receiving the message from those in the country sending the message. One example is the issue of "respect for the elderly." It is well-known that in Asian societies, in contrast with U.S. society, the elderly have traditionally been consistently revered. Asking a respondent in Korea to indicate his or her agreement with a statement such as "It is important to respect the elders in my family" functions as an assessment of that person's value for respecting the elderly in his or her family. A correlation was coded as positive if an increase in foreign TV consumption was associated with a preference for the values of the foreign country originating the message.

After coding the obtained articles, we found that beliefs were most often studied ($n = 11$), followed by values ($n = 7$), attitudes ($n = 6$), behaviors ($n = 2$), and knowledge ($n = 2$).

We analyzed each study to determine the effect size for each dependent variable measured in that study. The findings reported here are from those studies that provided either zero-order correlation coefficients in their results sections or some statistic that could be converted into correlation coefficients (e.g., F tests, t tests).[10] If a study had more than one measure of a given dependent variable, then the results were averaged across measures (Hunter & Schmidt, 1990). The individual study results for each of the five dependent variables are listed in Tables 8.2-8.6.

TABLE 8.2
The Impact of Foreign TV: Summary of Behavioral Effects

Author(s)	Sample[a]	Country	Behaviors(s)	r
Oliveira (1986)	96	Columbia	Use of American consumer products	.21
Kang & Morgan (1988)	226	Korea	Wearing jeans	.24

[a]Sample size corresponding to the specific relationship(s) is reported when available. Otherwise, total study sample size is reported.

---

[10]Partial correlations of standardized regression coefficients were used as best available estimates when no zero-order correlation coefficients or any other convertible statistics were reported.

8. A META-ANALYSIS

TABLE 8.3
The Impact of Foreign TV: Summary of Knowledge-Based Effects

Author(s)	Sample[a]	Country	Knowledge	r
Payne (1978)	694	United States	Knowledge of Canadian issues	.36
Payne & Caron (1982)	646	Canada	Knowledge of U.S. issues	.09

[a]Sample size corresponding to the specific relationship(s) is reported when available. Otherwise, total study sample size is reported.

TABLE 8.4
The Impact of Foreign TV: Summary of Value-Based Effects

Author(s)	Sample[a]	Country	Values	r
Tsai (1967)	160	Taiwan	General Western versus Eastern values	.08
Skinner (1984)	297	Trinidad	General U.S. values	.33
Kang & Morgan (1988)	226	Korea	Western versus traditional sex role values	.09
Zhao (1989)	990	China	General Western versus traditional values	.09
Wu (1989)	1,214	Taiwan	Western versus traditional sex role values	.06
Geiger (1992)	605	Venezuela	General U.S. Versus Venezuelan values	.03
Chaffee et al. (1995)	1,862	China	General Western versus traditional values	.22

[a]Sample size corresponding to the specific relationship(s) is reported when available. Otherwise, total study sample size is reported.

Meta-Analysis Results

For each dependent variable, we did an overall meta-analysis of the size of the effect. The results of these analyses are presented in Table 8.7, which gives the following key facts for each dependent variable: (a) the number of studies that measured that variable, (b) the total sample size across those studies, and (c) the average population correlation for those studies. The average population correlation is the generalized finding for the effect of foreign TV for the dependent variable.

TABLE 8.5
The Impact of Foreign TV: Summary of Attitudinal Effects

Author(s)	Sample[a]	Country	Attitude(s)	r
Tsai (1967)	598	Taiwan	Attitudes toward U.S. and American cultural products	.13
Payne & Peake (1977)	39	Iceland	Choice of U.S. to immigrate	.04
Payne (1978)	414	United States	Attitudes toward Canada	–.10
Payne & Caron (1982)	646	Canada	Attitudes toward the United States	.08
Oliveira (1986)	96	Belize	Attitudes toward consumption of U.S. products	.42
Kang & Morgan (1988)	226	Korea	Attitudes toward rock and roll	.12

[a]Sample size corresponding to the specific relationship(s) is reported when available. Otherwise, total study sample size is reported.

Table 8.7 also presents several statistics that assess the extent to which findings differ across studies. First, there is the standard deviation of population correlations across studies. From that, high and low estimates can be computed, assuming that the results are normally distributed across studies. Finally, there is the statistical significance test for homogeneity; the chi-square test. Many believe that if the homogeneity test is not significant, then there is no meaningful evidence of variation across studies. However, when the number of studies is small, this significance test—like all significance tests—can have a very high error rate. Given that the number of studies is small in our case, we will focus instead on the standard deviation as the best measure of homogeneity.

Table 8.7 lists the finding by level of definiteness. *Definiteness*, in this case, refers to the relative homogeneity of the correlations for the dependent variable. The findings for studies of behavior ($r = .23$, $z = 4.36$, $p < .01$) show no evidence of variation in the size of the effect across studies. That is, both studies show the same level of effect for behavior. The effect is positive and statistically significant, though modest. Foreign TV increases the purchase of foreign products, especially clothing and other consumer products. Homogeneity, however, does not denote that a meaningful effect has been detected. A correlation of .23 means that foreign TV accounts for only 5% of the variance in audience buying behavior.

TABLE 8.6
The Impact of Foreign TV: Summary of Belief-Based Effects

Author(s)	Sample[a]	Country	Belief(s)	r
Tsai (1967)	598	Taiwan	Beliefs about Americans	.18
Payne (1978)	414	United States	Various beliefs consistent with presentations on Canadian TV	−.01
Pingree & Hawkins (1981)	1,280	Australia	Beliefs about the United States and Australia	.05
Skinner (1984)	297	Trinidad	Beliefs about the United States	.25
Weimann (1984)	461	Israel	Beliefs about the United States	.38
Tan & Suarchavarat (1988)	279	Thailand	Beliefs about Americans	.07
Choi (1989)	222	Korea	Beliefs about the United States	.05
Wu (1989)	1,214	Taiwan	Beliefs about the United States	−.02
Ahn (1990)	705	Korea	Beliefs about the United States	.13
El-Koussa & Elasmar (1995)	481	Lebanon	Beliefs about the United States	.09
Elasmar & Akaishi (1995)	496	Japan	Beliefs about the United States	.05

[a]Sample size corresponding to the specific relationship(s) is reported when available. Otherwise, total study sample size is reported.

TABLE 8.7
The Impact of Foreign TV: Meta-Analytic Results

Impact	K	N	Mean Rho	SD Rho	Low	High	x^2
Behavior	2	322	.23	.00	.23	.23	00.07
Values	7	5,792	.15	.08	.05	.25	47.35*
Attitudes	6	2,019	.11	.08	.00	.21	20.77*
Beliefs	11	6,447	.09	.10	−.04	.22	75.59*
Knowledge	2	1,060	.19	.12	.04	.36	19.85*

*$p < .05$.

For the other four dependent variables, the average effect sizes are also positive, although there is variation across studies. The average correlations are as follows: for values, $r = .14$ ($z = 4.24$, $p < .001$); for attitudes, $r = .09$ ($z = 1.86$, $p > .05$); for beliefs, $r = .09$ ($z = 2.81$, $p < .01$); for knowledge, $r = .20$ ($z = 2.22$, $p < .05$).

Usually, interpretation of the average is better put off until a study is made of the cause for such variation. Thus, we did an analysis of potential causes of variation (moderators) for each of these four dependent variables.

The moderator variable that we considered most likely to be relevant is that of audience segment, specifically age. Are older viewers either more or less likely to be influenced? In the case of knowledge, such a moderator analysis was not possible because only two studies had investigated a knowledge effect, and both had used adult audiences (see Table 8.3). For the three remaining dependent variables, we could classify most studies in terms of the type of sample used: student or general population. The two types were used as proxies for age.

Table 8.8 presents the moderator analysis for values. The mean effect size was .16 for the general population and only .07 for students. The results for student samples were homogeneous across studies. The results for the general population showed some variation ($SD = .08$) across studies, though it is virtually certain that all effects are positive. The mean effects suggest that foreign TV has less effect on the attitudes of young students than on adults, although the difference is not statistically significant ($z = 1.5$, $p > .05$).

Table 8.9 presents the moderator analysis for beliefs. The mean effect size was .12 for the general population and only .09 for students. The results for student samples were less homogeneous ($SD = .09$) than those for the general population ($SD = .07$). It is virtually certain, however, that all effects are positive. The mean effects would suggest that foreign TV has less effect on the beliefs of students than on those of adults, although the difference is not statistically significant ($z = .428$, $p > .05$).

Table 8.10 presents the moderator analysis for attitudes. The mean effect size was .12 for both the general population and students. The results for student samples were homogeneous across studies. The results for the general population showed some variation ($SD = .10$) across studies, though most results are positive. The mean effects suggest that for attitudes, there are no differences between adults and students ($z = .01$, $p > .05$).

TABLE 8.8
Moderator Analysis for Values: Sample Type

Moderator	K	N	Mean Rho	SD Rho	Low	High	x^2
General population	4	3,754	.16	.08	.18	.27	31.97*
Students	3	1,600	.07	.00	.07	.07	00.21

*$p < .05$.

TABLE 8.9
Moderator Analysis for Beliefs: Sample Type

Moderator	K	N	Mean Rho	SD Rho	Low	High	x^2
General population	2	519	.16	.08	.06	.26	05.34*
Grade/high school/university	7	5,053	.06	.05	−.001	.13	20.51*

*$p < .05$.

TABLE 8.10
Moderator Analysis for Attitudes: Sample Type

Moderator	K	N	Mean Rho	SD Rho	Low	High	x2
General population	2	742	.12	.10	−.01	.25	09.94*
Grade/high school	3	8263	.12	.00	.12	.12	00.31

*$p < .05$.

We obtained similar results when we carried out a moderator analysis by grouping studies in terms of their geographic location. We considered the existence of other potential moderators (e.g., language), but the study characteristics did not permit their examination. In the following section we discuss the results of our meta-analysis and their implications.

DISCUSSION

The results of this endeavor reveal that empirical studies about the impact of foreign TV on a domestic audience are scarce. This result, by itself, is surprising, given the interest in this topic among policy makers and researchers. We found a total of 36 studies that met the most basic criteria set at the beginning of this research effort. Of these, 27 studies used direct measures of foreign TV exposure and were thus considered for the meta-analysis segment of this investigation. At the beginning of this endeavor, we identified two specific research questions and two expectations about our research results; we address these research questions and expectations below.

What Is the Average Effect Size of crossborder TV Across Studies?

Our meta-analysis revealed weak, positive correlations between exposure to foreign TV and viewers' knowledge, attitudes, beliefs, values, and behaviors.

Although the correlations for behavior ($k = 2$) were homogeneous, the correlations for the other four dependent variables were not. This means that effect sizes differed across studies. Based upon the concept that a message will be received differently by various audience members, we had expected such variation. Because it is usually preferred to put off the interpretation of the average correlations until further investigation of this variation, we carried out a moderator analysis, and age was identified as a potential moderator. The moderator analysis, however, revealed that the effects of foreign TV on students did not significantly differ from the effects on general audiences.

Besides the existence of an audience segment moderator, however, there could also be other explanations for variations in the correlations obtained. Among such explanations are artifacts and study imperfections. Chief among such artifacts is measurement error. The fact that only a few studies reported reliability coefficients in their findings makes it impossible to assess the relative influence of measurement error on the homogeneity of the correlations. This is especially true in the case of the predictor variable "foreign TV consumption." In most cases a single estimate of this predictor was used, which makes it impossible to estimate the measurement error associated with this variable.

Perhaps there are true differences across studies. These differences could be attributed to real disparities across samples or real discrepancies due to an interaction between geographic location and the timing of a study. Such possibilities can be investigated when more studies become available to permit further breakdown of results along geographic and chronological lines.

What Does the Size of the Average Effect of crossborder TV Mean to International Communication Scholars?

Although the source of variation in effect size across studies is unexplained, the results of this meta-analysis reveal a pattern of positive correlations for all effect types. Assuming that the average correlation is the best available estimate of effect size across studies, these findings can be summarized as follows:

1. Exposure to foreign TV increases the purchase of foreign products, especially clothing and other consumer products. The size of this increase, however, is very small, because foreign TV accounts for only 5% of the variation in foreign product purchasing.
2. Overall, exposure to foreign TV increases the tendency of audience members to hold values similar to those present in the country producing the foreign message. The size of the increase, however, is very small, because foreign TV accounts for only 2% of the variation in audience values.
3. Overall, there is no statistically significant relationship between exposure to foreign TV and the likelihood that audience members will hold positive attitudes toward the country originating the foreign message.
4. Overall, exposure to foreign TV increases the strength of audience beliefs about the country originating the foreign message. The size of this in-

crease, however, is very small, because foreign TV accounts for only .08% of the variation in beliefs. The reader needs to be cautioned that a positive correlation between exposure to foreign TV and beliefs about the United States, for example, does not necessarily mean that exposure leads to positive beliefs about the United States. This is true because the belief type could very well be normatively negative (e.g., violent society). In this case the positive correlation indicates simply an increase in normatively negative beliefs. The distinction between normatively positive beliefs and normatively negative beliefs could not be made in this study because it is very difficult to achieve a consensus on what constitutes negative or positive beliefs from a normative point of view.
5. Overall, exposure to foreign TV increases audience knowledge about the country originating the message. The size of the increase, however, is very small, because foreign TV accounts for only 4% of the variation in knowledge.

Based on the concept that foreign TV programs embody a tool of cultural imperialism, we had expected our meta-analysis to reveal that foreign television programs have strong effects on the domestic audience members who view them. The results summarized above reveal that this is not the case. At most, foreign TV exposure may have a very weak impact upon audience members. This result contradicts the assertions of Herbert Schiller and his colleagues, who have long warned against the dangers of cultural imperialism. Given this assessment, the very weak and positive correlations obtained in our meta-analysis cannot be used to support the tacit assumption made by policy makers that imported messages have strong and negative impacts upon the audiences in the importing countries. Our results are more consistent with the prediction made by Browne (1967) and echoed by Salwen (1991) that the effects are most likely to vary. Our results are also consistent with the assessments made by Yaple and Korzenny (1989) and Hur (1982), who argue that the effects are either nonexistent or very weak.

Although we found a pattern of positive correlations in our meta-analysis, not only is the size of these correlations very small, but we can also question the assumption of directional causality embedded in the literature. It is unclear whether exposure to imported television leads to the effect types or whether the existence of these effects, due to some other variables, leads individual to seek exposure to foreign TV.

A quick review of the theoretical framework utilized by the studies summarized in our meta-analysis reveals that all the theories identified are directional, with the arrow of causality pointing from TV to the individual. There is a very real possibility, however, that the arrow may actually point from the individual to the TV programs chosen by that individual. Television, after all, is not the only source of information about foreign countries. Family members (including those studying, working, or residing abroad), peers (including those who have family members abroad), religious leaders (including those affiliated with institutions abroad), dominant political ideologies within particular groups, as well as other factors, could very well influence veiwers' attitudes, beliefs, knowledge, and behaviors. These, in turn, may influence exposure to or avoidance of foreign TV programs. In this case, the actual exposure would be influence by knowledge, beliefs, attitudes, or behaviors, and not the other way around. Although this possibility is very real, it is not specifically addressed in any of the studies reviewed and is certainly not covered by any of the theoretical frameworks chosen by the researchers. Given the above reasoning, however, the very weak effects found in this meta-analysis could very well be indicative of the influence of existing knowledge, beliefs, values, or behaviors upon exposure to foreign TV programs.

The empirical studies in this area are apparently still at an early stage. The objective of this early research was to explore whether foreign TV has an impact. The use of standard media-impact theoretical frameworks across cultural contexts in the studies reviewed is indicative of this early research stage. The next stage needs to examine whether effects vary across subgroups along such cultural lines as differences in religion, language, or other cleavages within the cultural context being studied. This second stage will probably result in more culturally specific theories, which may enhance our understanding of the impact of foreign TV.

On the basis of our review of the studies composing this body of literature, we strongly recommend that researchers who conduct future studies do the following:

1. Clearly define predictor and criterion variables conceptually and operationally,
2. attempt to use similar predictor and criterion variables across studies and authors,
3. measure several controls to eliminate alternative explanation of results,
4. use multiple estimates for each variable, and
5. report reliability coefficients pertaining to each variable.

By providing a set of best available estimates for each effect type, we hope that this meta-analysis sheds light on the link between individuals' exposure to foreign TV and their attitudes, beliefs, values, behaviors, and/or knowledge. We also hope that the results of our meta-analysis based upon the available body of literature, provide researchers with a solid background for future studies and inspire other researchers to carry out periodic updates of this analysis.

REFERENCES

Note: Asterisks indicate studies included in the meta-analysis.
*Ahn, Y (1990). *Images of life in America: The relationships of Korean adolescents's U.S. television viewing and perceptions of American reality.* Unpublished master's thesis, Michigan State University, East Lansing.
*Barnett, G. A., & McPhail, T. L. (1980). An examination of the relationship of United States television and Canadian identity. *International Journal of Intercultural Relations, 4,* 219–232.

*Beattie, E. (1967). In Canada's centennial year, U. S. mass media probed. *Journalism Quarterly, 44,* 667–672.
Beltran, L. R. S. (1978a). Communication and cultural domination: USA-Latin American case. *Media Asia, 5,* 183–192.
Beltran, L. R. S. (1978b). TV etchings in the minds of Latin Americans: Conservatism, materialism and conformism. *Gazette, 24,* 61–85.
Bouwman, H., & Stappers, J. (1982). The Dutch violence profile: A replication of Gerbner's message system analysis. In G. Melischek, K. E. Rosengren, & J. Stappers (Eds.), *Cultural indicators: An international symposium* (pp. 101–125). Vienna: Verlag der Osterreichischen Akademie der Wissenschaften.
Browne, D. R. (1967). Problems in international television. *Journal of Communication, 17*(3), 198–210.
*Chaffee, S., Zhongdang, P., & Chu, G. (1995). *Western media in China: Audience and influence.* Paper presented at the annual meeting of the International Communication Association, Albuquerque, NM.
*Choi, J. (1989). *Use and effects of foreign television programming: A study of American armed forces television in Korea.* Unpublished doctoral dissertation, Michigan State University, East Lansing.
*Coldevin, G. O. (1976). Some effects of frontier television on a Canadian Eskimo community. *Journalism Quarterly, 53,* 34–39.
*Coldevin, G. O. (1979). Satellite television and cultural replacement among Canadian Eskimos. *Communication Research, 6,* 115–134.
*Coldevin, G. O., & Wilson, T. C. (1985). Effects of a decade of satellite television in the Canadian Arctic. *Journal of Cross-Cultural Psychology, 16,* 329–354.
*Day, P. (1975). Cultural imperialism in New Zealand. *Australian and New Zealand Journal of Sociology, 11,* 43–45.
Dizard, W. (1965). The political impact of television abroad. *Journal of Broadcasting, 9,* 195–214.
Elasmar, M. G. (1991). *Foreign TV impact: A systematic review of empirical studies.* Unpublished manuscript, Michigan State University, East Lansing.
Elasmar, M. G. (1993). *Analyzing the international direct broadcast satellite debate: Origins, decision-making factors and social concerns.* Unpublished doctoral dissertation, Michigan State University, East Lansing.
*Elasmar, M. G., & Akaishi, E. (1995). *The influence of American television on young Japanese females' beliefs about the United States.* Unpublished manuscript, Boston University.
Elasmar, M. G., & Hunter, J. E., & Straubhaar, J. D. (1995). *Quantifying the size of the impact of foreign TV on a domestic audience.* Paper presented at the annual meeting of the Broadcast Education Association, Las Vegas, NV.
Elasmar, M. G., & Straubhaar, J. D. (1993). *Toward a meta-analysis of foreign TV effects research.* Paper presented at the annual meeting of the Speech Communication Association, Miami, FL.
*El-Koussa, H. H., & Elasmar, M. G. (1995). *The influence of U.S. TV programs on the perceptions of U.S. social reality among students in Lebanon.* Paper presented at the annual meeting of the Broadcast Education Association, Las Vegas, NV.
*Elliott, L. S. (1994). *Comparing cultural influence of U.S. and Mexican television in Mexico.* Paper presented at the annual meeting of the Association for Education in Journalism and Mass Communication, Atlanta, GA.
*Geiger, S. F. (1992). *Social reality in the Third World: The influence of American television on Venezuelan values.* Paper presented at the annual meeting of the International Communication Association, Miami, FL.

Goldsen, R. K., & Bibliowicz, A. (1976). Plaza Sesamo: "Neutral language or "cultural assault." *Journal of Communication, 26*(2), 124–125.

Goonasekara, A. (1987). The influence of television on cultural values—with special reference to Third World countries. *Media Asia, 14,* 7–12.

*Granzberg, G. (1980). Psychological impact of television among Algonkians of Central Canada. In G. Granzberg & J. Steinbring (Eds.), *Television and the Canadian Indian* (pp. 321–359). Manitoba: University of Winnipeg.

Hadad, I. (1978). Media and international misunderstanding. *Phaedrus, 5,* 17–19.

Hedinson, E., & Windahl, S. (1982). Cultivation analysis: A Swedish illustration. In G. Melischek, K. E. Rosengren, & J. Stappers (Eds.), *Cultural indicators: An international symposium* (pp. 204–227). Vienna: Verlag der Osterreichischen Akademie der Wissenschaften.

Hunter, J. E., & Schmidt, F. L. (1990). *Methods of meta-analysis: Correcting error and bias in research findings.* Newbury Park, CA: Sage.

Hur, K. K. (1982). International mass communication research: A critical review of theory and methods. In M. Burgoon (Ed.), *Communication yearbook 6* (pp. 531–554). Beverly Hills, CA: Sage.

*Kang, G. J. & Morgan, M. (1988). Cultural clash: Impact of U.S. television in Korea. *Journalism Quarterly, 65,* 431–438.

*Kapoor, S., & Kang, J. (1993). *Cultural effects of U.S. television programs in India and Korea.* Paper presented at the annual meeting of the Speech Communication Association, Miami, FL.

Kerlinger, F. N. (1986). *Foundations of behavioral research.* New York: Holt, Rinehart & Winston.

Lee, C. C. (1980). *Media imperialism reconsidered.* Beverly Hills, CA: Sage.

Morgan, M., & Shanahan, J. (1992). Comparative cultivation analysis: Television and adolescents in Argentina and Taiwan. In F. Korzenny & S. Ting-Toomey (Eds.), *Mass media effects across cultures* (pp. 173–197). Newbury Park, CA: Sage.

Morgan, M., & Signorielli, N. (1990). Cultivation analysis: Conceptualization and methodology. In N. Signorielli & M. Morgan (Eds.), *Cultivation analysis: New directions in media effects research* (pp. 13–34). Newbury Park, CA: Sage.

*Oliveira, O. S. (1986). Satellite TV and dependency: An empirical approach. *Gazette, 38,* 127–145.

*Payne, D. E. (1978). Cross-national diffusion: The effects of Canadian TV on rural Minnesota viewers. *American Sociological Review, 43,* 740–756.

*Payne, D. E., & Caron, A. H. (1982). Anglophone Canadian and American mass media: Use and effects on Quebecois adults. *Communication Research, 9,* 113–144.

*Payne, D. E., & Peake, C. A. (1977). Cultural diffusion: The role of U.S. TV in Iceland. *Journalism Quarterly, 54,* 523–531.

*Pingree, S., & Hawkins, R. (1981). U.S. programs on Australian television: The cultivation effect. *Journal of Communication, 31*(1), 97–105.

*Saito, S. (1994). *Television and perceptions of American society in Japan.* Paper presented at the annual meeting of the Association for Education in Journalism and Mass Communication, Atlanta, GA.

Salwen, M. B. (1991). Cultural imperialism: A media effects approach. *Critical Studies in Mass Communication, 8,* 29–38.

Schiller, H. I. (1969). *Mass communication and American empire.* Boston: Beacon.

Schiller, H. I. (1991). Not yet the post-imperialist era. *Critical Studies in Mass Communication, 8,* 13–28.

*Skinner, E. C. (1984). *Foreign TV program viewing and dependency: A case study of U.S. television viewing in Trinidad and Tobago.* Unpublished doctoral dissertation, Michigan State University, East Lansing.

*Snyder, L., Roser, C., & Chaffee, S. (1991). Foreign media and the desire to emigrate from Belize. *Journal of Communication, 41*(1), 117–132.

Straubhaar, J. D., Heeter, C., Greenberg, B. S., Ferreira, L., Wicks, R. H., & Lau, T. Y. (1992). What makes news: Western, socialist, and Third-World television newscasts compared in eight countries. In F. Korzenny & S. Ting-Toomey (Eds.), *Mass media effects across cultures* (pp. 89–109). Newbury Park, CA: Sage.

*Tan, A. S., Dong, Q., & Li, W. (1994). *American television and movies in China: Exploring socialization effects from a functional perspective.* Paper presented at the annual meeting of the Association for Education in Journalism and Mass Communication, Atlanta, GA.

*Tan, A. S., Gibson, T., & Fujioka, Y. (1993). *American television in Japan and Russia.* Paper presented at the annual meeting of the Speech Communication Association, Miami, FL.

*Tan, A. S., Li, S., & Simpson, C. (1986). American TV and social stereotypes of Americans in Taiwan and Mexico. *Journalism Quarterly, 63,* 809–814.

*Tan, A. S., & Suarchavarat, K. (1988). American TV and social stereotypes of Americans in Thailand. *Journalism Quarterly, 65,* 648–654.

*Tan, A. S., Tan, G. K., & Tan, A. S. (1987). American TV in the Philippines: A test of cultural impact. *Journalism Quarterly, 64,* 65–72, 144.

*Tate, E. D., & Trach, B. (1980). The effects of United States television programs upon Canadian beliefs about legal procedures. *Canadian Journal of Communication, 6,* 1–17.

Tracey, M. (1985). The poisoned chalice? International television and the idea of dominance. *Proceedings of the American Academy of Arts and Sciences, USA, 114,* 17–56.

*Tsai, M. (1967). *A study of the effects of American television programs on children in Formosa.* Unpublished master's thesis, Michigan State University, East Lansing.

*Veii, V. S. (1988). *Foreign television entertainment programs viewing and cultural imperialism: A case study of U.S. television entertainment programs viewing in Windhoek, Namibia.* Unpublished doctoral dissertation, Michigan State University, East Lansing.

*Weimann, G. (1984). Images of life in America: The impact of American TV in Israel. *International Journal of Intercultural Relations, 8,* 185–197.

*Werner, A. (1981). Television and attitudes toward foreign countries: A report on a survey on Scandinavian children. *Political Communication and Persuasion, 1,* 307–314.

*Wu, Y. K. (1989). *Television and the value systems of Taiwan's adolescents: A cultivation analysis.* Unpublished doctoral dissertation, University of Massachusetts, Amherst.

Yaple, P., & Korzenny, F. (1989). Electronic mass media effects across cultures. In M. K. Asante & W. B. Gudykunst (Eds.), *Handbook of international and intercultural communication* (pp. 295–317). Newbury Park, CA: Sage.

*Zhao, X. (1989). Effects of foreign media use, government and traditional influences on Chinese women's values. *Revue Europeenne des Sciences Sociales, 27,* 239–251.

CHAPTER

9

An Alternative Paradigm for Conceptualizing and Labeling the Process of Influence of Imported Television Programs

Michael G. Elasmar
Boston University

When television made its debut in developing countries, it began by relying on imported programming content. This foreign TV content came primarily from developed countries. In the 1960s and 1970s, the United States was the main exporter of TV programs (Nordenstreng & Varis, 1973). The presence of foreign TV programs in domestic television schedules progressively raised concerns on the part of policy makers and international observers. These concerns became louder as television grew in popularity. The assumptions behind their concerns were as follows:

1. Television programs are imbedded with the values of the society in which they are produced.
2. When shows produced in society A are imported in society B, viewers in society B are exposed to the values of society A.
3. After being exposed to the television programs of society A and the values imbedded within them, viewers in society B will progressively adopt those values and lose their indigenous ones.

These assumptions have led policymakers in many countries to draft cultural preservation legislation that curtails the importation of foreign TV programs. The fear of cultural invasion through television has even prompted developed countries, such as France, to be critical of imported U.S. television (Tracey, 1993).

For this chapter, the topic of foreign TV is confined to entertainment programs displayed on a television set regardless of how they are received by the local viewers (e.g., traditional broadcast, cable, satellite, etc.). Further, the terms *foreign TV* and *imported TV* will be used interchangeably. This chapter focuses on three research questions:

Research Question I: Does foreign TV exposure affect local viewers?
Research Question II: If an effect is found, what is the process that results in this effect?
Research Question III: If an effect is found, how should the process of influence be labeled?

ANSWERING RESEARCH QUESTION 1: DOES FOREIGN TV AFFECT LOCAL VIEWERS?

International communication observers who are wary of the influence of foreign TV are especially concerned with its potential for influencing indigenous cultures. Culture is an elusive concept that is defined by some as encompassing all aspects of human life as experienced by those living in a specific geographical location. If defined as such, then any influence of foreign TV on domestic viewers (e.g., attitudinal, behavioral, etc.) will be considered a cultural influence. Many anthropologists have contributed to the definition of the term "culture." Herskovitz (1956) defined culture as "all the elements in man's mature endowment that he has acquired from his group by conscious learning or, on a somewhat different level, by a conditioning process—techniques of various kinds, social and other institutions, beliefs and patterned modes of conduct" (p.18).

Kroeber (1952) stated that it "is a way of habitual acting, feelings and thinking channeled by a society out of an infinite number and variety of potential ways of living" (p. 136). Hoebel (1971) contended that it is "more than a collection of isolated bits of behavior. It is the integrated sum total of learned behavior traits which are manifest and shared by the members of a society" (p. 208).

Can imported television content be a source of influence on the culture of local viewers who are exposed to it? As was noted in chapter 1, the dominant view among the vast majority of international observers is that imported television has a strong influence (homogenous and intense) on the culture of local viewers. Although one finds an abundance of articles consistent with this perspective, rare are the published manuscripts that question this de facto conclusion. Among those who did not readily accept the de facto influence argument is Browne (1967) who, as early as the 1960s, took into account the individual differences among viewers to explain the many factors that hinder foreign TV from having a homogenous impact on domestic audiences. He stated that "Experience should have already taught us that there is no universal visual language, any more than there is universal spoken or written language ... [which means that] if one picture is indeed worth a thousand words, those words will not mean the same thing to everyone" (p. 206).

9. AN ALTERNATIVE PARADIGM

This notion is supported by Salwen (1991) who maintained that foreign TV cannot be seen as a direct cause for the loss of individuals' indigenous cultures. "At the very least, factors inherent within cultures ... account for different responses to foreign media messages" (p. 36).

In addition to those who point out the barriers that foreign TV faces in achieving an effect on its audience, there are those who say that we are not ready to make any assessments simply because we don't know enough about the topic. Lee (1980) concluded that "research on the likely influences of alien television programs on the decline of traditional cultures and arts is inconclusive" (p. 103). A few years, later, Tracey (1985) asserted that "we have barely begun to scratch the surface of understanding the function and consequence of TV as an international cultural process" (p. 50).

Other researchers decided to draw conclusions about the effects of foreign TV after carrying out a narrative review of the existing empirical literature. Hur (1982), for example, concluded that "exposure to American television and film content by local populations has few cognitive and attitudinal effects, much less behavioral effects" (p. 546). A few years later, Yaple and Korzenny (1989) concluded that "media effects across national cultural groups are detectable but relatively small in magnitude, and that ... the environment, cultural situation, and context affect selectivity and the interpretation of content" (p. 313).

The overall assessments concerning the impact of foreign TV had, for a long time, been done in one of two ways: (a) by following a set of arguments heavily grounded in political ideology (i.e., most CI advocates); or (b) by carrying out a narrative literature review of selected empirical studies (e.g., Hur, 1982). Elasmar and Hunter (1997) used a more objective methodology—meta-analysis—to assess the entire body of quantitative studies about this same topic. After an extensive analysis of the results of past investigations, Elasmar and Hunter found that the effect varied across studies and across effect types (e.g., behavioral, attitudinal, etc.). Given the lack of homogeneity in the findings across studies, they concluded that "at most, foreign TV exposure may have a very weak impact upon its audience members" (p. 64).

The results of both narrative and quantitative reviews of the empirical literature suggest that finding an effect will depend on an interaction between audience characteristics and effect type (e.g., attitudinal, behavioral, etc.). The wide variation in effect sizes across individual studies also tend to demonstrate this interaction. For example, a study examining the influence of U.S. TV exposure on the adoption of Western gender role values among individuals in Taiwan found no foreign TV effect (Wu, 1989). Payne and Peake (1977) made a similar finding when exploring the intention of immigrating to the United States among people in Iceland. However, a study exploring the impact of U.S. TV exposure on the adoption of U.S. values by individuals in Trinidad found a moderate size effect (Skinner, 1984). A moderate to strong effect was also found by Oliveira (1986) when investigating the influence of U.S. TV on attitudes toward consuming U.S. products by individuals in Belize.

So, whereas one researcher might find no impact for foreign TV on particular viewers, another might find an impact when examining other viewers. Effects seem to vary across samples and even within samples. This suggests that a complex process of influence is at work. This conclusion is consistent with the findings of the various contributors of the current book. Overall, the previous chapters have suggested that the process of influence of foreign TV is indeed much more complex than critics of imported TV have traditionally portrayed it to be. A complex process of influence means that individuals will not respond homogenously to the same imported message. The finding that the intensity of the effect is not homogenous is consistent with the outcome that one would expect from a complex process of influence.

In summary, the empirical literature suggests that although foreign TV does not have a homogenous influence across individuals and effect types, it can be influential. If one adopts the term *culture* to label the many aspects of human life in a particular geographical location, then yes, it is possible that foreign TV may have some influence on some people and along certain cultural dimensions.

ANSWERING RESEARCH QUESTION 2: WHAT IS THE PROCESS OF INFLUENCE OF FOREIGN TV?

When critics of imported TV discuss its influence, they overwhelmingly do so under the rubric of cultural imperialism (CI) (Schiller, 1969, 1991). In their study, Elasmar and Hunter (1997) found that CI was also the second most frequently used theoretical framework in empirical studies about foreign TV influence. According to its proponents, CI is "a verifiable process of social influence by which a nation imposes on other countries its set of beliefs, values, knowledge and behavioral norms as well as its overall style of life" (Beltran, 1978, p. 184). The advocates of this perspective also claim that CI is an effect that stems from the documented flow of television programs from Western countries into Third World television schedules (Goonasekara, 1987). Note that critics of imported TV programs use the term CI to label both the process of influence and the outcome that is assumed to result from such a process. The contentions of CI are at the roots of all international legislation to protect indigenous cultures from influence through foreign television. The CI arguments are also used as a basis for international debates and resolutions about the same topic (for a discussion of these debates, see McPhail, 1987). Thus, for all practical purposes, the cultural imperialism theoretical framework (CI), as applied to imported TV, is the dominant paradigm when it comes to conceptualizing the effect of these TV programs on local viewers. Elasmar and Bennett's chapter in this book details the origin and evolution of cultural imperialism and extracts its assumptions about foreign TV. The focus in this section is on the process of influence of foreign TV. The following section will attempt to illustrate the process that is implicitly described in the writing of CI proponents.

9. AN ALTERNATIVE PARADIGM

In the 1940s, Lazarsfeld (1976) had defined international communication as a study of the "processes by which various cultures influence each other" (p. 485). Can such processes be illustrated? In contrast to chapter 1, the analysis in this chapter focuses on the individual audience member. Thus our discussion refers to processes occurring within humans. Although not widely prevalent in the international communication literature, process models are frequently used for illustrating attitudinal or behavioral outcomes in such areas as consumer behavior. Process models can be thought of as an externalization of a researcher's internal conceptualizations about influence. In order to evaluate CI as a process of influence of television on viewers, we need to identify and diagram its implicit building blocks. Graphically illustrating the implicit CI process allows the reader to better visualize otherwise internal conceptualizations and then better partake in the analysis. In the illustrations that follow, we adopt some basic conventions: the process of influence begins in time on the left side of the page and ends on the right; the building blocks of the process model are concepts, each of which is visually housed in a rectangle; and the arrows connecting the rectangles indicate presumed directional causality among the concepts.

Figure 9.1 illustrates the process of influence of foreign TV on local viewers as it is implicit in the CI literature.

The process of influence offered by CI contends that the mere presence of foreign programs in domestic TV schedules will necessarily result in strong (intense and homogenous) effects on local television viewers. Note that the CI literature only addresses the two components illustrated in Fig. 9.1. From a cognitive processing perspective, this model is incomplete. It lacks the building blocks that link "presence of foreign TV" to "impact on local viewers." These missing building blocks pertain to the following relationships: from availability of imported TV programs to exposure to them, from exposure to foreign TV programs to mentally processing their content, and from mental processing to being influenced by the foreign TV content. Instead of explaining the transition from availability of foreign TV programs to being influenced by these programs, the CI model makes several assumptions about this transition:

CI Assumption 1. The presence of foreign programs in domestic TV schedules will lead domestic audience members to watch these programs. Whereas CI assumes homogenous exposure, the body of literature suggests that when a choice is

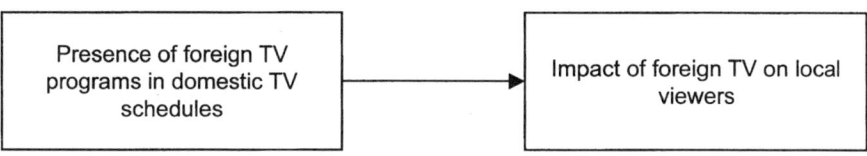

FIG. 9.1. Process of foreign TV influence implicit in the CI literature.

possible, most local viewers prefer TV programs that are either local or regional (Davis, chap. 7, this volume; Straubhaar, chap. 6, this volume; Straubhaar et al., 1992; Tracey, 1993).

CI Assumption 2. Foreign TV content will be similarly processed by all audience members who are exposed to it. This also assumes homogeneity of audience members along such dimensions as comprehension of stories being told and retention of story components. Further it also assumes that the story, as conceived by the program creators, will be correctly and homogenously decoded by the audience members living in a different cultural environment. This last assumption signifies a perfect transfer of meaning from the program creators to audience members across cultural contexts. There is an abundance of evidence that suggests that humans are not constant along such dimensions as comprehension and retention abilities (Renzulli & Dai, 2001). Further, research specific to the interpretation of foreign TV content has revealed wide variations in the interpretation of story content across audience members. This research has also shown that the transfer of meaning from the program creators in one country to audience members in another country is far from being perfect (Liebes & Katz, 1993).

CI Assumption 3. Foreign TV exposure will result in strong and homogenous effects across audience members. The body of literature reviewed in this book, although diverse along many dimensions, agrees with the observation that the effect of foreign TV varies in intensity across local viewers.

The process of influence imbedded in the CI arguments is very simplistic. Although parsimony is a virtue when it comes to building theories, in this case, the CI process does not help us explain the variation in the intensity of the effect of foreign TV among those who are exposed to it. Further, the implicit assumptions made by CI are not supported by the findings of pertinent empirical studies. We conclude that the process of influence implicit in the CI arguments is not adequate. In contrast to the CI process, the findings of the existing studies about the effect of foreign TV reveal that this relationship is quite complex. This prompts us to ask: Can we pool the findings of various empirical studies about the effects of foreign TV and related research areas and develop a more helpful and realistic process model of influence?

This section identifies the building blocks of a more complex process model for foreign TV influence that is compatible with the current body of literature about foreign TV. The building blocks of this model are organized in the following sequence: (a) availability of foreign TV; (b) exposure to foreign TV; (c) processing of foreign TV content; and (d) effect of exposure to foreign TV on local viewers. The logic of including these specific building blocks is as follows: availability of foreign TV is necessary for becoming exposed to it; exposure to foreign TV is necessary for mentally processing its content; and mentally processing its content is necessary for becoming influenced by it.

Availability of Foreign TV

Beginning in the 1970s, foreign television programs became quite prevalent in the domestic television schedules of countries around the world (Nordenstreng & Varis, 1973; Varis, 1993). Beginning in the 1990s, the advent of satellite technology for distributing television signals to small home receivers has made foreign TV programs more directly available to households worldwide. However, in the vast majority of countries, foreign TV will not be solely imported from a single country. And foreign TV, as a category, will not be the only type of TV content present because the vast majority of countries also produce domestic television programs (Straubhaar et al., 1992). So, we can reasonably conclude that foreign TV programs are available to most people living within the reach of a television signal but most viewers have a choice among foreign TV programs produced in various countries (including international and regional programs) and between foreign and domestic TV programs.

Exposure to Foreign TV

It is reasonable to expect that frequency of exposure to foreign TV will vary across viewers. To help explain this variation we adopt a version of the selective exposure framework. Zillman and Bryant (1985) stated that selective exposure "designates a behavior that is deliberately performed to attain and sustain perceptual control of particular events" (p. 2). The application of this notion to TV viewing is certainly not new in the field of communication research. In 1968, Katz reviewed the work of several researchers who had taken special interest in this issue and conducted studies about it. He identified perceived "utility" of a TV program and "interest" in the contents of a TV program as potential predictors of selectivity. Katz (1968) contended "there is no question that selectivity exists—i.e., that individuals are disproportionately exposed to communications which are congenial to their attitudes" (p. 788).

In the case of imported TV, we focus on the viewer's active decision to choose among national, regional, and international TV programs available to himself or herself. We presume that there are certain identifiable predictors of foreign TV selection. In a case study in Malaysia, Elasmar and Sim (1997) identified pre-existing affinity toward the United States as a predictor of U.S. TV program exposure. Their study identified two significant predictors of exposure to U.S. TV: having friends and/or family living in the United States and having learned about the United States through one's parents. Both predictors capture the idea of pre-existing affinity.

In the case of Brazil, Straubhaar (chap. 6, this volume) identified language compatibility, cultural proximity, and cultural capital as predictors of foreign TV selection (regional and international). He concluded:

> Cultural capital reinforces the use of [...] imported media and TV programming by giving elites and upper middle classes the ability to understand and enjoy program-

ming imported from outside their cultural–linguistic region. This kind of cultural capital is clearest with language ability [...] but also includes education, travel abroad, familiarity with the ways of life of other countries, education abroad, work with international companies, and the kind of family life that is produced by and reinforces these kinds of advantages. (chap. 6, this volume)

It is reasonable to propose that exposure to foreign TV is driven by various antecedent factors, some of which were identified earlier, others might include a variety of "perceived utilities of content for self" and "personal interest in various aspects of content" as Katz (1968) suggested. The drivers hypothesized to influence exposure are illustrated in Fig. 9.2. Other predictors are also likely to exist and will need to be identified in future studies.

Processing of Foreign TV Content

Once an individual is exposed to an imported TV program, this viewer picks up various content cues using his or her senses and then mentally processes this information. We argue that a person cannot be influenced by TV content unless he or she interprets it, stores it, and can recall it when needed. It is this mental processing that

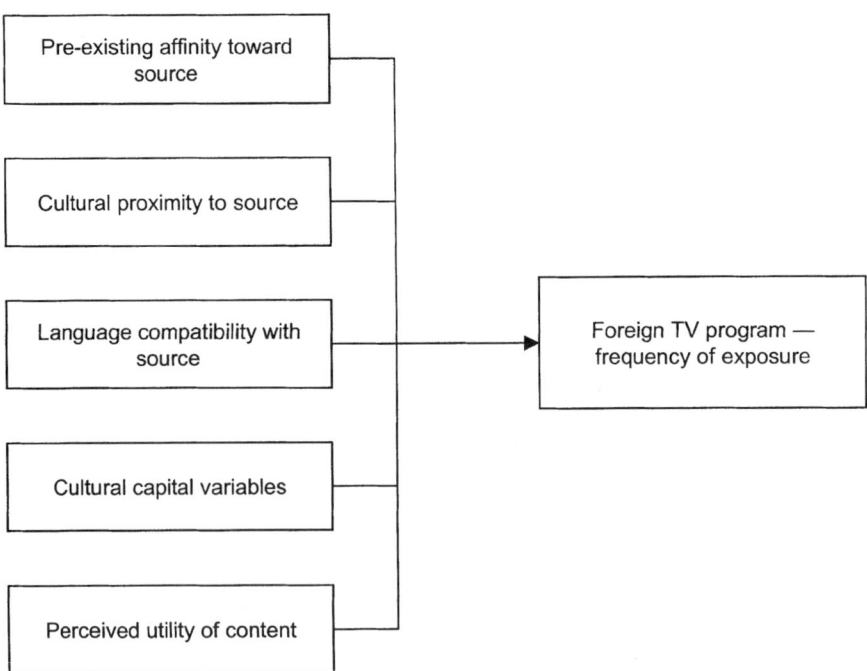

FIG. 9.2. Predictors of exposure to foreign TV.

9. AN ALTERNATIVE PARADIGM

results in comprehension, retention, and recall of the information presented. This area of research is usually concentrated in the field of cognitive psychology, although researchers in such fields as communication, education, social psychology, and political science are also interested in this same topic. Although this section cannot provide a comprehensive account of findings concerning cognitive processing, it focuses on results relevant for our understanding of how local viewers might mentally process imported TV messages.

Previous research on the interpretation of foreign TV programs has demonstrated the imperfection of the transfer of meaning between the creators of an imported TV show and its local viewers (Liebes & Katz, 1993). In a detailed study, Liebes and Katz (1993) have shown that viewers from different cultural backgrounds focused on and recalled different aspects of the same episode of the TV show *Dallas*. Liebes and Katz found that the differences in the cultural backgrounds of the viewers accounted for the variation in their cognitive processing of the same *Dallas* episodes. These findings suggest that cultural factors seem to trigger selective attention and selective retention of certain aspects of imported TV content. Further, that the viewers seemed to relate the program content they have viewed to pre-existing culture-specific values in order to interpret this content.

This interpretation of the findings of Liebes and Katz (1993) is consistent with the perspectives of researchers in the area of cognitive science who use the term *schema* to represent "individual cognitive elements such as objects, people, events, and so on, as well as systems composed of these elements, such as narratives, belief systems, and mental models of physical systems" (Read & Miller, 1994, p. 214). Individuals interpret incoming information by relating it to pre-existing schemas and interrelationships among schemas (Hawkins & Daly, 1988).

The various values that are imbedded in the cultural backgrounds of the participants in the study by Liebes and Katz (1993) can be thought of as schemas of values. The values related to the content of the episodes of *Dallas* that they viewed and the interrelationships among these values seem to have been used by the participants as a frame of reference for interpreting the *Dallas* stories. In this case, understanding the values held by viewers of imported TV (pertinent value types and intensity with which values are held) and the interrelationships among these values (relative strength of associations among discrete values) will be key in predicting the viewers' interpretations of the content of imported TV programs.

In a way, we are witnessing what seems to be an information sequencing effect: prior information structure (knowledge, beliefs and/or attitudes, as separate elements and interrelationships among elements—known as schemas) is affecting the interpretation of subsequent information. Evidence from the field of education supports the importance of this type of information sequencing for understanding new learning materials. In a synthesis of the existing body of literature on learning, Renzulli and Dai (2001) show that "prior knowledge of subject/topic" and "general attitude toward the subject" are antecedents of "new understanding of the subject/topic" (p. 25).

At this stage, we can argue that certain antecedent factors will help us explain the variation in the cognitive processing of imported TV messages. In addition to a viewer's values and the interrelationships among them, the following paragraphs present other potential factors that moderate the cognitive processing in which we are interested.

Imported TV content consists of the explicit televised message that the viewer observes (e.g., plot, characters, etc.) and the implicit notion communicated by certain content cues (e.g., program titles, foreign language spoken, dubbing, labeling of program by local TV station as foreign, etc.) that this message is not local. It is reasonable to wonder whether these cues about the perceived origin of the TV content might influence the viewer's processing of the program. In consumer behavior research, meta-analytic results show that the country where the product is said to be manufactured consistently influences an individual's evaluation of that product's quality (Verlegh & Steenkamp, 1999). According to Verlegh and Steenkamp (1999), prior positive information about country A influences an individual to positively evaluate the qualities of a product identified with country A. In general, this suggests that prior information (knowledge, beliefs, and/or attitude) about the country of origin influences the manner with which the individual processes subsequent information about products associated with that country.

The implicit cues about the national origins of an imported TV show might also trigger associations between this TV program and perceptions of the outgroup that has produced it. In this case, we wonder what we can learn about cognitive processing of information emanating from a group that is perceived by the viewer as outside his or her own. From the literature on intergroup prejudice, we learn that individuals belonging to group A and who hold negative perceptions of group B, will look for information that confirms their perceptions when interacting with group B (Stephan, 1987). In this case, even though they might be exposed to both positive and negative information about group B, group A members will tend to process the information that is consistent with their prejudices. Interestingly, meta-analytic results concerning this relationship show that repeat exposure to group B by individuals in group A who already hold positive (or neutral) attitudes toward group B will result in "strong exposure effects" that are positive in nature toward group B (Bornstein, 1993, p. 206).

From this body of research, we can conclude that, if a local viewer perceives an imported TV program to be produced by an outgroup, then prior information about that group (knowledge, beliefs, and/or attitudes) will influence the manner with which this viewer will process the content of the TV program. These findings also suggest that selective attention and selective retention mechanisms might be triggered by the prior information about the outgroup (knowledge, beliefs, and/or attitudes). In this case, prior information about the outgroup will prompt the viewer to pay more attention to certain parts of the TV program that are consistent with his or her prior information. Hence the importance of knowing the type of prior information held by the viewer about country A in order to predict how he or she will process the information associated with country A.

All the results just reported consistently suggest that prior information (knowledge, beliefs, and/or attitudes) about a communication source affects the way the audience member processes the messages emanating from that source. This consistency is also found by researchers examining the process of persuasion. The literature on persuasion reveals that audience members who like the communicator (whether appearing in person or via video) will be more influenced by his or her message (Chaiken & Eagly, 1983). In the current example, prior information is an impression of the communicator formed shortly before an audience member fully processes the communicator's message. If the impression is positive, then the audience member is more likely to accept the persuasive message. If the impression is negative, the audience member is less likely to accept the persuasive message. This finding suggests that viewers of imported TV who have neutral beliefs about the outgroup that has produced the TV program will likely formulate an impression of the program based on the first few minutes of its content. This initial impression will then influence the manner with which the viewer will process the rest of the program. In a case where the local viewer has neutral beliefs about the outgroup producing the program, the processes that Liebes and Katz (1993) have uncovered might come into play: The local viewer will relate the imported TV program's content to his or her pre-existing value system and this will result in the formation of an impression about this TV content.

The literature on persuasion also presents evidence that a person's involvement in the information presented to them will determine whether they are likely to be persuaded by this information. There are many perspectives on the actual processes that are triggered by the concept of "involvement" (see Cacioppo, Petty, Kao, & Rodriguez, 1986; Johnson & Eagly, 1989; Stiff, 1986). Despite the differences among researchers, they agree that the type and level of a person's involvement in message content seem to determine the degree to which that person will be persuaded by the message. In our case, the messages to which local viewers are exposed are not designed to persuade them. Persuasion would be a side effect because the imported TV programs were originally created to entertain the local viewers of the country where they were produced. In the present case, we are interested in the outcome of viewing this entertainment content by viewers living in a cultural environment that is different from the one in which it was originally created. A local viewer who finds a particular type of imported content useful for himself or herself (the concept of utility suggested by Katz, 1968) might indeed become more involved in it. For example, a teenager searching for guidance on how to approach the opposite gender, might find imported content to provide such guidance and that would be the utility of the imported content. Another example could be a teenager who realizes that some of his or her popular friends are learning how to dress from a particular imported TV show. The teenager might then find a utility in watching that show in order to learn from it, hoping that he or she will also become more popular. Note that in the latter example, the inspiration to watch imported TV programs comes from peers who have, themselves, found utility in the content of imported TV shows and are now unintentionally influencing others. Regardless of the origin of the utility found by the viewer, once he or she becomes involved in the imported TV show, the findings on "involvement" suggest that a viewer is more likely to be influenced by this program. Therefore, viewer involvement in the content of the imported message might turn out to be an important predictor for the influence of this foreign content on the local viewer.

The findings, so far, suggest that cognitive processing is moderated by the interrelationships among the information (explicit and implicit) in the imported TV program (content and source) and a variety of prior information held by the local viewer (i.e., knowledge, beliefs, attitudes, and values). This prior information seems to act as a powerful filter, triggering selective attention and selective retention processes. Strong evidence for this filtering process is presented by the body of knowledge concerning intergroup contact and acculturation. Both of these research domains focus on situations where the exposure of individuals to foreign information is much more intense than the mass media alone can achieve. Even so, the filtering process is clearly at work as information incompatible with existing beliefs, attitudes, and/or values seems to be disregarded.

In the case of the contact hypothesis, the researchers focus on whether members of group A, who hold negative perceptions of group B, change their perceptions of group B as a result of interpersonal interactions between the groups. Here, three decades of research yield a consistent trend: Overall, the mere exposure to information about group B through interpersonal interaction will not result in a significant change in beliefs about group B (Stephan, 1987). Pre-existing beliefs or attitudes that are strongly held are extremely hard to change despite one's immersion in information that might be contradictory to one's pre-existing beliefs and/or attitudes.

In the case of acculturation, studies of immigrants have shown that even those who have deliberately moved from their own cultural environment into another do not readily and homogenously internalize and adopt the values of the new culture (Berry & Sam, 1997). We can assume that most of these immigrants do not hold negative attitudes toward the new environment to which they moved. Even so, and even when totally immersed in this new environment, they seem to hang on to those values that they held strongly in their native cultures. Here again, change is very difficult to achieve: The values that are held strongly will be extremely hard to alter despite intense exposure to new values in the cultural environment into which an immigrant moves.

The difficulties encountered when attempting to change intergroup perceptions or traditional values suggest that the cognitive processing filters are in full action when individuals are prompted to change strongly held beliefs, attitudes, and/or values.

9. AN ALTERNATIVE PARADIGM

Understanding the cognitive processes at work in the case of foreign TV exposure is key for predicting the effects that stem from such exposure. Thus far, the various findings consistently point out the importance of prior attitudes toward the source and content of a message for understanding how this message will be processed and how this processing might potentially result in cognitive and/or attitudinal effects. Attitudes are also important for predicting behaviors. It is interesting to note that meta-analytic reviews of the literature show a clear bridge between cognitive processing and behavior (Kim & Hunter, 1993; Kraus, 1995). From a cognitive processing perspective, the best estimate of a behavior is a person's attitude toward that behavior (Kim & Hunter, 1993; Kraus, 1995). Of course, a behavioral effect is a function of the interrelationships among various knowledge, belief, attitude, and value types and intensities. But because the best predictor of behavior is one's attitude toward that behavior, then it becomes even more important for us to understand the interrelationships that result in attitudes in order to predict related behaviors.

Figure 9.3 shows the variables that mostly likely predict the selective processing (attention and retention) of imported TV programs.

The literature reviewed previously points out the special importance of pre-existing attitudes toward the content and source for determining how this

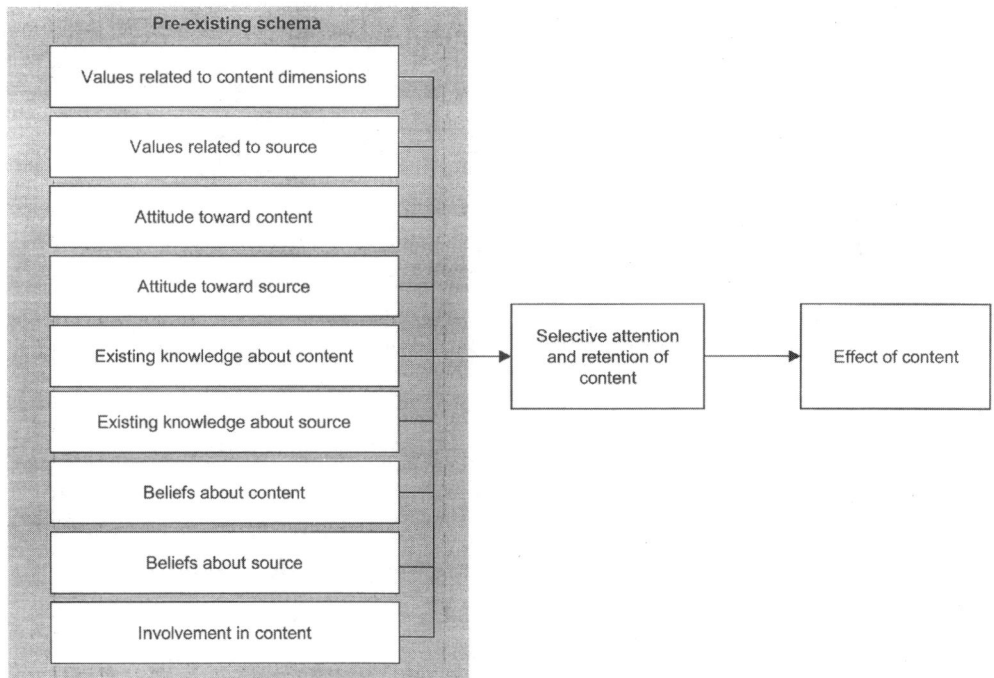

FIG. 9.3. Predictors of selective processing of foreign TV content.

content will be processed. A research program about the role of attitudes in predicting behaviors (Ajzen & Fishbein, 1980; Fishbein & Ajzen, 1975) has consistently shown the following structure: beliefs and norms predict their related attitudes. We can use this information to integrate the factors listed in Fig. 9.2 and Fig. 9.3 and propose a new process structure. Pre-existing beliefs, knowledge, and values as related to the source of foreign TV and its content most probably do influence a viewer's attitudes toward that source and content. Further, because selective attention and retention mechanisms cannot occur without exposure to the message, we can place exposure to foreign TV content before the cognitive processing component in the model. As a result, an integrated model of influence emerges. The illustration in Fig. 9.4 represents what I call a Model of Susceptibility to Imported Media (SIM).

Figure 9.4 shows that the components of a viewer's schema can be divided into two types: antecedents related to the source, and antecedents related to the content. Demographics, knowledge about country of origin, beliefs about country of origins, values related to country of origin and content, perceived utility of content, and involvement in content, as a set, predict attitudes toward country of origin and toward content. In turn, the attitude toward country of origin A and attitude toward content depicted in imported TV programs will predict exposure to imported programs from country of origin A. The model hypothesizes that all antecedents are at times additive and at times multiplica-

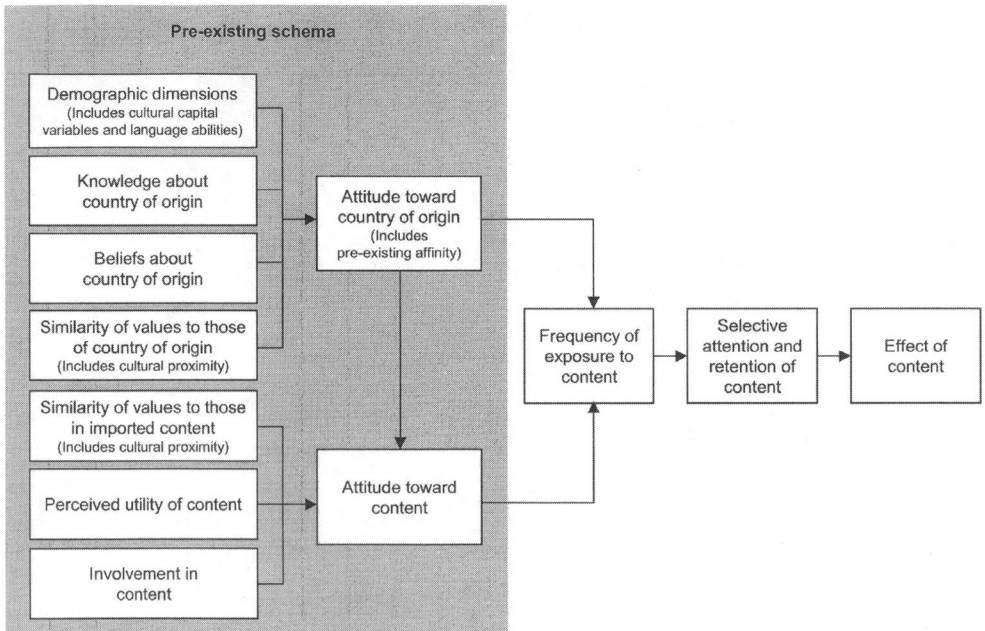

FIG. 9.4. The model of Susceptibility to Imported Media (SIM).

tive. All antecedents and interrelationships among them define the viewer's pre-existing schema. The pre-existing schema will determine how the content will be processed and, subsequently, the type of effect that the exposure to such content will produce.

Effect of Foreign TV Content on Domestic Viewers

Foreign TV might affect a local viewer in one or more ways. Elasmar and Hunter (1997) found the following effect dimensions in the empirical studies they synthesized: Knowledge, Beliefs, Attitudes, Behaviors, and Values. Elasmar and Hunter provided detailed definitions of these effects. In brief, whereas knowledge is factual, beliefs are perceptual and relative but not affective, attitudes are affective beliefs, behaviors refer to actions, and values refer to fundamental beliefs consistent with those traditionally held by most individuals in a particular society. Based on the findings of the various bodies of literature integrated into the process model presented in Fig. 9.4, we can rank in order the effect types from those most likely to occur to those least likely to occur given a set period of time as follows: Knowledge, Beliefs, Attitudes, Behaviors, and Values.

For all these effect types, the literature suggests that the most likely impact of foreign TV would be that of reinforcing pre-existing states. The least likely impact would be to radically change these pre-existing states.

Based on the overall model illustrated in Fig. 9.4, we can make some tentative predictions about the profile of the local TV viewer who will most likely be positively influenced by imported TV programs. A positive influence, in this context, means that the viewer will hold a positive attitude and/or acquire positive beliefs and/or engage in the behavior that is portrayed in these programs.

We conceive of the audience of imported TV programs as segmented along certain key viewer characteristics. The segment of viewers that is most likely susceptible for being positively influenced by imported TV programs is that which most closely fits these characteristics.

They are those who:

1. Have a pre-existing positive attitude toward the country that is perceived to be the source of the imported TV program. This is consistent with the findings concerning pre-existing affinity reported by Elasmar and Sim (1997): having friends and/or relatives in the United States and having learned favorable information from one's parents about the United States are positive predictors of exposure to U.S. TV and positive indirect predictors of a liking of U.S. fast food. This profile characteristic is also compatible with the findings on persuasion reported by Chaiken and Eagly (1983), the results concerning intergroup relations reported by Bornstein (1993) and the consumer behavior findings related to "country of origin" research reported by Verlegh and Steenkamp (1999);

2. Are compatible linguistically with the imported TV program. Straubhaar (this volume) found that linguistic compatibility was a clear predictor of exposure to international TV;

3. Have values that are compatible with the source and contents of the imported TV program. Straubhaar (this volume) found that cultural proximity and cultural capital predict a viewer's exposure to international TV program and facilitate his or her decoding of the message imbedded in that program. This requirement of a compatible value schema is also consistent with the findings about interpreting *Dallas* reported by Liebes and Katz (1993), and processing of new educational information reported by Renzulli and Dai (2001);

4. Are not negatively prejudiced against the source or content. This is consistent with the literature about the contact hypothesis summarized by Stephan (1987);

5. Perceive one or more "utilities" for self in the content of the imported TV program and are involved in such content. The concept of utility put forth by Katz (1968) combined with the concept of involvement that is central to the persuasion literature (see Cacioppo, Petty, Kao, & Rodriguez, 1986; Johnson & Eagly, 1989; Stiff, 1986);

6. Will frequently watch one or more imported TV programs stemming from the same foreign source. In this case, an interaction between exposure frequency to imported programs and a pre-existing affinity toward the source of those programs will produce the strongest effects (Bornstein, 1993).

These predictions are tentative, as the components of the SIM will still need to be empirically tested, as a whole, in future studies and subsequently refined and expanded.

ANSWERING RESEARCH QUESTION 3: WHEN AN EFFECT IS FOUND, HOW SHOULD THE FOREIGN TV PROCESS OF INFLUENCE BE LABELED?

The existence of a link between exposure to imported TV from country A and an effect detected among audience members in country B (e.g., Oliveira, 1986) is frequently used to simultaneously support three notions embodied in the CI arguments: (a) foreign TV is influential; (b) the mere presence of foreign programs in domestic TV schedules will influence local viewers; and (c) the exporting country is conspiring to achieve this influence. Previous sections in this chapter addressed the issue of influence and the process by which influence might occur. This section focuses on the adequacy of CI as a label for a potential process of influence. Labeling a process of influence is assigning a name to a theoretical explanation for the presence of a detected effect.

As a label, CI carries negative connotations. It embodies the revolting idea that group A is conspiring against group B in order to erode group B's culture and replace it with that of group A. The implicit reasoning is: If an effect is found, then it is

9. AN ALTERNATIVE PARADIGM

indicative of conspiracy. If this line of reasoning is correct, then there should be no other plausible explanation for a cross border effect other than that of a conspiracy.

The essence of the discussion now centers on labeling a process by which one culture can potentially influence another. We argue here that, when present, such influence processes are not new to human civilization. In fact, the label for such processes predates the introduction of audio-visual media. There is a widely established body of knowledge about this issue within the field of historical anthropology. In the field of communication, Rogers (1983) has extensively studied the diffusion of technological innovations within developed countries as well as those associated with development communication programs within developing countries. Our interest in this area is focused on unintended diffusion as contrasted to that associated with a communication or marketing campaign or other planned strategies designed to influence behavior. Thus our attention at this stage is directed toward the body of knowledge that predates the introduction of organized mass media systems.

Cultures Influencing Other Cultures With No Conspiracy

Culture diffusion or borrowing occurs when an individual "faced with a situation in which the shared habits of his own society are not fully satisfactory, copies behavior which he has observed in members of another society …" (Murdock, 1971, p. 325). How frequently does cultural diffusion occur? Smith (1933) contended that:

> …[e]very individual in a civilized society is indebted to his fellows not only for his speech and its content of ideas and beliefs, but also to a far-flung dependence on the world at large, past and present, for what the gift of language confers upon him. It is not only in speech, however, but in almost everything we use in our daily life and in most of the things we do that we also display our indebtedness to the world's civilization in its full range. (p. 8)

Echoing the concept of culture diffusion, Kroeber (1952) pointed to the existence of "a continuity of indirect causation from culture event to culture event through the medium of human intermediaries" (p. 132). Murdock (1971) agreed by stating that "it is doubtful whether there is a single culture known to history or anthropology that has not owed at least ninety per cent of its constituent elements to cultural borrowing" (p. 326).

Kroeber (1952) summed it up best by referring to cultural diffusion as "circular causality":

> The human beings who influence culture and make new culture are themselves molded; and they are molded through the intervention of other men who are culturalized and thus products of previous cultures. So it is clear that, while human beings are always the immediate causes of cultural events, these human causes are themselves the result of antecedent cultural situations, having been fitted to the existing cultural forms which they encounter. (p. 132)

Although it is not within the scope of this chapter to recount the various processes of influence that have shaped the existence of human kind, we can note one of them in the following for the purpose of providing an example.

Notable among diffusion processes is the spread of the phonetic alphabet. In a remarkable book summarizing the various anthropological investigations concerning the phonetic alphabet, Logan (1986) traced its origins to the Near East region. The formalization of this early phonetic alphabet is credited to the Phoenicians or Canaanites over 3,500 years ago (Drucker, 1995). The Phoenicians developed 22 notations, or as we know them today, letters, which, when put together, result in sounds that convey meanings (Swiggers, 1996). The Phoenicians were great traders with ship fleets roaming the Mediterranean. The motivation for inventing the first phonetic alphabet must have been to facilitate trade and expand earnings for the sea merchants who invented it (DeFrancis, 1989; Gaur, 1984). The cultural influence of that invention, however, is still very strongly felt today (Logan, 1986). In fact, Logan not only documents the diffusion of the alphabet, but also links its diffusion to the development of codified laws, science, and the rise of many civilizations. We confine our arguments here to the effect that the diffusion of the alphabet had onto forms of communication worldwide. If it weren't for that influence, for example, we would not be able to express our ideas in the form that the reader is now processing them. The Phoenicians were powerful traders at the time when their invention was diffused and influenced the cultures of those surrounding them (DeFrancis, 1989; Gaur, 1984; Swiggers, 1996). Their influence was transmitted through human intermediaries most probably in the context of trade (DeFrancis, 1989; Gaur, 1984). This is well illustrated by Logan (1986) in a quote by Herodotus in the fifth century B.C. In this excerpt, Herodotus narrated that:

> ... the Phoenicians ... introduced into Greece upon their arrival a great variety of arts, among the rest that of writing, whereof the Greeks till then had, as I think been ignorant. And originally, they shaped their letters exactly like all the other Phoenicians, but afterwards in course of time, they changed by degrees their language, and together with it the form likewise of the characters. (Herodotus, 5.58)

Logan's (1986) account of the diffusion of the alphabet over several millennia provides a great example of cultural influence. Although no one today labels the diffusion of the alphabet as cultural imperialism, it could easily be labeled as such: Homogenizing a system of communication, as the Phoenicians did, has some serious negative effects—it can be used for insulting others who can read and correctly interpret the insult; it can be used to defame others as many can understand the words used in the defaming statement; it can be used to declare wars as leaders can decipher the threats; and it most certainly did eradicate other systems of written and oral communication among non-Phoenicians who could have evolved but were not given a chance to develop. Accordingly, all those who use a variation or derivative of the Phoenician alphabet (including the readers of this chapter) would be a victim of the Phoenician cultural empire.

9. AN ALTERNATIVE PARADIGM

Of course, labeling the process of the diffusion and influence of the Phoenician alphabet as "cultural imperialism" or making accusations, as the ones just made, would be considered ridiculous and frivolous today. The wide prevalence of derivatives of the phonetic alphabet today is clearly a function of a process of cultural diffusion that long predates the invention of mass media. The diffusion of culture, then, has accompanied the evolution of human civilization and is not a function of conspiracy. Rather, it seems that diffused cultural items are functional to those who seek them. They seem to fill particular needs and seem to be adapted by the borrowers to fit their needs.

Writing in the early 1900s, long before the advent of worldwide information networks, Smith (1933) aptly stated that:

> ... [t]he diffusion of culture is not a mere mechanical process such as the simple exchange of material objects. It is a vital process involving the unpredictable behaviour of the human beings who are the transmitters and those who are the receivers of the borrowed and inevitably modified elements of culture. Of the ideas and information submitted to any individual only parts are adopted: the choice is determined by the personal feelings and circumstances of the receiver. Moreover, the borrowed ideas become integrated into the receiver's personality and more or less modified in the process of adaptation to his knowledge and interests. Such selection and transformation occur in a diffusion of culture not only from one individual to another, but even more profoundly in the passage from one community to another. The vehicles of transmission are affective human beings, and subtle changes are introduced into every cultural exchange in accordance with their personal likes and dislikes, no less than their ability and understanding and the circumstances at particular moments. (p. 10)

At the time that Smith (1933) wrote these words, the modes of information transmission were interpersonal. It is important to note that cultural diffusion as pointed out by Kroeber (1952) and documented by Logan (1986) involves people A adapting borrowed elements from people B and eventually transforming and customizing them to fit local needs. At some point, however, the elements customized by people B are transmitted to people C who adopt them and eventually also customize them. As the chain of diffusion continues, a circular pattern emerges: Eventually, people A will borrow the same elements they originally transmitted to people B after these elements have been subjected to a multitude of transformations and customizations.

An interesting example here concerns the diffusion of pita bread. Pita bread or flat bread has its origins in the Near East and its surrounding areas. Over the years, it was adapted by American fast food chains and has now become widely available in chains such as Kentucky Fried Chicken, Wendy's, and others in the United States in the form of a "sandwich wrap" (Fisher, 2002). This example shows that cultural diffusion can still originate from outside eminent countries and be diffused into eminent countries. Because the pita product stems from relatively weaker countries that are not centers of military or economic power, conspiracy theories cannot be sought to explain the introduction of this product into the United States. Its wide availability is the result of cultural diffusion, plain and simple. What is especially interesting to note here, however, is that the chains who have adopted the sandwich wrap are now serving a modified version of the Pita along with other American-style fast food at their branches in the Near East and elsewhere. The diffusion process has come full circle.

Whereas humans have, throughout history, channeled cultural diffusion, today, electronic media that span the globe at tremendous rates of speed can potentially contribute to the diffusion of culture. Cultural diffusion across borders, however, can and does occur independently of electronic media, as illustrated earlier by the diffusion of pita bread into the United States. However, when imported audio-visuals are found to influence some aspect of the receivers' culture, I propose to label the process of influence as Media-Accelerated Culture Diffusion (MACD).

CONCLUSION

The focus of this chapter was threefold: (a) whether imported television has an effect on domestic viewers; (b) to illustrate the process of influence that is likely to produce an effect; and (c) to label the process of influence when an effect is detected.

The perspective of most writers about the effects of imported TV is that these programs have strong (homogenous and intense) influence on the local viewers who are exposed to them. This notion is at the heart of the cultural imperialism (CI) theoretical framework. CI was found to be a label for the process of influence conceptualized by its proponents and a label for the effect stemming from this process. CI is the default and dominant paradigm for conceptualizing the impact stemming from the presence of foreign programs in domestic TV schedules.

This chapter illustrated the process implicit in the CI framework and evaluated its components. From a process model perspective, the CI paradigm assumes the existence of a simple relationship between the presence of imported TV programs and their influence of local audience members. The relationships implicit in the CI framework were said to be incomplete and not useful in explaining the variation in the intensity of effects stemming from exposure to imported TV.

By contrast to the CI perspective, the existing body of literature shows that the process of influence is a lot more complex than CI advocates believe it to be. The various attempts to summarize the empirical research literature agree that foreign TV does not have a homogenous influence across individuals and effect types, but it can be influential.

This chapter presented an alternative process model that accounts for the variation in the intensity of effects across the various studies about this topic. The model of Susceptibility to Imported Media (SIM) that we presented is derived from the existing findings of studies about foreign TV and related areas.

The similarity between the two models is in their attempt to explain the existence of a link between exposure to imported TV programs and subsequent influence on viewer attitudes, beliefs, behaviors, and/or values. Whereas CI asserts that such a link is strong and always exists, SIM argues that its existence and strength will vary depending on key antecedent factors and the interrelationships among these factors.

This chapter also tackled the task of labeling the process of influence when an effect is detected. In contrast to the cultural imperialism label that assumes forced influence, we proposed to label any effects stemming from exposure to imported TV as Media-Accelerated Culture Diffusion (MACD).

The SIM model and the MACD label are initiating a change in the existing paradigm. We certainly do not proclaim the SIM to be perfect. We encourage researchers to critique it, modify it, and develop ways of testing it empirically. In light of the ever-expanding global information networks, we hope that this chapter will refocus attention and inspire new programs of research on the potential impact of international television messages.

REFERENCES

Ajzen, I., & Fishbein, M. (1980). *Understanding attitudes and predicting social behavior.* Englewood, NJ: Prentice-Hall.

Beltran, L. R. S. (1978). Communication and cultural domination: USA–Latin American case. *Media Asia, 5,* 183–192.

Berry, J. W., & Sam, D. L. (1997). Acculturation and adaptation. In J. W. Berry, M. H. Segall, & C. Kagitcibasi (Eds.), *Handbook of cross-cultural psychology* (pp. 291–326). Boston: Allyn & Bacon.

Bornstein, R. F. (1993). Mere exposure effects with outgroup stimuli. In D. M. Mackie & D. L. Hamilton (Eds.), *Affect, Cognition and Stereotyping* (pp. 195–210). San Diego, CA: Academic Press, Inc.

Browne, D. R. (1967). Problems in international television. *Journal of Communication, 17,* 198–210.

Cacioppo, J. T., Petty, R. E., Kao, C. F., & Rodriguez, R. (1986). Central and peripheral routes to persuasion. An individual difference perspective. *Journal of Personality and Social Psychology, 51*(5), 1032–1043.

Chaiken, S., & Eagly, A. H. (1983). Communication modality as a determinant of persuasion: The role of communicator salience. *Journal of Personality and Social Psychology, 45,* 241–256.

DeFrancis, J. (1989). *Visible speech: The diverse oneness of writing systems.* Honolulu: University of Hawaii Press.

Drucker, J. (1995). *The alphabetic labyrinth: The letters in history and imagination.* London: Thames & Hudson.

Elasmar, M. G., & Hunter, J. E. (1997). The impact of foreign TV on a domestic audience: A meta-analysis. *Communication yearbook 20,* 47–69. Thousand Oaks, CA: Sage.

Elasmar, M. G., & Sim, K. (1997, April). *Unmasking the myopic effect: Questioning the adequacy of media imperialism theory in explaining the impact of foreign TV.* Paper presented at the conference of the Broadcast Education Association, Las Vegas, NV.

Fishbein, M., & Ajzen, I. (1975). *Belief, attitude, intention and behavior: An introduction to theory and research.* Reading, MA: Addison-Wesley.

Fisher, K. (2002, January 9). Baking pita in the middle of the night. *The Boston Globe,* p. E1.

Gaur, A. (1984). *A history of writing.* New York: Charles Scribner's Sons.

Goonasekara, A. (1987). The influence of television on cultural values—With special reference to Third World countries. *Media Asia, 14,* 7–12.

Hawkins, R. P., & Daly, J. (1988). Cognition and communication. In R. P. Hawkins, J. M. Wiemann, & S. Pingree (Eds.), *Advancing communication science: Merging mass and interpersonal processes* (pp. 191–223). Newbury Park, CA: Sage.

Herskovits, M. J. (1956). *Man and his works*. New York: Knopf.

Hoebel, E. A. (1971). The nature of culture. In H. L. Shapiro (Ed.), *Man, culture and society* (pp. 208–222). New York: Oxford University Press.

Hur, K. K. (1982). International mass communication research: A critical review of theory and methods. In M. Borgoon (Ed.), *Communication yearbook 6* (pp. 531–554). Beverly Hills, CA: Sage.

Johnson, B. T, & Eagly, A. H. (1989). Effects of involvement on persuasion: A meta-analysis. *Psychological Bulletin, 106*(2), 290–314.

Katz, E. (1968). On reopening the question of selectivity in exposure to mass communications. In R. P. Abelson, E. Aronson, W. J. McGuire, T. M. Newcomb, M. J. Rosenberg, & P. H. Tannenbaum (Eds.), *Theories of cognitive consistency: A sourcebook* (pp. 788–796). Chicago: Rand McNally.

Kim, M. S., & Hunter, J. E. (1993). Attitude–Behavior relations: A meta-analysis of attitudinal relevance and topic. *Journal of Communication, 43*(1), 101–142.

Kraus, S. J. (1995). Attitudes and the prediction of behavior: A meta-analysis of the empirical literature. *Personality and Social Psychology Bulletin, 21*(1), 58–75.

Kroeber, A. L. (1952). *The nature of culture*. Chicago: University of Chicago Press.

Lazarsfeld, P. (1976). The prognosis for international communications research. In H. Fischer & J. C. Merrill (Eds.), *International and intercultural communication* (pp. 474–484). New York: Hastings House.

Lee, C. C. (1980). *Media imperialism reconsidered*. Beverly Hills, CA: Sage.

Liebes, T., & Katz, E. (1993). *The export of meaning: Cross-cultural readings of Dallas*. Oxford: Polity Press.

Logan, R. K. (1986). *The alphabet effect: The impact of the phonetic alphabet on the development of Western civilization*. New York: Morrow.

McPhail, T. L. (1987). *Electronic colonialism: The future of international broadcasting and communication*. Newbury Park, CA: Sage.

Murdock, G. P. (1971). How culture changes. In H. L. Shapiro (Ed.), *Man, culture and society* (pp. 319–332). New York: Oxford University Press.

Nordenstreng, K., & Varis, T. (1973). Television traffic: A one way street. *Reports and Papers on Mass Communications* (No. 60). Paris: UNESCO.

Oliveira, O. S. (1986). Satellite TV and dependency: An empirical approach. *Gazette, 38*, 127–145.

Payne, D. E., & Peake, C. A. (1977). Cultural diffusion: The role of U.S. TV in Iceland. *Journalism Quarterly, 54*, 523–531.

Read, S. J., & Miller, L. C. (1994). Dissonance and balance in belief systems: The promise of parallel constraint satisfaction processes and connectionist modeling approaches. In R. C. Schank & E. Langer (Eds.), *Beliefs, reasoning and decision making* (pp. 209–236). Hillsdale, NJ: Lawrence Erlbaum Associates.

Renzulli, J. S., & Dai, Y. D. (2001). Abilities, interests and styles as aptitudes for learning: A person-situation interaction perspective. In R. J. Strenberg & L. Zhang (Eds.), *Perspectives on thinking, learning and cognitive styles* (pp. 23–46). Mahwah, NJ: Lawrence Erlbaum Associates.

Rogers, E. M. (1983). *Diffusion of innovations*. New York: The Free Press.

Salwen, M. B. (1991). Cultural imperialism: A media effects approach. *Critical Studies in Mass Communication, 8*, 29–38.

Schiller, H. I. (1969). *Mass communication and American empire*. Boston: Beacon.

Schiller, H. I. (1991). Not yet the post-imperialist era. *Critical Studies in Mass Communication, 8,* 13–28.

Skinner, E. C. (1984). *Foreign TV programs viewing and dependency: A case study of U.S. television viewing in Trinidad and Tobago.* Unpublished doctoral dissertation, Michigan State University, East Lansing.

Smith, G. E. (1933). *The diffusion of culture.* Port Washington, NY: Kennikat Press.

Stephan, W. G. (1987). The contact hypothesis in intergroup relations. In C. Hundrick (Ed.), *Group processes and intergroup relations* (pp. 1–37). Newbury Park, CA: Sage.

Stiff, J. B. (1986). Cognitive processing of persuasive message cues: A meta-analytic review of the effects of supporting information on attitudes. *Communication Monographs 53*(1), 75–89.

Straubhaar, J. D., Young, S., Campbell, C., Champagnie, K., Ha, L., Shrikhande, S., Elasmar, M. G., Ahan, T., Chen, M., Clark, S., & Takahashi, M. (1992, August). *Regional TV markets and TV program flows.* Paper presented at the meeting of the International Association for Mass Communication Research, São Paulo, Brazil.

Swiggers, P. (1996). Transmission of the Phoenician script to the West. In P. T. Daniels & W. Bright (Eds.), *The world's writing systems* (pp. 261–270). Oxford: Oxford University Press.

Tracey, M. (1985). The poisoned chalice? International television and the idea of dominance. *Proceedings of the American Academy of Arts and Sciences, USA, 114,* 17–56.

Tracey, M. (1993). A taste of money: Popular culture and the economics of global television. In E. M. Noam & J. C. Millonzi (Eds.). *The international market in film and television programs* (pp. 163–198). Norwood, NJ: Ablex.

Varis, T. (1993). Trends in the global traffic of television programs. In E. M. Noam & J. C. Millonzi (Eds.). *The international market in film and television programs* (pp.1–12). Norwood, NJ: Ablex.

Verlegh, P. W., & Steenkamp, J. B. (1999). A review and meta-analysis of country of origin research. *Journal of Economy Psychology, 20,* 521–546.

Wu, Y. K. (1989). *Television and the value system of Taiwan's adolescents: A cultivation analysis.* Unpublished doctoral dissertation, University of Massachusetts, Amherst.

Yaple, P., & Korzenny, F. (1989). Electronic mass media effects across cultures. In M. K. Asante & W. B. Gudykunst (Eds.). *Handbook of international and intercultural communication* (pp. 295–317). Newbury Park, CA: Sage.

Zillman, D., & Bryant, J. (1985). Selective exposure phenomena. In D. Zillman & J. Bryant (Eds.). *Selective exposure to communication* (pp. 1–10). Hillsdale, NJ: Lawrence Erlbaum Associates.

CHAPTER

10

The Impact of International Audio-Visual Media: An Expanded Research Agenda for the Future

Michael G. Elasmar
Boston University

The purpose of this chapter is to propose an agenda of research that will further our understanding of the role that international audio-visual media play in the diffusion of culture. The focus of this book has thus far been solely on television as an entertainment medium regardless of whether the imported content is received by the viewer via traditional broadcast, cable, satellite, and/or videocassette tapes. When planning future studies, researchers ought to consider extending the knowledge presented in this book by applying the model of Susceptibility to Imported Media (SIM) proposed in chapter 9 for investigating the following:

Agenda Item I: Exposure and effect of viewing imported entertainment television programs.

In addition to imported entertainment content, researchers ought to also consider testing the SIM for investigating imported content that is not entertainment, thus focusing on the following:

Agenda Item II: Exposure and effect of viewing imported news on television.

Although the most prevalent device for receiving imported audio-visual content is still the television set, beginning in the mid-1990s, an increasing number of people have also begun using the World Wide Web (Web), an information network that allows individuals to receive imported content via a computer. The information on the Web consists of entertainment, news, and other types of content. Although most Web users were initially located in developed countries, by the late 1990s individuals in developing countries were also increasingly using this new information medium. Thus, future studies also ought to consider applying the SIM model for investigating the following process:

> Agenda Item III: Exposure and effect of viewing information on foreign Web sites.

Although studying the exposure and effect of imported information via TV or the Web can be approached using quantitative methodologies, researchers ought to also explore the use of historical and anthropological strategies for illustrating the processes of culture diffusion that have taken place before the advent of television. This is important because television and the Web, as agents of international communication, are simply extensions of a process begun long ago, in the form of interpersonal contacts across people living in various geographical areas (Smith, 1933; Beal, Spindler, & Spindler, 1967). Understanding the role that the new agents of international communication play in culture diffusion will be enhanced by a thorough knowledge of the processes of culture diffusion that preceded them. Hence, researchers are also encouraged to document the following:

> Agenda Item IV: Historical diffusion of many of the cultural elements that constitute the building blocks of modern life in various locales.

The following sections of this chapter provide researchers with information that they might find useful when developing research programs that focus on each of the four agenda items mentioned.

Focusing on Television

There is no doubt that television is still the most prevalent device for receiving imported audio-visual information in the form of entertainment programs and news. Although this book has solely focused on the impact of entertainment programs, future researchers also ought to explore the impact of imported news and the interaction between exposure to imported news and imported entertainment. Even for the case of entertainment, there is a need to conduct many more studies in various countries. Ideally, several studies should be conducted in every country. Comparisons should then be conducted across study findings within every country and across countries. Doing so will provide plenty of data for the meta-analysts so that they are able to draw global conclusions about the processes and effects associated with the exposure to imported television content. Conducting multiple studies will also provide a unique opportunity for testing and refining the SIM framework

10. AN EXPANDED RESEARCH AGENDA FOR THE FUTURE

identified in chapter 9, and, by doing so, developing empirical-based theories concerning the process and effect of imported information.

Focusing on the World Wide Web

By the end of the second millennium, television had been a mass medium for close to 50 years. The following paragraphs rapidly trace the evolution of the audio-visual industries available to consumers. Doing so will highlight the changes to these traditional industries brought about in the mid-1990s with the introduction of the World Wide Web (Web) to the consumer. This section also points out the research implications of the changing media environment.

When television made its debut in various markets, from a consumer's viewpoint, it was an extension of the movie theater experience of the early 1900s because, as was the case for movies, the role of television was to simply display audio-visual information to an audience (DeFleur & Ball-Rokeach, 1989). As a medium, however, television brought with it significant changes to the movie theatre experience:

1. It involved a more private viewing context, as television sets were installed in individual homes and viewing was done either with family members or by oneself;
2. It enabled the distribution of the same message to a larger audience;
3. It significantly shrank the time between message release and simultaneous audience reception;
4. It dramatically increased the number of people involved in message production as the medium required much more content than the movie theaters had traditionally needed.

From its inception and until the 1980s, the television medium had very slowly expanded its program offerings, mostly as a function of progressively extending the television day to 24 hours. In the 1980s, however, television began witnessing an exponential growth in program offerings thanks to the advent of cable technology that allowed TV viewers to access many more channels than they previously could (Gross, 1990; Head & Sterling, 1991). Although this primarily happened in the United States, it slowly also began occurring in many regions around the world. Throughout the 1980s and 1990s, cable brought significant changes to the markets it had penetrated:

1. It offered audience members many more programs from which to choose;
2. It caused the television audience to become increasingly fragmented, preventing a single message from reaching as wide an audience as was previously possible;
3. It further increased the number of people involved in message production as more channels required more messages.

The building blocks of the television industry have traditionally consisted of producers of audio-visual programs (i.e., Hollywood studios, independent producers, etc.), the distributors of television signals (i.e., broadcast networks, cable networks), the exhibitors of television signals (i.e., local cable company, local broadcast network), the audio-visual programs themselves (e.g., entertainment, news, etc.), and the consumers of audio-visual content (i.e., the audiences) (Williams, 1987). Throughout the 20th century, the producers of audio-visual content were distinct from the audiences of that content. At the end of the 20th century, this distinction began to whither with the introduction of a new consumer application of computer technology.

It was in the mid-1990s that a new mode for distributing information and entertainment was introduced to the consumer market: The World Wide Web (Web). The Web uses the Internet as its backbone. The Internet is an intricate network of computers interconnected to facilitate the traffic of information (Comer, 1997). The roots of the Internet can be traced to the 1960s (Comer, 1997). However, it wasn't until the mid-1990s that the vast majority of consumers first heard about it and progressively began making use of it by accessing Web sites. As Web technology rapidly evolved, it enabled users to view audio-visual media similar in form to that which has traditionally been distributed via television. In a relatively short period after its inception, the Web enabled consumers to view audio-visual files via their computer screens.

The Web brought with it three very significant changes to the traditional communication process that television embodied and that had been unchanged for almost a century, beginning with the movie theatre experience, and ending with cable:

1. The Web gave the receiver of audio-visual programs the opportunity to also become the producer of such content. This was primarily due to the fact that producing content for Web distribution is simple and relatively cheap. Consumers can create their own Web sites and create their own audio-visual content which are then available to anyone who can access the Web from anywhere on earth.
2. The Web brought with it an almost immeasurable quantity of audio-visual content to which a user can choose to be exposed.
3. The Web allowed the integration of audio-visuals traditionally associated with television with mediated interpersonal communication traditionally associated with letters and the telephone.

Implications for Researchers. In addition to studying selection and exposure to Web content on foreign sites and the effects of such content on the individual, researchers also ought to focus on the motivations of local users for creating Web content in a foreign language (production of international Web sites by local users), and motivations for responding to content on foreign Web sites (whether it be in chat rooms, e-mail, or others). In other words, the researcher can no longer

10. AN EXPANDED RESEARCH AGENDA FOR THE FUTURE

solely focus on local audience members as receivers, as they can also be content producers. Given the characteristics of the Web, researchers also ought to focus on the feedback activities in which local audience members engage (e.g., responding to content posted on the Web via chat rooms and others). Further, researchers ought to study the process and impact of international exchanges of e-mail and instant chat messages over the Web.

In addition to the content production and interactivity features of the Web, researchers also need to take into account the following:

1. Traditional television exposure allowed for interpersonal exchanges among viewers physically located in the same room because the television screen was designed to accommodate more than one viewer at a time. In contrast, exposure to Web content via a computer screen is usually not a group activity and therefore does not lend itself to interpersonal exchanges among viewers physically located in the same room. Has this change affected the way a local user processes information from foreign Web sites?
2. The Web has further shrunken the time between message production and worldwide message dissemination. Has this change affected the perceived physical distances that exist among Web users living in various parts of the world? Has this change empowered local users who can now bypass the traditional gatekeepers for their countries and have unlimited access to information? Has this change also allowed for disinformation to quickly spread among local users?
3. The large amounts of information on the Web also signify that Web users are potentially fragmented. Is this the case worldwide, or do users in certain countries tend to congregate around particular Web sites on a regular basis? After assessing the level of user fragmentation, researchers ought to find if the Web can be used as a tool for international data collection that can facilitate the tasks of researchers associated with investigating the impact of exposure to imported information. Can the Web be used as a tool for data collection worldwide? If so, what problems are researchers likely to encounter when collecting information from international users via the Web?

The features of the Web will most likely prompt international communication researchers to modify and refine the model of Susceptibility to Imported Media (SIM) proposed in chapter 9 to make it suitable for an interactive environment.

Successfully Researching the Process and Effect of Exposure to Imported Information

Although the new media environment might require a refinement of the SIM model, the fundamental aspects of sound empirical research remain unchanged. Here are some specific recommendations that will ensure a high level of quality for future empirical research endeavors:

Researchers Need to Agree on Construct Definitions. When researchers adopt different definitions for the same concepts, they prevent the reader from reliably comparing across study findings. For example, if an author believes that she measured a behavior when in actuality she measured a belief, the reader of her article might combine her findings about what she considers to be a behavior with other findings concerning that behavior in order to draw a conclusion across studies. By doing so, the reader would be unknowingly combining the findings concerning two separate concepts and, by doing so, unknowingly reaching erroneous conclusions about the concept in which he or she is interested. Not adopting common definitions for identical constructs has negative implications for literature reviewers and for theory-builders in our field. It confuses the former and slows and frustrates the latter.

Researchers Need to Agree on Measurement. Two studies that examine an identical variable but use different measures might yield different results simply due to the variation in measurement. This has implications for finding relationships, such as the relationship between exposure to U.S. TV and attitude toward the United States. For example, if the construct is "attitude toward the United States" and one researcher uses a semantic differential scale developed by author A for measuring it, while another uses a semantic differential scale by author B for measuring this same construct, unless both scales have construct validity, the author's results concerning attitudes toward the United States are likely to not be comparable. Using different measures for the same construct will prevent solid conclusions from being drawn from these studies and slow the process of theory building in our field.

Researchers Need to Test Their Measures for Stability. Complex concepts, such as attitudes, knowledge, beliefs, and values, are hard to measure. As such, they will introduce to a study some amount of measurement error. Researchers can quantitatively estimate the amount of measurement error associated with a particular measure by using an internal consistency technique (e.g., computing Cronbach's Alpha). The problem is that such techniques for estimating a measure's reliability cannot be used unless the researcher's measures consist of more than a single estimate of the construct he or she is attempting to measure. In addition to the importance of simply assessing an instrument's stability, a lack of information about a measure's reliability also prevents a meta-analytic reviewer from correcting the results of individual studies for their inherent measurement error (see Hunter & Schmidt, 1990).

Researchers Need to Test Their Measures for Validity. Even among researchers who use multiple estimates for complex variables, many still combine their estimates and create composite scores without first carrying out appropriate validation tests. The most common validation test available to quantitative researchers today is factor analysis. It enables the researcher to test the various dimensions that might underlie a set of questions. Without statistical validation, a researcher runs the risk of combining multidimensional items and ending up with an invalid composite score of the construct he or she is trying to measure. When this happens, the composite scores computed by the researcher become distorted. The researcher will thus be unable to uncover the true relationships that exist among the constructs involved in his or her study.

Researchers Need to Take Into Consideration Respondent Burden. A trade-off exists between the amount of information that can be collected from human respondents and the accuracy of this information. The relationship is simple: The larger the amount of information requested, the larger the burden placed on the respondent, the more likely this respondent is to experience fatigue. The greater is respondent fatigue, the less accurate the responses will be. Researchers need to pay particular attention to this aspect of data collection because the attention span of the newer generations are shorter than those that preceded them. As such, researchers ought to carefully pretest any measuring instruments to ensure that the length of these instruments will not preclude the collection of accurate data.

Researchers Need to Agree on What Statistics to Report. Due to the variation in researchers' ages and diversity of training, they cannot be expected to automatically report the same statistics in their studies. Without guidance, some will use archaic and obscure notations that are no longer found in standard references today. Adopting conventions for reporting statistics will allow for more meaningful comparisons across studies. This is especially true for the meta-analytic reviewer who needs to convert statistics of effect–size into a common metric. Failure to report sufficient information about key statistics prevents the meta-analytic researcher from being able to convert them. Aside from making the findings of a study hard to interpret, the absence of key statistics also prevents the findings of a given article from being represented in a meta-analytic review.

Researchers Need to Think About Alternative Explanations Ahead of Time. Often, due to a researchers' intense interest in the specific variables appearing in his or her hypotheses, he or she fails to measure other important variables that do not seem to be directly related to his or her hypotheses. In this case, the researcher can test his or her hypotheses but cannot rule out alternative explanations for those findings. Often, the researcher draws conclusions and either ignores the possibility of alternative explanations or points out that a future study will need to test alternative explanations. Of course, not being aware of alternative explanations weakens the findings of a study, and proposing that they be tested in a future investigation only slows down the theory building process in our field. For example, finding that viewing television imported from the United States increases consumption of American fast food might be spurious. It could be that those who watch a lot of TV also tend to travel a lot and those who travel a lot tend to eat American fast food.

This alternative explanation cannot be ruled out unless the researcher has thought about it before the study and included appropriate measures for testing it as part of his or her study instrument.

Culture Diffusion Without Modern Communications

To a certain extent, early anthropologists have already charted the way by providing us with snapshots that illustrate the role that early forms of international communication played in the diffusion of certain cultural elements (e.g., see Smith, 1933, for an account of the role of intergroup communication in diffusing religion). With a few exceptions, these early efforts by anthropologists were never continued, as the focus of their successors shifted to investigating other aspects of their field unrelated to international communication. Being at an intersection of disciplines, international communication researchers can pick up where the early anthropologists left off by specifically focusing on the role that communication agents have historically played in the diffusion of cultural elements.

Aside from investigating the diffusion of cultural elements from eminent countries, researchers ought to also focus on the processes that have fueled elements specific to noneminent cultures to cross borders and diffuse into eminent cultures. Recent examples of such diffusions include the spread and adaptation of pita bread in the United States. The following is a very brief and anecdotal account of this diffusion process given for the sake of illustration.

Pita bread or flat bread or pocket bread has its roots in the Near East. Beginning in the 1980s, it progressively began appearing in major cities of the United States. By the late 1990s it had fully penetrated the U.S. market: (a) It could be found in most supermarket chains; (b) It was integrated into American fast food products, labeled as "a wrap" by the largest U.S. fast food chains; (c) It was even distributed in the form of flavored "pita chips," packaged in small bags and promoted as a tasty companion to sandwiches and soft drinks (Fisher, 2002). It is important to note that the pita bread was diffused in the United States at a time when the Near East, from where it came, was neither playing a leadership role nor had any entertainment communication flows toward the West. Pita bread was nevertheless diffused into the U.S. market. In addition to diffusing pita bread in its indigenous form, the diffusion process transformed pita bread into products that are more likely to appeal to the tastes of U.S. consumers (e.g., flavored chips).

Understanding the processes particular to the diffusion of similar cultural elements is key for separating the role of power from the process of cultural diffusion. This is so, because these cultural elements were diffused even though the countries from which they stemmed were not holding positions of significant political power during the time of their diffusion. To a certain extent, focusing on the processes of cultural diffusion from noneminent groups to eminent groups allows us to study the factors of diffusion while holding country power constant. Removing country power from the culture diffusion process will effectively allow us to observe the key diffusion factors that operate independently of power. These factors are usually obscured by "political power" in studies that focus on the diffusion of culture from powerful countries to others that are less powerful.

The items of the research agenda presented in this chapter are meant to stimulate the interest of researchers for conducting studies about the role of international communication in diffusing culture. This call for more research echoes the one made by Lazarsfeld in the 1940s (Lazarsfeld, 1976). As this book has shown, many studies have been conducted since Lazarsfeld defined international communication as a study of the "processes by which various cultures influence each other" (p. 485). Altogether, however, the body of available knowledge is still relatively small in size.

I hope that, in the coming decade, coordination and collaboration among researchers will yield a new volume of knowledge that updates this book and pushes forward our understanding of the process and influence of international communication at the onset of the third millennium.

REFERENCES

Beal, A. R., Spindler, G., & Spindler, L. (1967). *Culture in process.* New York: Holt, Rinehart, & Winston.

Comer, D. E. (1997). *The Internet.* Upper Saddler River, NJ: Prentice-Hall.

DeFleur, M. L., & Ball-Rokeach, S. (1989). *Theories of mass communication.* White Plains, NY: Longman.

Fisher, K. (2002, January 9). Baking pita in the middle of the night. *The Boston Globe,* p. E1.

Gross, L. S. (1990). *The new television technologies.* Dubuque, IA: Brown.

Head, S. W., & Sterling, C. H. (1991). *Broadcasting in America.* Boston: Houghton Mifflin.

Hunter, J. E., & Schmidt, F. L. (1990). *Methods of meta-analysis: Correcting error and bias in research findings.* Newbury Park, CA: Sage.

Lazarsfeld, P. (1976). The prognosis for international communications research. In H. Fischer & J. C. Merrill (Eds.), *International and intercultural communication* (pp. 474–484). New York: Hastings House.

Smith, G. E. (1933). *The diffusion of culture.* Port Washington, NY: Kennikat Press.

Williams, F. (1987). *Technology and communication behavior.* Belmont, CA: Wadsworth.

Contributors

Mary E. Beadle is Dean of the Graduate School at John Carroll University in Cleveland, Ohio and is a Professor of Communications. A former chair of the International division of the Broadcast Education Association (BEA), Dr. Beadle has published articles on the media and broadcast history and conducted communication seminars in Russia, Argentina and Paraguay. She recently edited a book on the contributions of women to local television and is co-author on a textbook for broadcast performance.

Kathryn Bennett completed a Master of Science Degree in Communication at Boston University where she also served as Project Manager at the Communication Research Center.

Linda Davis is Associate Dean of the William Allen White School of Journalism and Mass Communications at the University of Kansas. She is also on the faculty of the Center of Latin American Studies, and her research focuses on the business and culture of international media, especially television in Latin America. Prof. Davis has made presentations on Latin American television and/or international marketing communications in Chile, Mexico, Costa Rica, Australia and the U.S. With a master's degree in journalism from the UNC-Chapel Hill and a BS in advertising from the U. of Florida, Davis has worked in newspapers, radio and television and in news, advertising and public relations.

Michael G. Elasmar (PhD, Michigan State University) is Director of the Communication Research Center at Boston University (BU), a position he has held since 1994. He is also Associate Professor of Communication Research at BU and former chair of the International Communication Division of the Association for Education in Journalism and Mass Communication (AEJMC). His personal research programs include the impact of crossborder communication, a program he started in the 1980s, and the adoption patterns and effects of new communication technologies at home and in the workplace. He has published and/or presented over 40 manuscripts stemming from these two research programs, several of which have won prizes at international paper competitions.

Todd Gibson completed a Master of Arts degree in Communication at Washington State University.

John E. Hunter (PhD, University of Illinois) is Professor of Psychology at Michigan State University. He is co-author of three books: Meta-Analysis, Mathematical Models of Attitude Change, and Methods of Meta-Analysis. He is a Fellow of the Society of Industrial and Organizational Psychology, the American Psychological Society and the American Psychological Association. He has published more than 150 articles on a wide variety of topics, including personnel selection, organizational interventions, attitude change, psychometric theory, personality, group dynamics and other social processes.

David Payne is Vice President for Academic Affairs at Sam Houston State University. He has been a university dean or vice president for 20 years. He received his BS from Brigham Young University, his MA and PHD from the University of North Carolina. He has published widely in the areas of intercultural mass communication, organizational behavior, and university administration.

Joseph D. Straubhaar is Amon G. Carter Professor of Communication at the University of Texas' Radio-TV-Film Department. He previously taught at BYU and Michigan State University. His PhD in International Communication is from the Fletcher School of Law and Diplomacy, Tufts University. He worked as a Foreign Service Officer in Brazil and Washington. He has published extensively on international media studies.

Alexis Tan is Professor and Director, Edward R. Murrow School of Communication at Washington State University. He is the author of a textbook on communication theories and research, and of over 60 research articles, monographs and book chapters on communication processes and effects. He has done research in China, Taiwan, Mexico, the Philippines, Japan, South Africa, Russia, Thailand and Jordan. He has a PhD in mass communication from the University of Wisconsin-Madison.

Gerdean Tan is Associate Professor of Education in the College of Education, Washington State University. Her research focuses on multicultural education in the United States and other countries. She holds a PhD in Interdisciplinary Studies (Sociology, Anthropology and Education) from Washington State University.

Thimios Zaharopoulos is Professor and Chair of the Department of Mass Media at Washburn University of Topeka. As a former Fulbright Scholar to Greece, he has published extensively on Greek media and foreign media effects on Greek culture. He received his PhD in Journalism from Southern Illinois University, and has previously taught at the American College of Greece and Pittsburgh State University.

Author Index

A

Adams, P. V., 4, 14
Adoni, H., 39, 54
Ahan, T., 162, 163, 179
Ahn, Y., 147, 152
Ajzen, I., 170, 177
Akaishi, E., 147, 153
Alisky, M., 125, 127, 130
Alleyne, M. D., 119, 130
Alter, I., 39, 55
Altheide, D. L., 25, 27
Anderson, B., 77, 107
Ang, I., 91, 107
Antola, A., 79, 107
Antola, L., 61, 75, 118, 119, 122, 125, 130

B

Ball-Rokeach, S., 11, 14, 183, 189
Bandura, A., 30, 38
Barnett, G., 152
Beadle, M., 63, 75
Beadle, M. E., 63, 74, 75
Beal, A. R., 182, 189
Beattie, E., 153
Beltran, 111
Beltran, L. R., 1, 2, 8, 9, 14, 78, 107
Beltran, L. R. S., 135, 139, 153, 160, 177
Berger, P. L., 2, 7, 14
Berry, J. W., 168, 177

Berwanger, D., 117, 120, 130
Bhahba, H., 97, 107
Bibliowicz, A., 10, 13, 15, 135, 139, 154
Blumler, J., 91, 107
Bornstein, R. F., 166, 171, 172, 177
Bourdieu, P., 78, 82, 85, 107
Bouwman, H., 139, 153
Boyd, D., 105, 107
Boyd-Barrett, O., 78, 107
Broddason, T., 17, 27
Brown, A., 90, 107
Browne, D. R., 135, 151, 153, 158, 177
Bryant, J., 163, 179
Buck, E., 87, 109

C

Cacioppo, J. T., 167, 172, 177
Campbell, C., 79, 82, 91, 109, 162, 163, 179
Canclini N. G., 97, 107
Caron, A. H., 17, 22, 24, 28, 145, 146, 154
Castellon, L., 79, 82, 91, 109
Chaffee, S., 24, 26, 28, 145, 153, 155
Chaiken, S., 167, 171, 177
Champagnie, K., 79, 82, 91, 109, 162, 163, 179
Chaney, L., 57, 75
Chen, M., 162, 163, 179
Cherry, C., 42, 54
Chilcote, R. H., 91, 104, 107

Choi, J., 147, 153
Chu, G., 145, 153
Clark, S., 162, 163, 179
Coldevin, G. O., 153
Cole, R. R., 27, 28
Collins, R., 79, 82, 107
Comer, D. E., 184, 189
Copeland, G. A., 112, 115, 130
Crawford, M. L., 58, 59, 75
Curran, J., 9, 14
Cuthbert, M., 87, 109

D

Daalder, H., 4, 5, 14
Dai, Y. D., 162, 165, 172, 178
Daly, J., 165, 177
da Matta, R., 86, 107
da Távola, A., 102, 107
Day, P., 139, 153
DeFleur, M. L., 11, 14, 183, 189
DeFrancis, J., 174, 177
Dennis, E. E., 113, 118, 123, 127, 128, 131
Diamond, J., 2, 3, 4, 14
Direction of Trade Statistics, 58, 75
Dizard, W., 139, 153
Dominick, J. R., 112, 115, 125, 130, 131
Dong, Q., 30, 38, 155
Dorfman, A., 10, 14, 42, 54
dos Santos, T., 91, 104, 107
Drucker, J., 174, 177
Duarte, L., 44, 56
Dunn, T., 17, 27

E

Eagly, A., 167, 171, 177
Eagly, A. H., 167, 172, 178
Elasmar, M., 63, 64, 75, 78, 79, 82, 91, 107, 109
Elasmar, M. G., 1, 14, 43, 44, 54, 60, 61, 74, 75, 112, 130, 134, 147, 153, 159, 160, 162, 163, 171, 177, 179
Elber, L., 59, 75
Eleey, M. F., 39, 54
El-Koussa, H., 63, 64, 75
El-Koussa, H. H., 147, 153
Elliott, W. R., 45, 54
Elliott, L. S., 43, 54, 153
Emerson, R., 4, 5, 14

Evans, P., 78, 108

F

Featherstone, M., 93, 108
Fejes, F., 7, 9, 10, 14, 91, 108
Ferguson, M., 27
Ferraro, G., 57, 58, 75
Ferreira, L., 139, 155
Fieldhouse, D. K., 4, 15
Fishbein, M., 170, 177
Fisher, G., 41, 54
Fisher, K., 175, 177, 188, 189
Fiske, J., 9, 15
Fox, E., 78, 107, 124, 130
Franco, J., 118, 120, 124, 130
Friday, R., 58, 75
Fujioka, Y., 155

G

Galtung, J., 6, 11, 15
Gans, H., 27, 27
Gargúrevich, J., 124, 130
Gaur, A., 174, 177
Geiger, S. F., 145, 153
Gerbner, G., 25, 26, 27, 29, 30, 38, 39, 46, 54, 55, 60, 75
Gibson, T., 155
Golding, P., 27
Goldsen, R. K., 10, 13, 15, 135, 139, 154
Gonzales, I., 79, 109
Goodman, R., 44, 56
Goonasekara, A., 13, 15, 112, 130, 135, 154, 160, 177
Granzberg, G., 154
Greenberg, B. A., 139, 155
Gross, L., 25, 26, 27, 29, 30, 38, 39, 46, 54, 55
Gross, L. S., 183, 189
Guback, T., 40, 55
Guerevitch, M., 9, 14
Gunter, J., 13, 15

H

Ha, L., 162, 163, 179
Hadad, I., 13, 15, 135, 154
Hallin, D. C., 129, 130
Hamelink, C., 41, 55

AUTHOR INDEX

Hamelink, C. J., 78, 108
Hartman, P., 42, 55
Hawkins, R., 25, 26, 28, 60, 75, 142, 147, 154
Hawkins, R. P., 39, 45, 55, 165, 177
Haynes, R. D., Jr., 27, 27
Head, K., 33, 38
Head, S. W., 183, 189
Hedebro, G., 41, 55
Hedinson, E., 139, 154
Heeter, C., 139, 155
Hellwig, S., 58, 59, 76
Herman, E., 80, 108
Herold, J. C., 4, 15
Herskovits, M. J., 158, 178
Higgott, R. A., 7, 15
Hobson, J. A., 5, 6, 15
Hoebel, E. A., 158, 178
Höijer, B., 25, 27
Homans, G. C., 30, 38
Hoskins, C., 80, 89, 105, 108
Hunter, J., 60, 61, 74, 75
Hunter, J. E., 1, 14, 43, 54, 78, 107, 112, 130, 134, 138, 139, 144, 153, 154, 159, 160, 169, 171, 177, 178, 186, 189
Hur, K. K., 136, 151, 154, 159, 178
Hwa, L., 4, 14

I

Inalcik, H., 4, 15
Iwabuchi, K., 78, 83, 108

J

Jacks, L. P., 4, 15
Jacks, N., 101, 108
Jackson-Beeck, M., 39, 46, 54, 55
Janus, M., 7, 8, 11, 15
Jeffries-Fox, S., 39, 54, 55
Johnson, B. T., 167, 172, 178
Josepsson, B., 17, 27

K

Kahl, S., 44, 56
Kang, 154
Kang, G. J., 142, 144, 145, 146, 154
Kang, J., 60, 75
Kang, J. G., 46, 55

Kao, C. F., 167, 172, 177
Kapoor, S., 154
Karp, J., 92, 108
Katz, E., 6, 7, 15, 41, 44, 54, 55, 91, 107, 124, 125, 130, 162, 163, 164, 165, 167, 172, 178
Kerlinger, F. N., 137, 154
Kim, M. S., 169, 178
King, A. D., 2, 15
King, G., 61, 76
Korman, S., 3, 15
Korzenny, F., 136, 151, 155, 159, 179
Kottak, K., 80, 95, 96, 98, 108
Kraus, S. J., 169, 178
Kroeber, A. L., 158, 173, 175, 178

L

Langer, E. D., 4, 14
Lash, S., 93, 107
Lau, T. Y., 139, 155
Lazarsfeld, P., 161, 178, 189, 189
Lee, C., 7, 13, 15
Lee, C. C., 78, 108, 134, 136, 154, 159, 178
Lenin, V. I., 6, 15
Lent, J., 105, 107
Leslie, M., 87, 108
Li, S., 24, 25, 28, 32, 38, 60, 76, 155
Li, W., 155
Liebes, T., 44, 54, 55, 162, 165, 167, 172, 178
Limaye, M., 59, 75
Logan, R. K., 174, 175, 178
Lum, P., 79, 109

M

Maccoby, E. E., 87, 108
Man Chan, J., 84, 108
Mane, S., 39, 54
Marcus, D., 120, 130
Marques de Melo, J., 79, 106, 108
Marriott, J., 9, 14
Martin, J., 57, 75
Martin-Barbero, J., 86, 101, 108
Masmoudi, M., 11, 15
Mattelart, A., 10, 11, 14, 15, 42, 54, 93, 108
Mattos, S., 96, 108
Mattos, S. A., 96, 108

Mavromichali, I., 45, 55
McAnany, E. G., 7, 8, 11, 15
McBride Commission, 92, 108
McChesney, R., 80, 108
McNeil, W. H., 4, 15
McPhail, T. L., 13, 15, 40, 42, 55, 152, 160, 178
McQuail, D., 7, 9, 15, 40, 55
Merton, R. K., 31, 38
Milanesi, L. A., 96, 108
Miller, L. C., 165, 178
Millman, J., 120, 131
Mira, M. C., 100, 108
Mirus, R., 80, 89, 105, 108
Morgan, M., 25, 26, 27, 29, 30, 38, 39, 45, 46, 55, 56, 60, 61, 75, 139, 142, 144, 145, 146, 154
Morley, D., 85, 91, 108
Mosco, V., 90, 109
Murdock, G. P., 173, 178

N

Nelson, L., 30, 38
Noam, E. M., 11, 15
Nordenstreng, K., 9, 11, 15, 78, 89, 109, 111, 157, 163, 178

O

Obregon, R., 89, 109
Olalquiaga, C., 129, 130
Oliveira, O. S., 91, 109, 140, 144, 146, 154, 159, 172, 178

P

Paldan, L., 11, 12, 16, 91, 109
Parameswaran, R., 80, 88, 109
Paraschos, M., 44, 45, 56
Park, H., 28
Paterson, C., 78, 88, 109
Paterson, R., 116, 119, 130
Payne, D. E., 17, 19, 20, 22, 24, 27, 28, 145, 146, 147, 154, 159, 178
Peake, C. A., 17, 19, 28, 146, 154, 159, 178
Perse, E., 59, 75
Petty, R. E., 167, 172, 177
Phillips, W. A., 4, 16

Pingree, S., 25, 26, 28, 39, 45, 55, 60, 75, 142, 147, 154
Pool, I. de S., 80, 109
Porto, M., 78, 109
Potter, W. J., 45, 55
Prada, R. R., 124, 125, 130
Prosser, M., 40, 55

Q

Quataert, D., 4, 15

R

Read, S. J., 165, 178
Read, W., 40, 42, 55
Read, W. H., 81, 109
Reeves, G., 119, 127, 130
Renzulli, J. S., 162, 165, 172, 178
Rionda, G., 61, 75
Roach, C., 2, 4, 9, 10, 16
Roberts, C., 9, 14
Robinson, D., 87, 109
Robinson, J., 33, 38
Rodolfo, L., 4, 16
Rodrigues, A., 84, 85, 109
Rodriguez, R., 167, 172, 177
Roetter, C., 11, 16
Rogers, E., 61, 73, 75, 76, 79, 89, 109, 110
Rogers, E. M., 79, 107, 114, 117, 118, 119, 122, 124, 125, 127, 130, 173, 178
Rokeach, M., 33, 38
Roser, C., 24, 26, 28, 155
Rowell, N. W., 4, 16
Rubin, A., 59, 64, 75
Ruch, W. V., 58, 59, 75
Rusk, J., 33, 38

S

Saito, S., 154
Salinas, R., 11, 12, 16, 91, 109
Salwen, M. B., 135, 151, 154, 159, 178
Sam, D. L., 168, 177
Samovar, L., 58, 59, 76
Sarti, I., 41, 55
Schement, J., 73, 76, 79, 109

AUTHOR INDEX

Schement, J. R., 114, 117, 119, 124, 127, 130
Schiller, H., 9, 15
Schiller, H. I., 1, 2, 8, 10, 11, 16, 41, 55, 111, 135, 136, 154, 160, 178, 179
Schmidt, F. L., 138, 139, 144, 154, 186, 189
Schmucler, H., 93, 108
Schnitman, J., 7, 8, 11, 15
Selnow, G., 35, 38
Shanahan, J., 60, 61, 75, 139, 154
Sherman, B. L., 112, 115, 130
Shrikhande, S., 162, 163, 179
Shrum, L. J., 76
Signorielli, N., 25, 26, 27, 29, 30, 38, 39, 46, 54, 55, 56, 139, 154
Sim, K., 44, 54, 63, 171, 177
Simnett, W. E., 5, 16
Simpson, C., 24, 25, 28, 32, 38, 60, 76, 155
Sinclair, J., 7, 16
Singhal, A., 89, 90, 109
Siwek, S., 77, 81, 105, 110
Skinner, E. C., 140, 145, 147, 155, 159, 179
Slater, D., 45, 54
Smith, A., 42, 56
Smith, G. E., 173, 175, 179, 182, 188, 189
Smith, M., 123, 130
Smythe, D. W., 41, 56
Snow, R. P., 25, 27
Snyder, L., 24, 26, 28, 155
Sodre, M., 100, 109
Somavia, 111
Sparks, V. M., 20, 28
Spindler, G., 182, 189
Spindler, L., 182, 189
Sproule, J. M., 10, 16
Sreberny-Mohammadi, A., 13, 16, 40, 44, 56
Stappers, J., 139, 153
Statistical Abstract of the U.S., 63, 76
Stearns, P. N., 4, 14
Steenkamp, J. B., 166, 171, 179
Stefani, L., 58, 59, 76
Stephan, W. G., 166, 168, 172, 179
Sterling, C. H., 183, 189
Stevenson, R. L., 27, 28, 112, 125, 126, 131
Stiff, J. B., 167, 172, 179
Stilling, E. A., 46, 56
Straubhaar, J., 44, 56, 61, 74, 76, 79, 80, 82, 83, 87, 88, 91, 96, 102, 109

Straubhaar, J. D., 105, 107, 112, 113, 114, 115, 116, 123, 129, 130, 131, 134, 139, 153, 155, 162, 163, 172, 179
Suarchavarat, K., 24, 25, 28, 32, 38, 60, 76, 142, 147, 155
Swiggers, P., 174, 179

T

Takahashi, M., 162, 163, 179
Tan, A., 24, 25, 26, 28, 30, 31, 32, 37, 38, 60, 76
Tan, A. A., 24, 25, 26, 28
Tan, A. S., 142, 147, 155
Tan, G., 30, 31, 32, 37, 38
Tan, G. K., 24, 25, 26, 28, 155
Tate, E. D., 155
Taylor, D., 59, 75
Tomlinson, J., 2, 5, 16, 43, 44, 56
Torres, C., 120, 131
Townsend, M. E., 5, 16
Tracey, M., 12, 16, 83, 109, 123, 131, 135, 136, 139, 155, 157, 159, 162, 179
Trach, B., 142, 155
Tsai, M., 145, 146, 147, 155
Tuchman, G., 28

U

Udornpim, K., 90, 109
Ulanovsky, C., 62, 76
Umble, D., 31, 38

V

Valencia, R., 79, 109
Vanden Heuvel, J., 113, 118, 123, 127, 128, 131
Varan, D., 24, 25, 28
Varis, T., 11, 15, 40, 55, 78, 89, 109, 111, 116, 118, 128, 131, 157, 163, 178, 179
Veii, V., 44, 56
Veii, V. S., 140, 155
Verlegh, P. W., 166, 171, 179
Verlinden, C., 5, 16
Victor, D., 59, 75

Vink, N., 88, 110
Viscasillas, G., 87, 109, 116, 123, 124, 131

W

Walker, M., 7, 16
Wallerstein, I., 12, 16, 110
Waterman, D., 79, 110
Wedell, G., 6, 7, 15, 41, 55, 124, 125, 130
Weimann, G., 24, 25, 26, 27, 28, 60, 76, 147, 155
Wells, 111
Wells, A., 7, 16
Werner, A., 142, 155
Wert, M. C., 112, 126, 131
Wicks, R. H., 139, 155
Wiesner-Hanks, M. E., 4, 14
Wildman, S., 77, 81, 105, 110
Wilkinson, K., 83, 84, 110
Williams, F., 184, 189
Williams, J. F., 4, 16
Wilson, T. C., 153
Wimmer, R. D., 125, 131
Windahl, S., 139, 154
Woollacott, J., 9, 14
Wu, Y. K., 145, 147, 155, 159, 179

Y

Yaple, P., 136, 151, 155, 159, 179
Youn, S.-M., 79, 82, 91, 109
Young, S., 162, 163, 179

Z

Zaharopoulos, D., 88, 110
Zaharopoulos, T., 43, 44, 45, 56, 60, 76
Zhao, X., 25, 28, 142, 145, 155
Zhongdang, P., 145, 153
Zillman, D., 163, 179

Subject Index

Page numbers followed by *f* indicate figures.

A

ABIPEME social classification system, 93–94
Acculturation, 139, 168
Action-adventure films, 80
Action-adventure series, 37, 81
Adolescents, perceived foreign influence and television viewing among, 18–21, 39–54, 60, 148–149
Advertising, in foreign media, 44–45, *see also* Consumerism
Affective beliefs, 143
Africa, 92
Age
    acceptance of democratic values and, 36, 37
    as moderator variable, 148, 150
    perceptions of American social reality and, 63, 72, 73
    as source of cultural capital, 87, 88
Agenda setting, cross-cultural television and, 20, 23
America, 34
American communication behavior, 58–59
American cultural stereotypes, 32, 58, 59
American culture, adoption of, 31
American Express, 63, 66
American family system, exposure to American television and acceptance of, 43, 52
American food, 44
American magazines, 34, 40, 69
American media, capitalism and, 10
American movies, 34, 36, *see also* Feature films
American music, 34, 35, 36, 62
American newspapers, 34, 35, 36
American social scientists, modernization and, 7–8
American television
    in Ecuador, 111–129
    genres of, 34
    in Iceland, 17–19, 111, 159
    in Mexico, 32
    perception of foreign consumer goods and, 48–49
    in Quebec, 21–24
    in Russia, 32–36
    socialization effects of, 31, 37–38
    in Taiwan, 32
    in Thailand, 32
    themes of, 33–34, 35

see also United States
American values, exposure to American television and acceptance of, 33–37, 43, 52, see also Values
Anglophone Canadian television, 21–24
Arabic language market, 83
Argentina
    age and perception of American social reality, 72, 73
    cultivation effects of television in, 59, 60–61
    education and perception of American social reality, 72, 73
    English proficiency and perception of American social reality, 72, 73
    gender and perception of American social reality, 66–67, 73
    influence of newspapers, magazines, Internet, and television, 69–70
    influence of television on perceptions of American social reality, 62–74
    international trade in, 58
    light vs. heavy television viewers in, 67–69, 74
    media in, 61–62
    perceptions of North Americans, 58–59
    personal contact and perception of American social reality, 65–66, 70–72, 73, 74
    preference for local television in, 122
    as television exporter to Ecuador, 67, 116, 117, 121, 122, 127
    travel to United States and perception of American social reality, 72
Artifacts, 150
AT&T, 63, 66
Attitudes, media effects on, 24
Attitudes toward United States, imported American television and, 19, 21, 22
Attitudinal effects, of cross-border television, 143, 146, 147, 148, 149, 150, 169, 171
Audience
    classification of, 142
    conception of television, 91, 135–136
    effect of foreign television on domestic, 13, 171–172
    homogeneity of, 162
    socialization effects of American television on, 29–38

B

Baywatch, 80, 87–88
Behavioral-based effects, of cross-border television, 143–144, 147, 149, 171
Behavioral exchange theories, 31
Belief-based effects, of cross-border television, 143, 147, 148, 149, 150–151, 171
Beliefs about United States, foreign television and, 147, 151
Belize, 159
Beverly Hills 90210, 48
Borrowing, 173–176
Brand awareness, 51, 97
Brazil
    access to television in, 92
    case study, 93–107
    cultural capital of poor Brazilians, 97–100
    culturally defined markets and, 83–85
    cultural proximity and, 85–89, 122, 123
    cultural shareability and, 89–93
    culture and media commonalities across class boundaries in, 95–96
    dubbing in, 83
    exposure to foreign television in, 163–164
    global cultural genres and men in, 88
    globalization via television in, 96–97
    language defined markets and, 81–83
    middle class cultural capital in, 102–103
    national programming in, 81
    politically charged novelas in, 120
    regional television production and, 43
    as television exporter, 62, 79, 81, 89, 106, 116, 117

SUBJECT INDEX

upper middle/upper class cultural capital in, 103–104
working class cultural capital in, 100–102
Broadcast satellite technologies (DBS), 92, *see also* Satellite television
Buco, 63

C

Cable television, 61–62, 91, 92, 103, 183
Cablevision-TCI, 62
Camp Ruski Mir, 32
Canadian television
    effect in Minnesota, 19–21
    effect in Quebec, 21–24
    export of, 140
Capitalism
    American media content and, 10
    imperialism and, 5–6
Carnival, Brazilian national culture and, 95, 96
Cartoon Network, 62
Cartoons, 81
Celeste Siempre Celeste, 121
Center Nations, 11–12
Chat rooms, 185
Chile, 62, 122
China, 92
Chinese language market, 83, 84
CIDEM, 114
Circular causality, 173
Class, *see* Social class; Socioeconomic status
CNN, 34, 62, 69, 73, 74, 103
Coding rules, in meta-analysis, 138–139
Cognitive functional theory, 30–31, 37–38
Coke, 96, 97
Cold War, 7
Colombia, 116, 120
Colonialism, 2, 3, 4–5, 8, 40
Comedy programs
    American, 34, 35, 37
    rarity of production in small countries, 125–126
    values and viewing, 52
Comics, 101
Communication technology
    economic capital and access to, 78, 91–92, 105
    importation of, 40–41
Communication Yearbook, vii
Conquests, cultural imperialism and, 3–4
Conservation International, 99
Conspiracy theory
    cultural imperialism and, 2, 3
    dependency theory and, 9
    imported television and, 13–14
    modernization hypothesis and, 7–8
    strength of media effects in, 27
    transnational corporations and, 10–12
Consumer goods, perception of foreign, 46, 48–49, 51, 53
Consumerism
    American television and promotion of, 41
    in Brazil, 96
    foreign television viewing and, 13, 134, 135, 143, 144, 146
Contact hypothesis, 168
Content cues, 166
Control variables, 26
Costa Rica, 113, 126
Critical-cultural paradigm, 9, 10
Critical theory, 91
Cross-border effect studies, meta-analysis of, 133–152
Cross-cultural business communication, 57–59
Cross-cultural influence, 172–173
Cross-cultural magazines, 23
Cross-cultural mass media, impact in Iceland, 17–19
Cross-cultural radio, 23
Cross-cultural research, methodological problems, 25–26
Cross-cultural television
    impact in Minnesota, 19–21
    impact in Quebec, 21–24
Cultivation hypothesis, 25, 29–30, 35, 36–37, 59–61, 74
    Greek environment and, 39, 43, 44–46, 53–54
Cultural affinities, 88–89
Cultural archetypes, 89–90
Cultural capital, 74, 77–78
    cultural proximity and, 85

Feature films, 34, 36, 80, 81, 92, 103, 120
Females, television consumption among Greek adolescent, 47–48, *see also* Gender
Flow patterns
  global, 78–80
  in Latin America, 129
  one-way, 27, 40, 43, 79
Foreign television
  availability of, 163
  conceptualizing impact of, 134–136
  cultural capital and limits on individual preferences for, 92–93
  cultural imperialist assumptions about, 13–14
  defined, 1, 137
  effect of content on domestic viewers, 158–160, 171–172
  exposure to, 163–164
  labeling effect of, 172–176
  limited or unknown effects of, 135–136
  processing of content, 164–170
  process of influence of, 160–172
  produced by outgroup, 166–167
  research agenda for studying, 181–182
  selectivity and, 163–164
  as source of national ills, 134–135
Fox network, 62
France
  fear of imported television in, 157
  as television exporter, 67, 81–82, 116
Francophone Canadian television, 21–24
Frankfort School, 9
Freedom Forum Media Studies Center, 113
Free press, in Ecuador, 123, 125
French language market, 83
Full House, 116, 121

G

Game shows, 100
Gender
  acceptance of democratic values and, 36, 37
  foreign media and perceptions of American social reality and, 62, 66–67, 73
  influence of American television and, 43, 44, 60
  as source of cultural capital, 87–88
  television consumption and, 47–48
General Hospital, 119
General population, as focus of cross-border television studies, 142, 148
Genres, television, 34, 88, 142
Geographic location, control of television exposure and, 18
German language market, 83
Germany, 62, 67, 83
"Ghost," 34
Global culture
  Brazilian poor and, 98
  class and, 88
  middle class Brazilians and, 102–103
  social class and, 85, 86
  upper middle class/upper class Brazilians and, 103–104
Global elite, 78
Global television flows, 27, 40, 43, 78–80
Globalization
  cultural imperialism and, 42–43
  television and, 96–97
Great Britain, 67, 81–82
Greece
  cultural imperialism, cultivation, and, 44–46
  ethnocentrism in, 43–44
  gender images in imported media in, 88
  perceived foreign influence and television viewing in, 39–54, 60
  perception of foreign cultural influence in, 46, 49–52, 53
Guatemala, 125–126

H

Heavy television viewing, vs. light, 67–69, 74
Heterogeneity, 139
Hindi language market, 83
History, cultural imperialism and, 2–3
Hong Kong, 81–82, 89
Household access, to television, 91–92, 105

SUBJECT INDEX

Household conditions, perception of American, 64, 68, 69, 71
Hypodermic model, 12, 43

I

Iberia, 83
Iceland, 17–19, 111, 159
Identity
 cultural proximity and, 85
 local, 77
 regional, 77
 supranational, 77
 television and synthesis of, 77–78
 see also Cultural identity; National identity
Identity-definition function, 42
Ideology, supporting cultural imperialism paradigm, 4–6
Imperialism, 5
 structural theories of, 11–12
 see also Cultural imperialism
Imported television, 1, *see also* Foreign television
Independent variable, measurement of, 142–143
India, 81, 83, 88
Indigenous culture
 foreign media influence on, 44, 45, 158–160
 legislation to protect, 13
Individual access, to television, 91–92, 105
Indonesia, 84
Information
 media effect on, 19, 22, 23, 24
 processing foreign television content and prior, 165–167, 168, 170
 researching effect of exposure to imported, 185–188
 social class and access to, 94–96
Information sequencing effect, 165
Inter-group behavior, historical, 2, 3
Internal consistency technique, 186
International behavior, cultural imperialism and, 3–4
International communication, defined, 161, 189
Internationalized culture, 41–42

International television, 1, *see also* Foreign television
International trade, cross-cultural business communication and, 57–58
Internet
 research agenda for exposure and effect of, 182, 184
 use of in Argentina and perceptions of American social reality, 66, 69, 70
 see also World Wide Web
Interpersonal contact
 as control variable, 26
 effect on agenda setting, 23–24
 influence of, 34, 35, 36, 37
 perceptions of American social reality and, 63, 65–66, 70–72, 73, 74
Interpersonal cultural transmission, 175
Involvement, foreign television processing and, 167
IPSA Group Latin America, 121
ISEG (Institute for Government Economics), 63
Israel, 60
Italy, 62, 67

J

Japan, 81–82, 89, 90, 116
Jose Litwin and Associates, 63

K

Knowledge-based effects, of cross-border television, 143, 145, 147, 151, 171
Knowledge of United States, impact of imported American television on, 19, 22, 23
Korea, 60
Kung Fu, 69, 74, 121

L

Lampsi, 48
Language compatibility
 foreign television effects and, 171

foreign television exposure and, 164
Language defined markets, 77, 81–83
Language proficiency
   as control variable, 26
   global culture and, 103–104, 105
   impact of media and, 23–24
   influence on media use, 34, 35, 37, 44
   television selection and, 82–83
   see also English proficiency
Latin America
   criticism of American media content in, 10
   dependency hypothesis and, 8–10
   national production in, 123–124
   perceptions of North Americans, 58–59
   regional television production, 43
   see also individual countries
Latin American cultural-linguistic television market, 79
   subgroups in, 85
Latin American programs, preference for in Ecuador, 115, 121–124
Learning, effect of television on, 30
Legislation, to protect indigenous culture, 13
Levis, 96
Light television viewing, vs. heavy, 67–69, 74
Lloyds Bank, 63
Local culture
   Brazilian poor and, 97, 99
   social class and, 85, 86, 88
   working class Brazilians and, 100
Local identity, 77
Local television, preference for, 162, *see also* Cultural proximity
Loving, 48
Lower class audiences, local culture and, 86, *see also* Poor; Working class

M

MACD, *see* Media-Accelerated Culture Diffusion
Magazines, 23, 34, 40, 69
Magic bullet theory, 12
Mainstreaming, 25, 30
Malay language market, 83

Malaysia, 163
Males
   global culture genres and, 88
   television consumption among Greek adolescent, 47–48
   see also Gender
Maria Soledad, 127
Marimar, 121
Marxist critical-cultural paradigm, 9, 10
Mass media
   modernization and, 7–8
   neo-colonialism and, 12
   role in cultural imperialism paradigm, 2, 3
   strength of effects, 26–27
   strong effects theory of, 10–11, 12, 14, 136, 162
   as tools for control, 9–10
McBride Report, 112f
Measurement error, 150
Measurement scales, 186
Media
   American, 10, *see also* under American
   Argentina and, 61–62
   consumption of among Greek adolescents, 47–48
   electronic, 9–10, 70
   media effect, 19, 22, 23, 24, 30
   privatization of, 43
   social class and access to, 94–96
   as source of cultural capital, 86–87
   as tools for control, 9–10
   transnational corporations and power of, 10–12
   see also Mass media; Print media
Media-Accelerated Culture Diffusion (MACD), 176, 177
Media imperialism, 78
Melrose Place, 48
Mercado Iberoamericano de la Industria, 128
Message production and dissemination, 183, 185
Meta-analysis, 138–139, 159, 187
Meta-analysis of cross-border effect studies, 133–152
   average effect size, 149–152

SUBJECT INDEX 209

conceptualizing impact of foreign television, 134–136
implications for research, 150–152
method, 137–139
results, 139–149
study expectations, 136
Methodological problems, in cross-cultural research, 25–26
Mexico
access to television in, 92
influence of American television in, 32, 60
preference for local television in, 122, 123
regional television production and, 43
as television exporter, 62, 79, 81, 89, 116, 117, 121, 122, 126, 127, 140
Middle class, Brazilian, 94–95
cultural capital, 102–103
Middle East, 116
Migrants, access to television by Brazilian, 99–100
Migration, television exposure and, 19
Minnesota, impact of cross-cultural television in, 19–21
Moderator variables, 148–149
Modernization hypothesis, 7–8, 9, 40, 139
Moscow Institute of Steel and Alloys, 32
Motivation
to accept American culture, 31
to watch foreign television, 46
Movies, *see* Feature films
Movimento dos Sem Terra (Movement of the Landless), 99
Mozambique, 90, 92
MTV, 62
MTV Brazil, 104
Music
American, 34, 35, 36, 37, 62
Brazilian, 101, 104
national culture and, 95, 96

N

Nanny, The, 62
National Communication Association, vii
National culture, 85, 86
in Brazil, 95–96
Brazilian poor and, 97, 98, 99–100
class and, 88

National identity, 77
building through television, 126–127
impact of cross-cultural television on, 20
television access in Brazil and, 98–100
see also Cultural identity
National Science Foundation, 17–18
National television production, 90–91, 105
in Ecuador, 115, 127–128
in Greece, 46, 48
in Latin America, 123–124
media privatization and, 43
preference for, 80–81, 105–106, 115, *see also* Cultural proximity
NBA Basketball, 48
Negative perceptions, of United States, 65, 69, 71
Neighborhood associations, as source of cultural capital, 86
Neighborhoods, as source of cultural capital, 85–86
Neo-colonialism, 11–12
Neo-Marxism, cultural imperialism and, 6, 7
News agencies, American, 40
Newspapers, 34, 35, 36
News programs
American, 37
CNN, 34, 62, 69, 73, 74, 103
in Ecuador, 119–121, 123, 124–125
effect of imported, 181–182
Newsweek, 34, 69, 73–74
New World Information Order, 112f
New York Times, The, 34
New Zealand, 111
Non-Aligned movement, 13
Nongovernmental organizations (NGOs), 99
Norte, 63
North Americans, perceptions of, 58–59

O

One-way hypothesis, 27, 40, 43, 79
Oshin, 90
Otis Elevator, 63

P

Packard Electric, 63
Panama, 126
Panamericanism, 84
Pan-ethnic Latin audience, 84
Pasado y Confeso, 128
Peer networks, as source of cultural
    capital, 85–86
Perceived Realism Index (PRI), 64
Perceptions, 143
Periphery Nations, 11–12
Personal networks, as source of cultural
    capital, 85–86
Persuasion, foreign television processing
    and, 167–168, 171
Peru, 122
Phonetic alphabet, spread of, 173–175
Pita bread, diffusion of, 175–176, 188
Playboy, 34
Plaza Sesamo, 135
"Police Academy," 34
Political ideology, assessing impact of
    foreign television and, 159
Political power, cultural diffusion and,
    188–189
Poor, Brazilian, 94, 95
    cultural capital of, 97–100
Portugal, 79
Portuguese language market, 83
Positive perceptions, of United States, 65,
    69, 71
Prestige, ownership of foreign consumer
    goods and, 46, 49, 51–52, 53
"Pretty Woman," 34
PRI, see Perceived Realism Index
Prime time viewing, in Ecuador, 117–118,
    119
Print media
    exposure to among working class
        Brazilians, 101–102
    magazines, 23, 34, 40, 69
    newspapers, 34, 35, 36
    perceptions of American social reality
        and, 62, 66, 69, 70
Process models, 161
Producer–audience interaction, 79

Professional associations, as source of
    cultural capital, 86
Professionals, as focus of cross-border
    television studies, 142
Professions, perception of American, 64,
    69, 71
Psychological Abstracts, 137f
PsycINFO, 137f
Puerto Rico, 117
Purchasing power, foreign television
    viewing and, 143, 144, 146, 150

Q

Quebec, impact of cross-cultural
    television in, 21–24

R

Radio
    Anglophone Canadian, 23
    in Argentina, 62
    influence of imported American, 34, 36
    as localizing force, 97–98
    working class Brazilians and, 101
Ratinho (Little Mouse), 100
Readers Digest, 34
Realism, perception of television, 45–46,
    53, 62
Reality shows, 96
Record Network, 87, 100
Regional culture, class and, 88
Regional identity, 77
Regional markets, 79, 81, 82–83
Regional television production, 105, 106
    role in Ecuador, 114, 115
    media privatization and, 43
    preference for, 162, see also Cultural
        proximity
Religion, as source of cultural capital, 86
Research agenda, on impact of
    international audio-visual
    media, 181–189
Resonance, 25
Respondent burden, 187
Rockwell International, 63, 66
Rural poor, access to television among
    Brazilian, 98–99, 100

SUBJECT INDEX

Russia, American television in, 32–36

S

Satellite television, 18, 91, 92, 103, 163
SBT (Sistema Brasileira de Televisão), 87, 100, 102
Schema, 165
Selective exposure framework, 163
Selectivity, 163
Self-esteem, 31
Self-selection, 26
Sesame Street, 13, 135
Siete Lunas y Siete Serpientes (Seven Moons and Seven Serpents), 128
"Silence of the Lambs," 34
SIM, *see* Susceptibility to Imported Media
Simplemente María, 89, 125
Simpsons, The, 62
Sitcoms, 48
Soap operas, 48, 88, 90, 119, 125
Soccer, national culture and, 95, 96
Social approval, 31
Social change, mass media and, 7–8
Social class
  access to information and, 94–96
  cultural proximity and, 78, 91
  culture and media commonalities across boundaries of, 95–96
  defining Brazilian, 93–94
  family and, 85
  preferences for global, regional, national, or local culture and, 85, 86, 88
Social cognitive theory, 30, 37
Social learning theory, 39, 139
Social stereotypes, of Americans, 32, 58, 59
Socialization effects, 139
  of American television on international audience, 29–38
Socioeconomic status
  as control variable, 26
  foreign media influence and, 44
  vs. impact of media, 23–24
Sociological Abstracts, 137f
Soviet Union, 7
Spain, 62, 67
Spanish language market, 83

Speech Communication Association, vii
Sports, national culture and, 95, 96
Sports clubs, as source of cultural capital, 86
Sports programs, 34, 35, 37, 48, 88
Stability measures, 186
Star Trek, 116
Statistical validation, 186–187
Statistics, reporting, 187
Stimulus-response model of media effects, 30
Strong effects theory, of mass media, 10–11, 12, 14, 136, 162
Structural analysis, dependency theory and, 10
Structural theories of imperialism, 11–12
Students, as focus of cross-border television studies, 18–21, 39–54, 60, 142, 148–149
Success principle, 31
Suchard-Kraft Foods, 63
Superman, 121
Superpowers, 6–7
Supranational culture, 86
Supranational identity, 77
Susceptibility to Imported Media (SIM), 170, 176–177, 181, 185

T

Taiwan
  access to television in, 92
  effect of foreign television in, 32, 60, 159
  television production in, 85
Talk radio, 62
Talk shows, 96, 100
Tamil language market, 83
Telefonica de Argentina, 63
Telefteo Antio, 48
Telenovelas
  Brazilian, 83, 88, 98, 100, 102, 119
  Ecuadorian, 123
  Greek, 48
  as imports to Ecuador, 117, 118, 119–121
  Mexican, 119
  national culture and, 95, 96